BED & BREAKFASTS AND COUNTRY INNS OF NEW ENGLAND

A YANKEE® BOOKS TRAVEL GUIDE

BED & BREAKFASTS AND COUNTRY INNS OF NEW ENGLAND

by Deborah Patton

Camden, Maine

To Sam, an inspiration in staying power.

Address inquiries to Yankee Books, P.O. Box 1248, Camden, Maine 04843

Text redesign and production • Amy Fischer, Camden, Maine
Cover design • Dale Swensson, Mt. Desert, Maine
Composition • High Resolution, Camden, Maine
Printed and bound • BookCrafters, Chelsea, Michigan
Cover Photo • Caroline & Jim Lloyd

Library of Congress Cataloging-in-Publication Data

Patton, Deborah.

Bed & breakfast and country inns of New England / by Deborah Patton.

p. cm

Rev. ed. of: Bed & breakfast inns of New England. ©1987.

ISBN 0-89909-225-X : $10.95

1. Bed and breakfast accommodations—New England—Guide-books.
2. New England—Description and travel—1981—Guide-books.
I. Patton, Deborah. Bed & breakfast inns of New England. II. Title. III. Title: Bed and breakfasts and country inns of New England.

TX907.3.N35P38 1990 90–49114
647.9474—dc20 CIP

10 9 8 7 6 5 4 3 2 1

CONTENTS

INTRODUCTION

On the Back Roads Again. 9
How to Use This Guide 11
The Best of New England. 12

MAINE

Bar Harbor/Cottage Inns of Bar Harbor 14
Camden/Edgecombe-Coles House. 17
Camden/The Elms 19
Camden/Windward House 21
Cape Neddick/Cape Neddick House. 23
Cape Neddick/Wooden Goose Inn 25
Center Lovell/Westways Country Inn 27
Deer Isle/Pilgrim's Inn 29
Freeport/Isaac Randall House 31
Fryeburg/Oxford House Inn. 32
Hull's Cove/Inn at Canoe Point 34
Kennebunkport/Captain Jefferds Inn. 36
Kennebunkport/Captain Lord Mansion 38
Kennebunkport/Welby Inn. 40
Northeast Harbor/Grey Rock Inn. 41
Portland/Inn at ParkSpring 42
Wiscasset/Squire Tarbox Inn 43

NEW HAMPSHIRE

Center Sandwich/Corner House Inn 46
Cornish/Chase House 47

Etna/Moose Mountain Lodge 49
Fitzwilliam/Amos A. Parker House 51
Fitzwilliam/Hannah Davis House. 54
Intervale/The Forest 56
Intervale/Riverside Country Inn 58
Jackson Village/Ellis River House 59
Jackson Village/Nestlenook Inn 61
Jackson Village/Wildcat Inn 63
Jaffrey/Benjamin Prescott Inn. 64
Jaffrey/Gould Farm 66
Jefferson/Stag Hollow Inn 68
Laconia/Ferry Point House 70
Lyme/Lyme Inn 72
Marlborough/Thatcher Hill Inn 73
Nelson/Tolman Pond Farmhouse 75
New London/Maple Hill Farm 77
Newport/Inn at Coit Mountain. 79
Orford/White Goose Inn. 80
Shelburne/Philbrook Farm Inn. 82
Sugar Hill/The Homestead 84
Sunapee/Seven Hearths Inn 86
Tamworth Village/Gilman Tavern 87
Temple/Birchwood Inn. 89
Tilton/The Black Swan Inn. 91

VERMONT

Craftsbury/Craftsbury Inn 94
Craftsbury Common/Inn on the Common 95
Danby/Quail's Nest Inn 97
Dorset/Cornucopia of Dorset 98
East Poultney/Eagle Tavern 100
Fair Haven/Vermont Marble Inn 102
Goshen/Blueberry Hill Inn. 104
Ludlow/Governor's Inn. 106
Manchester/1811 House 107
Manchester/Wilburton. 109
Middlebury/Swift House Inn 110
Middletown Springs/Middletown Springs Inn. 112
Newfane/Four Columns Inn. 113
Quechee/Quechee Bed & Breakfast 115
South Woodstock/Kedron Valley Inn 116
Vergennes/Strong House Inn 118
West Dover/West Dover Inn 119
Weston/1830 Inn on the Green 120
Woodstock/Canterbury House 121
Woodstock/Charleston House 123
Woodstock/Jackson House. 124

MASSACHUSETTS

Barnstable Village/Charles Hinckley House 128
Chatham/Captain's House Inn of Chatham. 130
Dennis/Isaiah Hall B&B Inn 132
Eastham/The Over Look Inn 134
Edgartown/Daggett House 136
Edgartown/Governor Bradford Inn 138
Edgartown/Point Way Inn 140
Falmouth/Mostly Hall 142
Great Barrington/Elling Guest House 144
Great Barrington/Littlejohn Manor. 145
Lenox/Walker House 147
Lenox/Whistler's Inn 149
Nantucket/Century House 151
Nantucket/Cliff Lodge 153
Nantucket/Corner House 154
Nantucket/Fair Gardens 156
Nantucket/Four Chimneys Inn 157
Nantucket/Great Harbor House 158
Newburyport/Morrill Place 159
Northfield/Northfield Country House 161
Rockport/Inn on Cove Hill 162
Sheffield/Staveleigh House 164
Stockbridge/The Inn at Stockbridge 166
Vineyard Haven/Captain Dexter House 167
Vineyard Haven/Thorncroft 168
West Tisbury/Lambert's Cove Inn 170
Yarmouth Port/Wedgewood Inn 172

RHODE ISLAND

Block Island/Blue Dory Inn 176
Newport/Admiral Benbow Inn. 177
Newport/Brinley Victorian Inn. 178
Newport/Cliffside Inn 180
Newport/The Inn at Castle Hill 182
Newport/Inntowne 184
Newport/Queen Anne Inn 186
Westerly/Shelter Harbor Inn. 188

CONNECTICUT

Bethlehem/Eastover Farm. 190
Deep River/Riverwind Inn 192
East Haddam/Austin's Stonecroft Inn 194
Essex/Griswold Inn 196
Greenwich/The Homestead 198

Kent/The Country Goose 200
Kent/Flanders Arms. 202
Litchfield/Tollgate Hill Inn 204
New London/Queen Anne Inn 206
New Preston/Boulders Inn 208
Norfolk/Greenwoods Gate 210
Norfolk/Manor House 212
Pomfret/Cobbscroft 214
Warren/Evie's Turning Point Farm. 216
Westport/Cotswold Inn 218

INDEX

ABOUT THE AUTHOR 220

INTRODUCTION

ON THE BACK ROADS AGAIN

HOW DO YOU even begin to make sense of the thousands of bed and breakfast country inns in New England? You may have been lucky enough to land in one or two good places quite by accident. Chances are you religiously return to these inns, even to the same rooms.

With all the pretty places in the Northeast, it's easy to be lured into a charming place by virtue of the architecture. But in the inn world particularly, looks are deceiving. What you think you see is not necessarily what you're going to get. And the last thing you want when you're on holiday (or on business) is the type of surprises that all too many country inns offer beneath the veneer of country decor and Colonial charm.

Good news! This guidebook has done your homework for you. Based on an experienced and well-traveled viewpoint, it includes the best inns that New England has to offer. It is a highly edited guide in that the 114 inns that made it into this book are truly special. This book is not intended as a reference guide to all the inns in New England. Rather, it is a collection of places that will meet the same high standard of authenticity and integrity. Whether the inns are plain or fancy, expensive or modest, you will find all of them share one or more of these characteristics: fabulous hosts, stunning decor, perfect location, and terrific food. When all four come together in a single inn, the results can be memorable.

In the four years since the research on the original edition of this bed and breakfast guide was published, the entire bed and breakfast industry has undergone a shakeout. Many couples who escaped their corporate jobs to find new meaning and fulfillment in the country found that running a bed and breakfast was a lot of work—not to mention a lot of demands from demanding travelers. In short, it was more than they were either prepared for or trained to deal with. These people came to the realization that they grossly underestimated their dreams; they have since cashed out of the business and returned to city life—or at least life that is less service-oriented.

Fortunately, most of the inns included in the first edition of this book are still thriving and have gotten better over the years. Their innkeepers have discovered a true sense of personal satisfaction with making life pleasant for other people, taking care of them with a sense of personal style and good humor.

For those of you who like to keep score, of the innkeepers of the 106 inns included in the original edition, two couples divorced (one remarried), one innkeeper found a husband while renovating her inn, and one innkeeper had a baby, the start of a second family. In counterpoint, four owners died (thankfully unrelated to innkeeping). In one case, an octogenarian couple's sons are keeping their parents' forty-year innkeeping tradition alive as second-generation innkeepers move into high gear, taking care of second generation guests.

Of the original 106 inns, some changed owners or were closed; these have been replaced with some wonderful new finds. The caliber of the 114 inns in the book is exceptional. This is a book for people with a spirit of adventure, for those who like to discover forgotten back roads and who aren't afraid to take the out-of-the-way routes through New England. It's for people who want to stay at inns with personality and a point of view, and for those who appreciate the personal effort and care it takes to make a good bed and breakfast inn great. And it's for everyone who is a romantic.

It used to be that staying in bed and breakfast homes was a great way to travel on a shoestring budget. Although there are still many families who open their homes to visitors, making rooms available as the kids grow up and leave home, these are frequently amateur ventures, sometimes used as tax shelters or simply to offset mortgage costs. Breakfasts are often whatever the family is eating, and the accommodations are just like home — only more so. That kind of bed and breakfast experience is not what this book is about.

This book is about bed and breakfast *inns* in New England. These inns are professionally run business ventures, and their innkeepers take their work seriously. All the inns adhere to local and state safety and fire codes.

Bed and breakfast inns are a wonderful way to travel. Their intimacy will convert you forever to wanting the personal touch they provide — so much so that you'll probably go out of your way to experience their singular brand of hospitality and to be treated in the considerate, highly personal, and civilized style that is the signature of great bed and breakfast inns.

Rates: All rates quoted are for double occupancy, including breakfast, unless otherwise noted. The rates do not include any state taxes and service or gratuities surcharges. Rates vary from season to season, and seasons differ from location to location. Be sure to clarify what innkeepers consider to be their "off-season."

A wide range of rates is included in this book. Generally speaking, many of the more expensive inns are located within convenient driving distance of New York City and Boston to allow for a weekend visit. A few of the inns in this guide, because of their prices, fall into the category of "special event" or "splurge" accommodations. Be forewarned: these inns can become addictive. You might find yourself creating special events to justify frequent return visits. But don't assume that the most expensive inns are the best. To the contrary, some inns with modest rates are among the more charming.

All inns accept cash and traveler's checks. In addition, some accept personal checks or one or more of the major credit cards: MasterCard (MC), VISA (V), American Express (AE), Diners Club, and Discover (D). Payment policy information has been specified for each inn.

The rates quoted are accurate as of June 1990.

Reservations: Reservations can be made by contacting the inns directly. Although there are reservation services and associations that serve some of the inns listed in this book, you can make reservations yourself by telephone or letter. Plan ahead! These inns are popular and frequently are booked well in advance. Some of them also have minimum weekend or holiday stays, so clarify individual policies.

Children: Most inns do not welcome young children. Right or wrong, innkeepers reason that guests come to their inns to get away from the kids. Some of the inns listed in this book specify age requirements for child guests. Innkeepers at these inns are particularly firm about their policies. Be safe and ask about such policies when you make reservations. A handful of inns will accept children—even babies! They are duly noted.

Food: Most of the innkeepers in this book try a little harder at the breakfast table. Many of them got into the business because they love to cook. Most of the inns in this guide fall into the "semigourmet" category, even those that offer only a simple Continental breakfast. Pastries, muffins, and breads are homebaked, and fresh fruit or freshly squeezed orange juice is often available. If breakfast is not your favorite meal, or if you have a special diet, mention this to your host so you won't disappoint a self-described gourmet innkeeper.

A few of the inns also offer dinner, which is noted in their rates. These inns are included because they are special places, generally in out-of-the-way locations. It makes sense to include dinner as part of the package so you don't have to wander the back roads looking for a decent evening meal.

THE BEST OF NEW ENGLAND

Although all the 114 inns in this guide are exceptional, the following 17 inns are superb examples of bed and breakfast innkeeping at its best and deserve special recognition for such.

Maine
Camden/Edgecombe-Coles House
Cape Neddick/Wooden Goose Inn
Kennebunkport/Captain Jefferds Inn
Wiscasset/Squire Tarbox Inn

New Hampshire
Jefferson/Stag Hollow Inn
Marlborough/Thatcher Hill Inn
Tamworth Village/Gilman Tavern

Vermont
East Poultney/Eagle Tavern
Manchester/1811 House
Woodstock/Jackson House

Massachusetts
Barnstable Village/Charles Hinckley House
Nantucket/Corner House
Yarmouth Port/Wedgewood Inn

Rhode Island
Newport/Inntowne

Connecticut
Deep River/Riverwind Inn
Norfolk/Greenwoods Gate
Pomfret/Cobbscroft

MAINE

THE STATE O' MAINE

Maine's bed and breakfast inns are akin to the best summer camps imaginable (many close for the winter). The locations are stunning, activities are abundant, weather is perfect . . . and even the food is good. Although Maine has its fair share of full-service country inns, the bed and breakfast places listed here are especially attractive. You can find just about any experience or atmosphere you want: stately mansions in old seaports, Colonial farmhouses, former summer cottages of the rich and famous — even Victorian townhouses. The few inland places are as charming as those on the coast (where you'll find the highest concentration of inns), and all will seduce you into many return visits to experience their distinctive personalities.

FOR A TRULY DELIGHTFUL SUMMERTIME INN EXPERIENCE, MAINE'S INNS ARE HARD TO BEAT. ABOVE: CAPTAIN JEFFERDS INN, REVIEWED ON PAGE 36.

THE COTTAGE INNS ARE PERFECT GETAWAYS IN ANY SEASON.

Bar Harbor • Cottage Inns of Bar Harbor

DON JOHNSON MAY well create the next innkeeping dynasty in Bar Harbor now that the Jackson family has left the business. Don has a very stylish approach to innkeeping, and the Maples and Ridgeway cottages, along with his Inn at Canoe Point (see page 34), show that you don't have to be old-fashioned to be in the bed and breakfast business. Don's decorating viewpoint is contemporary, but not cold. His rooms are clean-line, refreshing, and masculine without being impersonal. They are spare, but not empty, with just enough detail to keep you interested. He has converted the two Victorian summer homes to handsome inns, blending country with sophisticated living. He is a genius at the understated. A perfectly placed painting on a bookshelf. Unusual dried greens in a Mingesque vase. Designer sheets that make a statement. An antique bureau updated with contemporary crystal candlesticks. Or, modern wicker furnishings in a nostalgically old room. His inns are always filled with subtle surprises. The overall effect is one of simplicity, an oasis of serenity in the bed and breakfast world.

Don also chooses wonderful innkeepers. At Maples Cottage, Katy Wood and her husband, Jed, are in residence. Katy is a youthful, savvy hostess whose studies in tourism and marketing are preparing her for her own future innkeeping business. In the meantime, she is getting excellent training with Don and she will take care of you with genuine sincerity and interest. She oversees both cottages, and will help you find the perfect haven in any of the six rooms in the Maples. Whether you choose the immensely popular Birch Point Suite with its own sitting room and fireplace; Schooner Head with its tailored yellow-striped walls and green iron bed; the Briars with its handsome, dark mahogany furnishings—one of the more striking rooms in any inn; Edgemere with its deep burgundy colors and paisley sheets; or equally attractive Chatwold and Brook End, you won't be disappointed.

Nor will you be disappointed by any of the six rooms in Ridgeway, the other cottage, back-to-back with Maples. Ridgeway is a work in progress, blending Don's approach with a more countrified look.

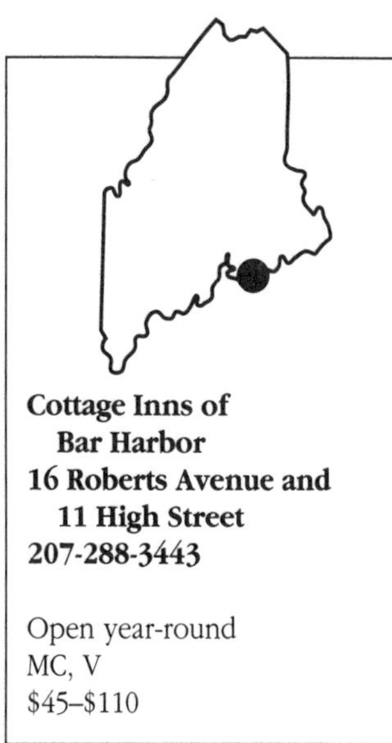

Cottage Inns of Bar Harbor
16 Roberts Avenue and 11 High Street
207-288-3443

Open year-round
MC, V
$45–$110

The effect is no less attractive, whether it's Wingwood with its blue floral walls and queen-size tall-post bed; Homewood with its sleigh bed and light peach decor; or one of the two third-floor rooms, Greenway Court enticing in deep green and pink with a beautiful half-moon window and king-size bed; or Stanwood, typical Don Johnson decor with blue pinstriped walls and Queen-sized bed. Each of the twelve lovely rooms in these cottages is named after one of the historic summer houses in Bar Harbor.

Breakfast for guests in both cottages is served by candlelight at Maples with contemporary tables and fashionable blue-and-white china. Fresh fruit is followed by homemade coffee cakes and entrées such as spinach quiche and broiled tomatoes, French toast with blueberry sauce, cranberry-walnut pancakes, or vegetable-cheese strata.

When you are ready for lunch or dinner, try a popular place in town owned by local personality Fred Pooler. The **Brick Oven** (21 Cottage Street, 207-288-3708) is filled with Fred's antique toy collections and his imaginative approach to diorama and mechanical-display decor. This environment will entertain restless children of all ages who have already enjoyed any of the well-prepared multi-national dishes Fred offers.

Directions: From I-95 north, take exit 15 in Augusta to Route 3 east. From Ellsworth take Route 3 into Bar Harbor. Turn left on Cottage Street, go 4 blocks to Roberts Avenue. Turn right, Maples Cottage is on the left. For Ridgeway, follow above directions, but continue past Roberts Avenue and turn left onto Mt. Desert Street. Go 1 block, turn left onto High Street.

DON JOHNSON HAS CREATIVE DECORATING INSTICTS THAT MAKE HIS INNS UNIQUELY DIFFERENT.

Edgecombe-Coles House • *Camden*

THE SCENERY AND SURROUNDINGS ARE EVERY BIT AS APPEALING AS EDGECOMBE-COLES HOUSE ITSELF.

WHEN YOU PERCH yourself on top of Mount Battie, you may feel the poetry escaping from within, just as Edna St. Vincent Millay did when she sat in this same spot in 1910 and was stirred to write "Renascence." Or you might lose yourself in some nature trance, immersed in the spectacular view of Maine's wooded coastline and Camden's charming harbor. You can also take a more active role, hiking the trails of Camden Hills State Park, enjoying the crisp air and pristine skies.

The only thing better than spending a morning on Mount Battie is starting your day at Edgecombe-Coles House, just down the road. Secreted away behind an imposing privet, surrounded by lilac bushes and a circular driveway, strategically placed on a rise with a full view of Penobscot Bay, this marvelous inn offers sanctuary to guests in all seasons. Terry and Louise Price, former San Franciscans, have created an inn to showcase their lovely furniture collection, enhanced by decor that is both pleasing and comfortable. The house is filled with the Prices' collection of primitives, prints, early American furniture, Oriental rugs, antique toys, country pieces, lace and crochet works, beautiful beds, and flattering colors. The two front rooms, with their spectacular views, are, understandably, the most popular. One offers a king-sized brass bed and apricot decor, the other a queen-size white iron bed and pink and blue pastel colors. The remaining four rooms are equally lovely (albeit without the same view) and offer the same tranquil privacy that distinquishes this handsome inn. One room features a mosquito net as an innovative alternative to the traditional lace canopy. The combination of net and nostalgic floral spread makes this room look more Ralph Lauren than Ralph Lauren's safari collection.

Terry helps guests to fuel up for the day with a hearty breakfast. Selections include Dutch babies, popoverlike pancakes; seafood omelets; roast beef hash with eggs and hollandaise sauce; blueberry muffins; strawberry waffles; scrambled eggs with bacon and cheese; Amaretto French toast; and fresh fruit. If you stay both nights of the weekend, the second morning's menu might include blueberry pancakes served with bacon; homemade breads; and fresh jams and preserves. You'll enjoy these well-prepared feasts in the company of other happy guests in the Prices' stylish dining room, with its collection of marvelous oil paintings, or outdoors in the summer garden.

Edgecombe-Coles House
64 High Street (Route 1)
Camden, 04843
207-236-2336

All major credit cards
Open year-round
\$70–\$145

Directions: From I-95 north, take exit 22 at Brunswick to Route 1 north. The inn is .7 mile north of downtown, on the left.

The Elms • *Camden*

THE ELMS IS ROMANTIC AND RESTFUL, WITH GENUINE HOSPITALITY TO BOOT.

ALL TOO FREQUENTLY, your lasting impression of a given inn is your first impression when the innkeeper opens the door. In this case, be sure to visit the Elms, as Joan James's gracious, graceful greeting reflects her inn's personal charm and attention to detail. Joan bought this Federal-era house on one of her vacations to Maine, after a restorative windjammer cruise. The inn is particularly lovely, a salute to Joan's tenacity and good taste.

Each of the six rooms (four have private baths, two share) has its own journal so that you can add your comments and observations to those of previous guests. It makes for some pleasant bedtime reading. The Paisley Room is lush in deep rose and maroon, with its namesake wallpaper motif. The black iron bed makes this dramatic room all the more so. The Pink Room, in counterpoint to Paisley, is light in rose-and-ivory striped wallpaper, with its own ivory iron bed. Or, you may prefer the Blue Room with its blue-and-beige bargello-print walls. The Honeymoon Suite on the third floor shimmers in pale paisley, a romantic escape for any couple. There are two more

THE LUSH DECOR GIVES THE ELMS A COMFORTABLE, PLEASING ENVIRONMENT.

rooms in the carriage house, one in salmon, the other in blue. Before her venture into innkeeping, Joan was an interior decorator for a retail store (as well as a personnel professional), and her prowess is obvious.

Breakfast is served in the handsome dining room. Minimuffins and homebaked breads join entrées such as French toast stuffed with peaches and cream, strata with Canadian bacon, frittatas, omelets, and French toast with oranges. The living room is equally attractive with its oversize cooking hearth, bay window, and Queen Anne chairs. The overall effect of this inn is feminine—but not intrusively so—warm, and comforting. The candles lit in every window beckon you, and the welcome here is genuine and lasting.

Directions: From I-95 north, take exit 22 in Brunswick to Route 1 north. The inn is just before downtown, on the right.

The Elms
84 Elm Street (Route 1)
Camden, 04843
207-236-6250

Open year-round
MC, V
$50–$85

Windward House • *Camden*

WINDWARD HOUSE IS one of those inns that captures your imagination as you approach it. The immaculate gardens, sparkling, fresh paint, even the summer straw hats with ribbons indicating the current wind direction give you hope. Follow your intuition and reserve a room at this cheerful inn. Owners Mary and Jon Davis and innkeeper Megan Roberts are lovely hosts, and a stay here makes a visit to Camden even more pleasant.

THERE IS A SUNNY QUALITY TO THIS IMPRESSIVELY HANDSOME INN.

A refreshing room here is the Tea Room, one of the few sitting areas in New England with California decor, complete with its dhurrie rug, a light touch that gives a lift to the more traditionally decorated Greek Revival interior. This is a pleasant place to relax before breakfast. The dining room is pretty, too. Its large table is surrounded by a handsome silver coffee-and-tea service and a display of seasoned wedding gifts. Guests share a homebaked meal, including fresh fruit, blueberry crunch, spanakopita with phyllo and spinach, vegetable-egg bake, and waffles. It's no surprise that Mary was once in the catering business.

The five bedrooms are fresh and pretty. The Rose

THE BEDROOMS IN WINDWARD HOUSE ARE STATELY AND ELEGANTLY DECORATED.

Windward House
6 High Street (Route 1)
Camden, 04843
207-236-9656

Open year-round
MC, V
$65–$95

Room has unusual wallpaper with deep rose and green accents and a canopy-size queen bed. The Brass Room has its expected bed and a twin-sized curly maple canopy bed. The Antique Canopy Room has just that with lovely oak furniture. The Mount Battie Room is sweet in lavender and pink, and the Camden Room is light aqua with a handsome iron queen-size bed. The Elijah Glover Suite, named after the original house builder, is a beautiful three-room suite. The inn is filled with updated country decor that is sophisticated and fresh.

The living room is a great gathering place. An entire Maine village crafted from wood decorates the mantel. Windward House has one more surprise for you. The downstairs bathroom doubles as sort of a hydroponic greenhouse with a profusion of plants innovatively housed in the antique tub.

Directions: From I-95 north, take exit 22 in Brunswick to Route 1 north. The inn is 2 blocks north of downtown, on the left.

THE RESTORED CAPE NEDDICK HOUSE OFFERS ONE OF THE BEST VALUES ON THE MAINE COAST.

Cape Neddick House • *Cape Neddick*

IF YOUR HUSBAND IS in the demolition business and he happens to inherit his uncle's one-hundred-year-old Victorian home (which has seen much better days) and two barns, located in a small Maine coastal village, the logical choice might be to put him to work tearing down and rebuilding a house perfect for the bed and breadfast business. That's exactly what John Goodwin decided to do with his inheritance. John's demolition business also has come in handy in locating great finds with which to furnish the inn.

Today, Cape Neddick House, run by John and his wife Dianne, has reclaimed its rightful Victorian appearance, and the six-room inn is particularly appealing to guests who appreciate a fair deal and good food. Dianne, a former geriatrics nurse, runs the inn with her an infectious sense of perfection and enthusiasm. She loves to show guests the before-and-after scrapbook (a staple in most inns) and share stories about her family's adventure in the bed and breakfast business.

Dianne's forte, besides being a bubbling hostess, is in the kitchen, and you can expect fabulous breakfasts to go with your overnight accommodations (a Continental breakfast is also available for a slightly lower price). Her tailor-made kitchen is larger than most people's living rooms. Its colorful fruit stencils are echoed on her apron (and yours, too, if you purchase one to wear at home after your visit here).

Cape Neddick House
Route 1
Cape Neddick, 03902
207-363-2500

Cash or personal check only
Open year-round
Off-season, \$49; fall, \$59; in season, \$69

homemade sweets are among the offerings at tea. Breakfast is even more amazing; restraint is not in the Wooden Goose's vocabulary. There are eighteen different breakfast menus, and you'll not be disappointed if your morning is assigned delicacies such as cranberry bread, raisin muffins, poached pears with Grand Marnier custard sauce, a julienne potato nest filled with steamed broccoli and poached eggs with hollandaise, carrots poached in apple jelly and white wine, eggs Oscar (with the traditional asparagus, béchamel, and hollandaise in puff pastry), sausage-mushroom strudel, or French bread topped with poached eggs and mushroom-béchamel sauce and steamed vegetables. Guests are served this early-morning feast on the sun porch, with crisp linens, silver, crystal, and fine china.

Leave your diet and self-discipline at home.

After such a bacchanal, you might have to stagger back to bed for a nap. More stalwart guests may choose to take in Maine's fabulous antique stores or head for the beach to bask in sublime laziness.

A visit to the Wooden Goose is an experience not to be missed. Leave your diet and self-discipline at home and take in the atmosphere, luxury, and wonderfully pampered treatment you'll receive at this exceptional inn.

Directions: From I-95, take the York/Ogunquit exit to Route 1 north. The inn is about 3½ miles along on the right.

"YOU CAN GET SERIOUSLY LOST IN THE LUSHNESS OF THE WOODEN GOOSE."

Westways Country Inn • *Center Lovell*

ONCE A RETREAT FOR BUSINESS EXECUTIVES, WESTWAYS PRESERVES THE SPIRIT OF THE GATSBY ERA.

SOME BUSINESSMEN IN the 1920s prided themselves on owning expensive playthings to keep them busy between executive meetings: Pierce-Arrows, Long Island mansions, private train cars, summer palazzos in Italy, and weekend flats in Pamplona. William Fairburn, original owner of the Diamond Match Company, had his own style of retreating from the demands of the business world. On the cutting edge of employee relations, Fairburn offered amenities in the twenties that have become commonplace in current-day executive headquarters. He created an upper-crust executive boys' camp on the shores of Kezar Lake, to which he imported his management team from New Jersey for periodic meetings.

Today Westways, the understated, shingled, green-trimmed lodge Fairburn built, is a wonderful inn that takes you back to the Gatsby era as soon as you enter the 120-acre compound. It serves as a reminder of days when business was conducted with a great deal of style and finesse. The lodge is surrounded by a series of smaller buildings housing the Fives (British handball) Court, whose wood paneling and arched ceiling make it something of a cathedral to sports; the Recreation Hall, with ping-pong, billiards, and two amazing inlaid-wood bowling alleys (you have to spot your own pins); and the boathouse, perched over Kezar Lake. Also on the grounds are tennis courts, a baseball diamond, and stables (the story has it that the horses were brought to the lodge promptly at one in the afternoon for the daily fox hunt). There is boating in the summer and cross-country skiing in

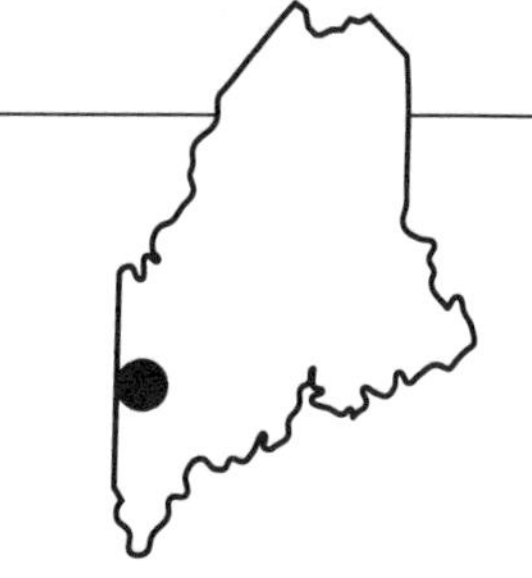

Westways Country Inn
Route 5
Center Lovell, 04016
207-928-2663

AE, MC, V
Closed November and April
$145–$175; incl. dinner, $165–$195

The bedrooms are just as they were in the twenties, with vintage bath fixtures and Fairburn's obvious penchant for European decor.

the winter, making Westways a completely self-contained vacation in any season.

The bedrooms are just as they were in the twenties, with vintage bath fixtures and Fairburn's obvious penchant for European decor. He imported Italian craftsmen to create the reproduction furniture in the master suite and living room. It's somewhat surprising to see Renaissance-esque heavy wooden furniture in such a rustic lake-front lodge. Fairburn's bedroom has a handsome display of wood paneling, Italian furniture, a wonderful old bathroom, and a spectacular view of the lake. The West Room is stocked with maple furniture, and the Blue Room is beautiful and spacious, with lovely antiques and a custom-made carpet. The servants' quarters are bright, cheery, and comfortable.

Downstairs in the living room is an astonishing collection of late-eighteenth-century original Japanese woodcuts, a nice balance to the abundance of European reproduction prints scattered throughout the rest of the lodge. Guests relax in the living room before the massive fieldstone hearth and can enjoy four-course dinners in the comfortable dining rooms or on the porch overlooking the lake. A country breakfast is served each morning in the same rooms. Offerings include special omelets such as sautéed apple and cinnamon, spinach-mushroom-cheese, and smoked trout with Brie. Cheerful manager Nancy Trip is alway on hand to help guests plan their busy day and to greet them when they return to the lodge ready for another serene, silent night in this extraordinary retreat.

Directions: From I-95 north in Maine, take exit 8 in Portland to Route 302 west to Bridgton. Continue past the Moose Pond Causeway. Just before the entrance to Pleasant Mountain Ski Area, turn right onto Knights Hill Road, toward Lovell. Turn right onto Route 5 north. Continue through the village of Lovell to the stone gate entrance to the inn, 7 miles along on the left. From I-95 in New Hampshire, take the Spaulding Turnpike to Route 16 north. Turn onto Route 302 east, then onto Route 5 north in Fryeburg. The inn is 16 miles north of Fryeburg.

Pilgrim's Inn • *Deer Isle*

IF YOU WERE TO award a prize to the innkeepers with the most unrelated past careers (they've all had some sort of past life), Dud and Jean Hendrick would surely win. He, the former lacrosse coach at Dartmouth, and she, a former guidance counselor at a prep school in Maryland, met when Dud was on the road recruiting high-school athletes. As things do, one led to another, and they married soon after. The romance continues today, and Pilgrim's Inn is the realization of their dream to spend as much time together as possible.

THE INN'S SIMPLE BEAUTY BLENDS PERFECTLY WITH ITS STUNNING LOCATION, FACING NORTHWEST HARBOR.

You and your traveling companion will share that dream when you visit this subtle inn. Its appearance is deceptively simple: spare decor, bare floors, restrained Colonial architecture (the inn was built in 1793), and understated detailing. The location itself is stunning, with a millpond at the back of the house and Northwest Harbor in the front. There's nothing more seductive than watching the relection of the front-yard trees shimmering in the afternoon sunlight.

The unpretentious rooms are decorated with Laura Ashley linens, yet the overall feeling is decidedly Colonial. Beautiful antiques, beam ceilings (on the third floor, the beams show up in the middle of two rooms, an architectural detail some guests find irresistible), hooked and braided rugs, and authentic colors all contribute to the strikingly simple effect. The inn also serves as a gallery for many local artists. Each room has contemporary prints or photography, color-coordinated with the decor. Much of the work is available for sale, so the collection is constantly changing. There is also an everchanging exhibition of artwork in the upstairs parlor-cum-gallery.

The height of luxury is to book yourself into Pilgrim's Inn for the summer season of **Haystack Mountain School of Crafts** (P.O. Box 87B, Deer Isle, 04627, 207-348-6946). This famous crafts school has a stunning location on the water and offers courses in everything from papermaking and ceramics to weaving and glass blowing. It's worth a visit even if you don't enroll, although you may find yourself inspired to become a weaver or potter after you've toured this extraordinary facility.

The heart of the Hendricks' home is downstairs. The comfortable sitting room is a popular gathering spot for guests, and the pulse point of the inn is Jean's kitchen. When you visit here, you're in for a complete experience: tranquil lodging and fabulous

Pilgrim's Inn
Main Street
Deer Isle, 04627
207-348-6615

Cash or personal check only
Closed third week in October to third week in May
Private bath (incl. dinner), $150; shared bath (incl. dinner), $130

PILGRIM'S INN'S DECOR INCLUDES NUMEROUS CONTEMPORARY FEATURES, BUT THE OVERALL FEELING REMAINS COLONIAL.

cuisine, perfect for an inn in such an isolated location. You'll join other guests before dinner to taste healthful starters such as vegetables with pesto dip, mussels marinara, smoked salmon spread, and the inn's famous homemade pretzels. Dinner, served in the handsome barn-sided dining room with its raffia rug, fresh flowers, and handthrown ceramics, is a hearty affair offering anything from pork stuffed with apples and prunes, paella, pasta with roasted peppers and scallops, to salmon with lime beurre blanc. All ingredients are fresh, and the vegetables come from the Stanley Joseph garden farm on Cape Rosier.

You'll be treated to one of Jean's many breakfast menus, which include French toast stuffed with apricots, apples, and Triple Sec; scones; eggs; cherry cobbler; sour cream coffee cake; cranberry-nut muffins; blueberry pancakes; and the inn's staple, homemade granola with fruited yogurt. This sort of early-morning fueling up might encourage you borrow to one of the inn's bikes and race around the island to work off those great-tasting calories. Lunch is not on the docket at the inn, but you can stop off at **Fisherman's Friend** (Route 15, Stonington, 207-367-2442) for a light bite and some of the best cream pies you'll ever taste. Tennis, golf, sailing, and water sports also are available. Or you might choose to relax on the inn's sprawling lawn, admiring the gorgeous landscape, passing the afternoon with the athletic Hendricks and their springer spaniel, Mr. BeauDandy. Pilgrim's Inn is a superb place to stay and worth every dollar of its tariff.

Directions: From I-95, take exit 15 in Augusta. Follow Route 3 east to Bucksport, then take Route 15 south through Blue Hill. Continue south over the Deer Isle Bridge and into the village of Deer Isle. Turn right onto Main Street. The inn is on the left.

AFTER YOUR NEXT SHOPPING TRIP TO L.L. BEAN, CHECK IN TO FREEPORT'S ISAAC RANDALL HOUSE.

Isaac Randall House • *Freeport*

WHEN YOU'RE SCHEDULING your next foray to L.L. Bean to stock up on the season's latest essential gear and outerwear, plan to spend the night at Issac Randall House. The sweet feminine look to this welcoming inn is a nice contrast to Freeport's burgeoning commercialism. Glynrose and Jim Friedlander run the inn, housed in an 1832 farmhouse. The soul of their home is the bustling kitchen (originally the house's summer kitchen), where guests share a long trestle table amidst the Friedlanders' copper pot collection, which hangs from nineteenth-century beams.

Jim's breakfasts are reason enough to congregate here. They feature his excellent French toast, blueberry pancakes, fruit breads, homemade granola, and renowned Amaretto coffee. Glynrose and Jim (formerly an urban planner) create a comfortable environment that keeps loyal guests returning as often as possible.

The nine bedrooms are on the romantic side, with plenty of floral designs, canopy beds, lace, ribbons, pastels, painted cottage furniture, pretty quilts, wreaths, and tender touches. Many of the rooms overlook the inn's six acres, which provide tranquil, bucolic panorama. The new loft room offers cable television and a telephone perfect for business travelers. Pets are allowed to stay with their families in two of the rooms, and children are welcome throughout the inn.

Once you've discovered this inn, you'll have one more reason to become a loyal customer of Laura Ashley, Ralph Lauren, Benetton, Anne Klein, and the host of other fashion and home stores that have helped L.L. Bean put Freeport on the map.

Directions: From I-95 north, take exit 19 (Freeport) to Route 1 north. Continue 1 mile to the light. Turn left onto Independence Drive. The inn is 1/3 mile along on the left.

Issac Randall House
Independence Drive (off Route 1)
Freeport, 04032
207-865-9295

Cash or personal check only
Open year-round
Off-season, \$45–\$85;
in season, \$65–\$100

Fryeburg • **Oxford House Inn**

OXFORD HOUSE INN IS A PERFECT PLACE TO STAY IN THE NORTH CONWAY, NEW HAMPSHIRE, AREA.

WHAT EVERY COMPULSIVE bargain hunter needs after an exhaustive day of weeding through the racks of North Conway, New Hampshire's, bevy of discount stores is a good meal, a pleasant place to sleep, and friendly company. If this situation sounds even remotely tempting, drive east across the Maine border to spend the night at Oxford House Inn, a lovely 1913 home with a superb restaurant. Run by Phyllis and John Morris, young innkeepers who found happiness managing their own place after an extended stay running the Scottish Lion in North Conway, the inn reflects an easygoing professionalism.

What is so refreshing and oftentimes surprising here is the fabulous food. John, a self-taught chef, is a master in the kitchen, and you will find the meals served in the three handsome dining rooms among the better available to travelers. His specialties are poached salmon with pommery mustard sauce, fresh scallops in puff pastry, and a hearty grilled pork tenderloin with black currant sauce. A four-course dinner starts with homemade crackers and moves on to a fresh salad with wonderful homemade dressings. Next comes the entrée served with homemade breads, and finally come the sinfully delicious desserts. If you dine on the enclosed back porch, you'll enjoy watching the sun set behind the White Mountains. The new Granite Lounge offers guests a friendly place to relax for after-dinner drinks watching any of the Inn's many videotapes.

When you're ready to march upstairs to end the day, each of the five rooms offers a distinct personality and singular brand of comfort. The master suite is quite large and attractively furnished in Victorian antiques. One room has nostalgic rose-print walls, the sleeping porch is simple and straightforward, and the sewing room is pleasing. There is also a plaid-theme country room.

Breakfast is another John Morris masterpiece: scones, blueberry buttermilk pancakes, and French toast stuffed with cream cheese and homemade marmalade are just a few of his specialties.

The Oxford House is a charming inn, the prices are reasonable, and it's a perfect place to stay while visiting the North Conway area.

Directions: From I-95 north in New Hampshire, take the Spaulding Turnpike north to Route 16. Follow Route 16 north into Conway. Continue on Route 113 east, then onto Route 302 east. The inn is on the left, 1 mile after the Maine state line. From I-93 south, take Route 112 east to Conway. Follow above directions.

Oxford House Inn
105 Main Street (Route 302)
Fryeburg, 04037
207-935-3442

All major credit cards
Open year-round
Private bath, $85; shared bath, $65

Hull's Cove • Inn at Canoe Point

SET ON A ROCKY SHORELINE, INN AT CANOE POINT IS A WONDERFUL HIDEAWAY.

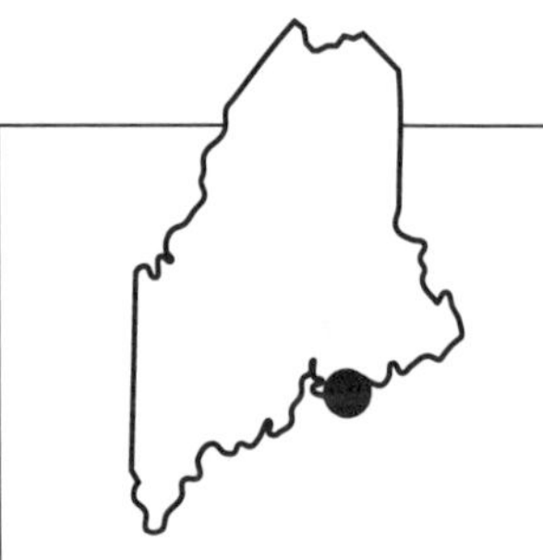

Inn at Canoe Point
Route 3
Hull's Cove, 04644
207-288-9511

Cash or personal check only
Open year-round
$60–$180

IT'S SO REFRESHING to find a bed and breakfast inn with contemporary decor, uncluttered design, and modern style. This is not to say that Inn at Canoe Point is starkly modern, but it is the stuff that many amateur decorators aspire to. Owner Don Johnson is just such an amateur decorator, and his inn reflects a measured approach to decor and a welcome relief from all those lace-laden country inns. Canoe Point's site adds to the attractiveness of this inn. Perched on a rocky beach and overlooking Frenchman's Bay, the location is truly sensational. Breakfast during the summer is served on the deck—you literally float over the waves above the inn's shoreline.

Each of the six bedrooms is uniquely decorated. Among the most tempting is the Master Suite, with its own fireplace, deck, and clean-line design. The Garden Room is a great getaway room with loads of windows overlooking the bay, serene in pale beige, its bed virtually a piece of architecture and with its own private entrance and fireplace. Anchor Room has its expected wall-covering motif plus its own deck and bridge to the side hill. The Garret Suite on the third floor is a private apartment for traveling friends or families. All of the bedrooms have wonderful comforters and designer sheets.

The downstairs sitting room is cheery especially in

winter when there is a blazing fire in the enormous granite fireplace. During cold weather, breakfast is served here with fresh fruit, blueberry pancakes, French toast, cheddar quiche, or homemade breads, on a given morning.

As you leave this minature Tudoresque cottage, the impressive fieldstone fireplace in the foyer will remind you of a time when the original owners of this 1889 house lived in a somewhat more formal atmosphere.

Perched on a rocky beach and overlooking Frenchman's Bay, the location is truly sensational.

Directions: From I-95 north, take exit 15 in Augusta to Route 3 east. From Ellsworth, take Route 3 approximately 15 miles toward Bar Harbor. Just beyond the village of Hull's Cove, turn left at the inn sign (Acadia National Park entrance is on right). Follow drive to inn.

Kennebunkport • Captain Jefferds Inn

If you're seduced by the look of the place, you can take some of it home from the small shop run out of the garage.

IF YOU HAVE A longing for majolica, twig and root furniture, primitives, early American furnishings, and wicker—and you appreciate being surrounded by a priceless collection of such—Captain Jefferds Inn is your bed and breakfast fantasy. As soon as you enter this astonishing house, you'll be assaulted by Warren Fitzsimmon's expansive collection of majolica; it is crammed into every cupboard and on every available shelf. Even a jaded majolica fan will have reason to pause. It would take inn guests an entire season to see it all. And when the ceramics have been exhausted, it's time to tour the rest of Warren's many collections of superb furniture and objects.

It can safely be said that Warren does not live in a vacuum. This dense inn is a feast for the eyes. Yet the collections are not so intrusive as to give guests claustrophobia. In fact, there is plenty of space for visitors to spread out.

The handsome yellow living room has comfortable, flower-splashed seating; the solarium is stocked with a striking collection of deco wicker; the back porch is cool and breezy; and the dining room is serene in gray-blue with an unusual landscape-painted mirror over the mantel. Each piece of furniture, each lamp, each painting, and each detail is calculated to please, a tribute to the decorating prowess of Warren, who retired from his Southampton, Long Island, antique business to run the Captain Jefferds.

The twelve bedrooms in the main house are just as well-stocked as the other rooms in the house. Everything from painted cottage furniture to antique wicker to American country and root furniture can be found. A visit here is a continual visual surprise. Beautiful antique linens cover the beds, and the colors are peaceful and flattering. One room on the third floor even has an antique copper shower in the middle of the bedroom. The downstairs two-bedroom suite is a wonderful haven, especially if you love country and early American decor. Dollhouses, American art, pottery lamps, hobo art, weather vanes, and assorted other folk art treasures give the suite a distinct personality. If you're seduced by the look of the place, you can take some of it home from the small shop run out of the garage. And if you want to stay at the inn for an extended run, the carriage house has three apartments.

As if the surroundings were not enough, Warren presents a breakfast feast of eggs Benedict, blueberry

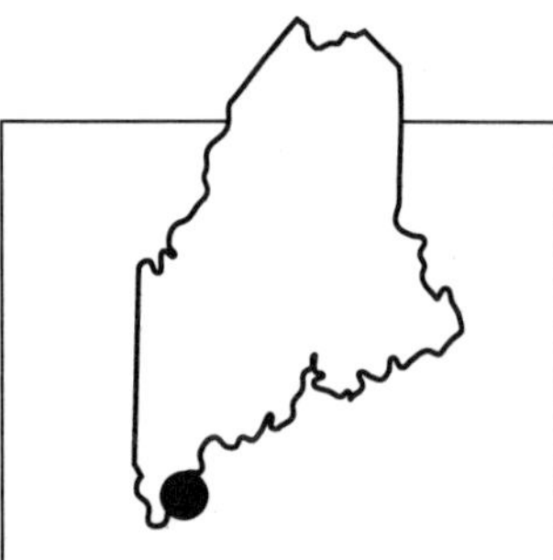

Captain Jefferds Inn
Pearl Street
Kennebunkport, 04046
207-967-2311

Cash or personal check only
Closed November and January–March
$75–$110

THE CAPTAIN JEFFERDS INN IS "A FEAST FOR THE EYES."

crêpes, New England flannel (hash and poached eggs), French toast with Grand Marnier and fresh fruit, and frittatas. There's no danger of not being sated at the Captain Jefferds. Your host is charming and entertaining, the environment is unique, and the location is perfect for quick visits to town or a drive to see the nearby summer cottages of the rich and famous, including George Bush's carefully guarded compound.

Directions: From I-95, take exit 3 to Route 35 south. Follow signs to Kennebunkport (about 6 miles). Turn left at the traffic light and continue on Route 9 east over the bridge to the monument on the square. Turn right onto Ocean Drive. Continue 4 blocks, then turn left onto Pearl Street just past the Arundel Wharf restaurent. The inn is on the next corner.

Kennebunkport • Captain Lord Mansion

IF YOU'VE BEEN HAVING a tough week — business deals are not taking place on schedule, the kids are getting to you, the hot weather has you out of sorts, or you just need to get out of the house — come to Captain Lord Mansion. Here you'll be treated like the king or queen you know, deep inside your heart, you are.

This elegant structure, built in 1812, was home to the Lord family until 1972 and continues to retain its upper-crust look and feel (after being reclaimed from is former service as a boarding house). The mansion was built on a scale to impress Captain Lord's community; the ceilings are high, the rooms are large, and the exterior is notice-me yellow. Bev Davis and husband Rick Litchfield created this inn to fulfill their dream of becoming their own bosses after corporate careers in fast-food marketing. As a result of their backgrounds, they are masters at making sure the inn is run smoothly and professionally.

Rick has prepared a fascinating account of the history of the house and of the Lord family, and there's plenty of that history to look at while you're visiting. Portraits of generations of Lords are sprinkled throughout the inn. Among these are wonderful period pieces of Julia Fuller (great-great-great-granddaughter of Nathaniel Lord, the original "captain") and her handsome husband, Harrison, both of whom look like they just stepped out of an F. Scott Fitzgerald novel.

Each of the sixteen bedrooms is named after one of the Lord family's ships. They are extraordinary rooms, and it will take many visits to determine which is your favorite. As Bev and Rick are wont to say, "We're in the business of selling sleep," and

THE CAPTAIN LORD MANSION WAS BUILT ON A SCALE TO IMPRESS — AND IT DOES.

you'll find a stunning collection of comfortable beds available to you. All the furnishings are oversize, a necessary accommodation for such a large-scale house. The wallpaper is beautiful, the details perfect, and the painted wood-grain doors a collector's dream. The window glass is handblown, and the original Indian shutters are still in place. Each bedroom has its own bath. The ocean breezes of Kennebunkport keep the house cool in the summer, and fireplaces in nearly all the bedrooms keep things cheery during the winter months. Bev also runs a little shop stocked with books, holiday ornaments, antique decorative treasures, handmade clothes, jams, glassware, doorstops, maps, and ceramics.

Breakfast—a ceremony of sorts—is conducted in two seatings. Guests are summoned to the kitchen by Oriental chimes, played with a flourish by the gregarious Rick. Everyone is seated Walton-family-style at two long tables and served homemade muffins, breads, and Rick's famous soft-boiled egg. They are perfectly cooked and presented in eggcups, a novelty for some guests who receive instant lessons in the fine art of eating a soft-boiled egg in public. There's a supply of eggcups, egg cutters, and related paraphernalia available in the shop for those who want to share the experience when they get back home.

Bev and Rick have another more intimate inn, Captain's Hideaway. This secluded cottage has two luxurious rooms with fireplaces and Jacuzzi baths. A gourmet breakfast is served by candlelight, to keep the romantic look intact in the morning.

Captain Lord Mansion is within an easy walk of the town's many restaurants and shops. Its widow's walk offers a fabulous view of the surrounding area. The yard is a peaceful place to relax (iced tea is always on tap for guests during the summer), the rooms are absolutely beautiful, and the ambiance is pure quality. After you've visited, you'll receive an annual New Year's letter from Bev and Rick, bringing you up-to-date on the inn's doings, the couple's two young daughters, and what's happening in Kennebunkport — and inviting you to experience the inn during the serene winter months. If you're smart, you'll sign up right away.

Directions: From the I-95, take exit 3. Follow 35 south. Follow signs to Kennebunkport (about 6 miles). Turn left at the traffic light and continue on Route 9 east over the bridge to the monument on the square. Turn right onto Ocean Drive. Take the fifth left, onto Green Street. The inn's parking lot is 2 blocks along on the left.

IN A HOUSE THIS LARGE, IT'S NO SURPRISE THAT ALL THE FURNISHINGS ARE OVERSIZE.

Captain Lord Mansion
Ocean Avenue
Kennebunkport, 04046
207-967-3141

MC, V, D
Open year-round
Off-season, $65–$155; in season, $115–$175

Kennebunkport • Welby Inn

WELBY INN OFFERS TRAVELERS A HIGHLY PERSONAL AND INTIMATE LODGING EXPERIENCE.

KENNEBUNKPORT HAS MORE than its share of mansions, elegant homes, sea captain's inns, and vacation complexes. But when you're in the mood for something quaint, highly personal, and a little more intimate — something along the lines of a gambrel-roof cottage — come to Welby Inn. This unpretentious establishment is run by a most appealing couple, Betsy and David Knox.

Both Betsy and David are sincere, lovely people who are keenly interested in their guests. Betsy is a botanical illustrator; her paintings and note cards are available for sale at the inn. Her passion for flowers is evident in the flower portraits in each of the bedrooms and in the lovely floral arrangements throughout the house and the gardens.

The seven bedrooms (all with private baths) are cheerful and light. There's an easy feeling to the place that reflects David and Betsy's approach to innkeeping. Guests can relax in the pleasant yard in summer or before the fireplace in the charming Victorian living room in winter. Breakfast is served in the large wood-paneled dining room or on the enclosed side porch, overlooking the gardens. The Knoxes prepare delicious breakfasts of homemade specialties, usually enhanced with floral garnishes (such as nasturtiums, petunias, and impatiens). On a given morning you can expect to enjoy baked stuffed French toast with blueberry sauce; cinnamon-batter puffs with lemon bread; popovers stuffed with herb-cheese scrambled eggs; blueberry coffee cake; and fresh fruit.

A visit to Welby Inn is a gentle experience, one that loyal guests enjoy repeating. You will, too.

Directions: From I-95, take exit 3. Follow Route 35 south and signs to Kennebunkport (about 6 miles). Turn left at the traffic light and continue on Route 9 east, over the drawbridge into Kennebunkport. At the monument on the square, turn right onto Ocean Avenue. The inn is ½ mile along on the left.

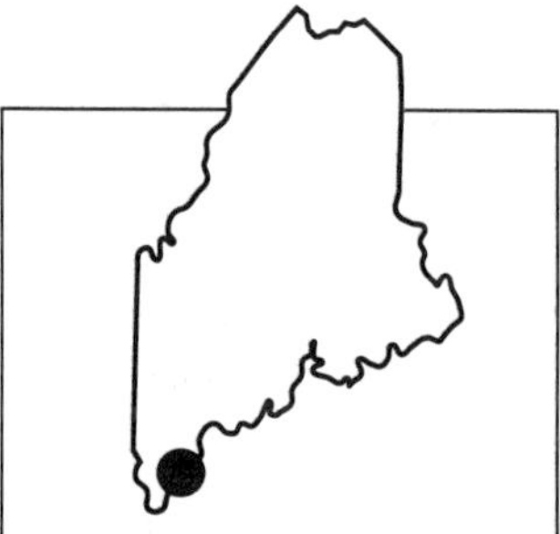

Welby Inn
Ocean Avenue
Kennebunkport, 04046
207-967-4655

AE
Open year-round
$68–$88

Grey Rock Inn • *Northeast Harbor*

ONCE YOU BECOME A regular here, you, too, will no doubt plead with owner Janet Millett to sell you the Tree House cottage on her property so that you can become a permanent resident of Grey Rock Inn. It's tempting, because this is one of the most attractive inns in New England, a beautiful aerie perched on a ledge overlooking Northeast Harbor.

Janet gradually opened her home as an inn as her six children grew up and left the nest. Each of the inn's nine rooms has been decorated with her highly personal touch, and every detail is perfect. You won't be disappointed by the beautiful pink-and-green-floral upstairs room, with its canopy tall-post beds and its sensational view. Or by the room with dogwood wall covering, an iron-and-brass bed, and a country bathroom. Or by the smaller bedroom, with its unique wallpaper (butterflies floating in a silver field), matching silver candles, and lace-linen runners on the handsome furniture.

No matter what size the room, the inn is filled with romance and a femininity that will melt the heart of the most resolute man's man. The highlight is the downstairs suite. It is as though you've entered another era when you pass through its double doors. A canopy bed, a large Japanese screen, some extraordinary carved furniture, a handsome fireplace, and the room's immense size make this a must-see, must-have.

In the living room wicker and English furnishings join forces with Victorian lace to create a tranquil mood. The view is superb, and admiring it is the perfect way to end the day. It's also just right to wake up to. Janet serves breakfast here at beautifully set tables. Guest enjoy fresh fruit, cheese-and-blueberry Danish, honey buns, blueberry turnovers, pecan buns, and croissants, all baked in the Millett kitchen.

Grey Rock is on the edge of Acadia National Park. Janet's sons Adam and Karl are happy to direct guests to the many activities this recreational treasure has to offer. Guests seeking a more serene experience can relax at the inn under Janet's care and the spell of Grey Rock's storybook charm.

Directions: From I-95, take the Bangor exit to Route 1A east, then take Route 3 south. Follow Route 198 past the 25-mph sign. The inn is on the right, but continue past the entrance and turn around to approach from the south.

THE ATTRACTIVE GREY ROCK INN IS LOCATED ON THE EDGE OF ACADIA NATIONAL PARK.

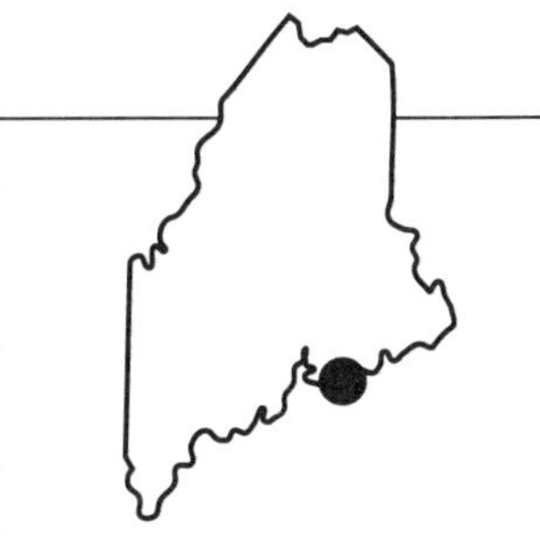

Grey Rock Inn
Route 198
Northeast Harbor, 04662
207-276-9360 (summer); 207-276-5526 (winter)

Cash or personal check only
Closed November to May
$110–$145

Portland • Inn at ParkSpring

PARKSPRING OFFERS A FABULOUS LOCATION FOR PORTLAND'S CULTURAL ACTIVITIES.

PORTLAND HAS UNDERGONE a restoration renaissance at the waterfront, and the Old Port Exchange gives one all the more reason to visit this historic town. The Inn at ParkSpring is located within walking distance of the waterfront, and it is near the Portland Museum of Art and Performing Arts Center.

Once you enter the front door, you are part of history in townhouse living, circa 1880. The seven rooms are quiet, calming, and demonstrate creative use of limited space—especially in the private baths. Some of the rooms are pastel, some Victorian, some a mix, and all are pleasant and comfortable. The downstairs rooms, converted from parlors, have beautiful marble fireplaces and tall-post beds. The Museum Room is especially pretty in apricot and green. The Murphy Room in the rear has the predictable pull-down bed topped with a surprising paisley-fabric fantasy tent. The pull-out sofa accommodates the balance of a traveling family.

The living room is handsome, filled with magazines and music. Breakfast is served in the kitchen, with cereals, fresh fruit, and homemade breads and pastries. Owners Judi and Bob Riley are generally in and around the inn. They have a staff of professional young women who manage the inn and give you a sincere welcome and thorough orientation to all that Portland has to offer. Take their advice and dine at **Alberta's Cafe** (21 Pleasant Street, 207-774-0016), a short walk away. This popular place has terrific food that is as innovative and delicious as it gets, all served in a very casual, yet energetic environment.

Directions: From the south, take I-95 and then I-295 north to exit 6A (Forest Avenue south). Bear right and turn right at traffic light on Route 77 south. Continue through Deering Oaks Park. Stay in left lane, turn left at third light onto Congress Street. Continue 1 block, turn right onto Park Street. Continue 1 block to intersection of Park and Spring streets. Park on Park Street.

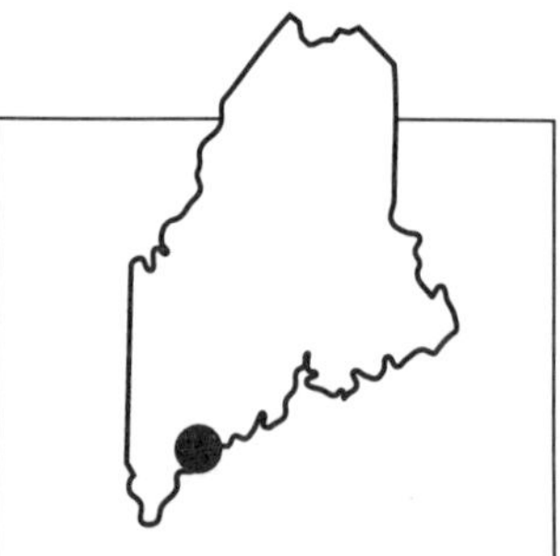

Inn at ParkSpring
135 Spring Street
Portland, 04101
207-774-1059

AE, MC, V
Open year-round
$60–$90

Squire Tarbox Inn • *Wiscasset*

IF YOU CAN'T TRAVEL to the French countryside for your vacation, do the next best thing and visit Squire Tarbox Inn, a Yankee variation on a Burgundy country inn, complete with a goat farm. This charming 1825 inn has a very Colonial 1763 barn converted to simple sleeping rooms with exposed beam ceilings that are among the more popular quarters at the inn. The former pigsty has a cathedral ceiling and is especially in demand. The entire inn offers a delightfully different country experience.

Whatever your inn expectations, the Squire Tarbox — located nearly at the end of one of Maine's coastal fingers — is a delight. Owners Karen and Bill Mitman come with impressive credentials; formerly with the Copley Plaza in Boston, they've traded in their corporate passkeys for the freedom and adventure of this engaging inn.

The Mitmans have intentionally kept life at the inn country-simple, which makes an experience here all the more authentic.

One of the best things about this remarkable place is Karen's family of prize-winning goats. She makes her own goat's cheese, which is generally found on the dinner menu and served to guests with drinks before dinner. She also packages the delicious cheese and ships it off to guests for their holiday gift orders. The goats are so popular among visitors that it's not unusual to find women in their dinner dresses and men in coat and tie in the barn helping Karen with the 9:15 P.M. milking. The affectionate goats, with their floppy ears and innocent eyes, are irresistible.

The inn itself is situated on a saltmarsh, and a deck overlooks the peaceful woodlands. The dining room has a Colonial charm, with the original cooking hearth serving as the centerpiece, especially on colder evenings. A fabulous dinner is served here, all the more reason to make the Squire Tarbox your destination for an extended stay. The buffet breakfast is just as delicious with a variety of homebaked breads and coffee cakes.

The rooms in the main house are country-simple, with tiny floral prints, fresh flowers, antique beds, uncomplicated furnishings, fireplaces, and private baths. The Mitmans have intentionally kept life at the inn country-simple, which makes an experience here all the more authentic. There is a cozy sitting room in the main house and a more casual gathering room in the barn, complete with player piano to break the ice among strangers. Lots of bird watchers visit here, and the local feathered community provides ample diversion. There is also plenty to do in the area: the Maine

Squire Tarbox Inn
Route 144
Wiscasset, 04578
207-882-7693

AE, D, MC, V
Closed November to mid-May
$65–$125; incl. dinner, $110–$170

Maritime Museum, crafts and antique shops, harbors and beaches, as well as the Mitmans' "samplers" noting good diversions for rainy days.

A VISIT TO SQUIRE TARBOX INN IS THE NEXT BEST THING TO A VACATION IN THE FRENCH COUNTRYSIDE.

Directions: Follow I-95 to Brunswick. From Brunswick, take Route 1 north through Bath. Turn right onto Route 144. The inn is 8½ miles along on the right.

New Hampshire

Rustic Renditions

New Hampshire has more bed and breakfast inns than any other state in New England. There are a zillion of these places, and the inns in this chapter are culled from New Hampshire's collection of rustic and not-so-rustic places. Each region in the state is represented, from White Mountain farmhouses to Lakes Region summer homes to Monadnock Region country houses. The inns in New Hampshire tend to be on the modest side, and therefore they usually are very affordable. These are authentic, simple, and rustic places, owned, for the most part, by innkeepers from New Jersey and California! There is a lot of driving involved in visiting these places. Sampling them all will keep you busy for months.

VARIETY AND AFFORDABILITY CHARACTERIZE NEW HAMPSHIRE'S BED AND BREAKFAST ESTABLISHMENTS. ABOVE: CHASE HOUSE, REVIEWED ON PAGE 47.

Center Sandwich • Corner House Inn

THIS INN IS LOCATED ON THE QUIET END OF SQUAM LAKE IN A TOWN FILLED WITH CRAFTS SHOPS.

THE NEXT TIME YOU'RE in Center Sandwich admiring (or most probably purchasing) local crafts (this little town is a celebration of goldsmiths, weavers, ceramicists, quilters, silversmiths, painters, and metalworkers), be sure you've booked ahead to spend the night at Corner House Inn. This lovely 1849 house is centrally located at the crossroads in town, perfect for window-shoppers who enjoy an evening stroll to get a head start on the next day's shopping. Although the inn is best known as a restaurant, there are four pretty rooms upstairs that offer a haven on the quiet end of Squam Lake (which gained overnight recognition as Golden Pond in the popular film).

This wonderful house is filled with local crafts, a decorative salute to Center Sandwich artisans. The rooms are stocked with antiques, and innkeeper Jane Kroeger's light decorating touch is in evidence in rooms that are country-simple and uncluttered. She and her husband, Don Brown, are on hand to greet and take care of you.

Breakfast is served in one of the four dining rooms, within the surroundings of a barnyard crafts decor, and you can depend on a hearty country offering of yogurt and fruit with omelets or pancakes to fuel you up for strolling about the October country fair, touring the lake, visiting local shops (the League of New Hampshire Craftsmen was founded here), and enjoying the quiet off-season in this happy town. You'll enjoy the Corner House for its sweet innocence, Don and Jane's friendly welcome, and the convenient location.

Directions: From I-93 north, take exit 23 onto Route 104 east. In Meredith turn right at the traffic light onto Route 25 north. In Moultonboro, turn left onto Route 109 north. The inn is at the junction of Routes 109 and 113. From I-93 south, take exit 24 onto Route 3 south. In Holderness turn left onto Route 113 north.

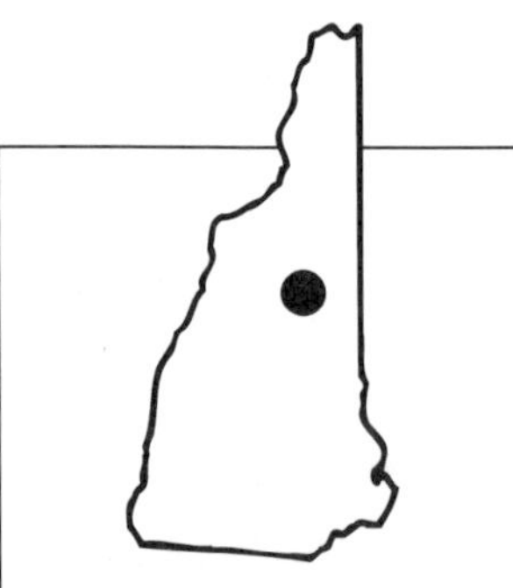

Corner House Inn
Routes 113 and 109
Center Sandwich, 03227
603-284-6219

AE, MC, V
Open year-round
Private bath, $70; shared bath, $60

Chase House • *Cornish*

PETER BURLING IS SOMETHING of a local legend. He rehabilitated Cornish's Trinity Church, reclaimed Chase House, is active in politics, and is committed to the little town of Cornish. Chase House is his contribution to preserving a piece of the past: he sponsored its restoration and continues to protect its history. This handsome 1770 house was the boyhood home of Salmon Portland Chase, who served in President Lincoln's cabinet and who was a Supreme Court Chief Justice. He helped to found the Republican party and is the Chase in the Chase Manhattan Bank. You'll no doubt recognize him on the next $10,000 bill you use. All of this rich past started in this simple, unprepossessing Colonial house.

Today, the six-room inn is run by Marilyn and Hal Wallace, resident innkeepers. It has been decorated to retain the look and feel of its era. The result is that Chase House is one of the more attractive Colonial inns in New England. Historic colors, wide-plank floors, tall-post beds, lace canopies, period-authentic Oriental bird-print wallpapers, and antique furnishings make Chase House a voyage to the past.

Breakfast is served in the snug dining room with

CHASE HOUSE IS A TRUE CLASSIC — INSIDE AND OUT.

AUTHENTICITY IN DECOR ADDS TO CHASE HOUSE'S CHARM.

fresh fruit compote, eggs any style, blueberry pancakes, French toast, homemade breads, and cereals to refuel you.

Seasonal activities include cross-country skiing, hiking, visiting Peter's other restoration projects in the village, and exploring the Connecticut River across the road, all of which will keep you busy during the day. Visit Chase House for a restful interlude and for an appreciation of the value of preserving the past in order to give travelers a glimpse of Colonial life.

Directions: New York, take I-91 north to exit 8. Take Route 131 east across the Connecticut River to Route 12A north. Inn is 4 miles on right. From Boston, take I-93 north to I-89 to exit 20. Take Route 12A south 17 miles. Inn is on left.

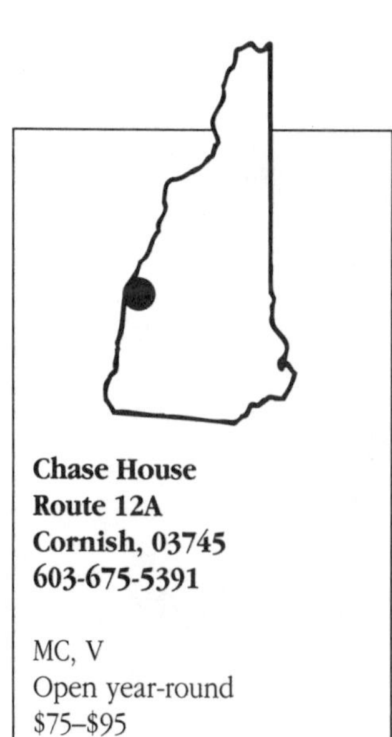

Chase House
Route 12A
Cornish, 03745
603-675-5391

MC, V
Open year-round
$75–$95

Moose Mountain Lodge • *Etna*

MOOSE MOUNTAIN LODGE is better than Heidi could have imagined, even in her wildest dreams. This mountaintop idyll is a haven for everyone who visits, no matter what the season. In winter you can ski right out the back door. In summer you can hike in the surrounding forest. And in fall the festival of colors leaves you breathless. Whenever you visit Moose Mountain, the fifty-mile panoramic view, with a focus on Mount Killington and Sugarbush, is spectacular. The front porch might become your weekend headquarters, as you immerse yourself in the stunning location and the serenity it offers.

This mountaintop idyll is a haven for everyone who visits, no matter what the season.

The surroundings are equaled by the friendliness of Peter and Kay Shumway. This handsome, athletic couple loves to introduce guests to the unique joys of Moose Mountain—so much so that they run a shuttle up the winding road leading to the inn in the winter. Unless you have four-wheel drive, the ascent is sometimes impossible.

Once you've reached this rustic, twelve-room log cabin inn, you'll find plenty of reasons not to leave. There is a ski shop on site to outfit cross-country skiers, and the Shumways' ski guide is only too happy to lead you on a day-long adventure through their back woods. Your children can also receive their first cross-country ski lessons here, making the lodge experience even more memorable. Kay's robust cooking also will help you stay healthy and fit; bountiful dinner buffets (for guests only) and delicious breakfasts are designed for active people who tend to fuel up on high-carbohydrate meals. The food here is so popular, Kay has published her own cookbook which is a favorite among guests. For the more contemplative, there's always the view to enjoy and the chance to develop friendships with the Shumway's pet goat, Kirby, and their happy weimaraner, Ulla.

The lodge is truly an exceptional inn. Its log cabin charm (the inn was constructed from local timber) has been keeping guests returning since 1938. Everyone is seduced by the enormous stone fireplaces, the handmade log furniture (the massive tree beds are beautiful), the cozy living room, the dining room that comfortably seats at least twenty at one elongated table, the bedrooms with their gorgeous views, and the moose-head trophies eyeing everyone from their stairwell command posts.

The rooms are decorated in blues, soft roses, and

Moose Mountain Lodge
Moose Mountain Highway
Etna, 03750
603-643-3529

MC, V
Closed April and May, November through December 26
Incl. dinner, $160–$170

AFTER YOU'VE HUNG UP YOUR SKIS, YOU CAN COME INSIDE TO THE RUSTIC CHARM OF MOOSE MOUNTAIN LODGE.

Its log-cabin charm (the inn was constructed from local timber) has been keeping guests returning since 1938.

mauves, and the wood paneling gives off a warm glow. Everyone shares three bathrooms (there are also two streamlined Scandinavian baths downstairs), and a comfortable camaraderie develops among each group of guests. The relaxed atmosphere, the hearty decor, and the Shumways themselves will lure you into visiting Moose Mountain as often as you can. Kay is an inspiring knitter, and you may find yourself under her spell attempting the same ambitious projects that she completes with impressive results. The lodge is also a terrific place for well-behaved children (over five years old) to experience mountain life, run off their perpetual energy in the hundreds of acres surrounding the cabin, and make the hills come alive with their own sounds of music.

Directions: From I-89, take exit 18 to Route 120 north. After ½ mile turn right onto Etna Road (Higbea Motel on the left). Follow Etna Road into Etna Village. One-half mile past the Etna post office, turn right onto Rudsboro Road. Turn left after 2 miles onto Dana Road. After ½ mile, just past the big red barn, turn right up the mountain onto Moose Mountain Highway. Continue 1 mile to the lodge.

Amos A. Parker House • *Fitzwilliam*

FREDA HOUPT COULD have been touring mainland China on bicycle with her daughter. She could have continued to work toward retirement as a successful corporate travel agent. Freda could have taken it easy in Chicago, fulfilling her grandmotherly responsibilities to her four children. Instead, she took a chance and purchased a beautiful eighteenth-century home in Fitzwilliam fifteen minutes after she first saw it, putting herself in the bed and breakfast business, literally overnight. She claims that spontaneity has never been her hallmark, but she seems to be making up for lost time. She has recently been known to buy valuable antiques on the spot. Her lovely home bears witness to this newfound impulsiveness, as it is filled with tasteful treasures. Her carpet collection is stunning, and high-spirited Freda is only too willing to take you on a house tour to view this intriguing Middle Eastern art form room by room. She loves antiques, has learned a lot about them, and will share her enthusiasm and knowledge with anyone who expresses an interest.

Freda has a well-developed sense of humor (they don't call her "Mame" in vain), a world traveler's sophistication (a fringe benefit of travel agency life), and a genuine midwestern warmth. She is bound to laugh you through your visit here. You will sample

THE APPEAL OF FITSWILLIAM'S AMOS A. PARKER HOUSE IS SIMPLE YET IRRESISTIBLE.

THE ORIGINAL 1780S ONE-ROOM FARMHOUSE HAS BEEN MADE INTO A SURPRISINGLY DELIGHTFUL SITTING ROOM.

Freda's fabulous cooking in her elegant dining room on Spode china. You'll want to return here often to sample her breakfast creations, such as French bread stuffed with praline sauce, sweet potato muffins, apple-raisin-nut or apple-cranberry compote, and spinach soufflé with mushroom-Newburg sauce. She puts enthusiasm and appeal into everything she does, and you'll feel perfectly at home keeping up with her good-natured, entertaining conversation.

Amos A. Parker House is a testimony to Freda's good judgment in interior decor. There are plenty of spaces where you can find a private nook in the "What a Great Room," with its vista of the back "forty." The same is true of the outdoor deck, the more formal living room, and the surprise of the house, the original 1780s one-room farmhouse, now a sitting room. Paneled in barn siding, it is a winner, filled with dried flowers, books, comfortable seating, and Freda's collection of needlework supplies. It's hard to leave this haven for any of the nearby sights and activities. Still, Freda will ask about your special interests when you make your reservation and suggest activities available within an hour's drive of Fitzwilliam.

When you return to the house to spend the night, you'll have a difficult time choosing from among the five bedrooms. The front double, with a fireplace and private bath, has a four-poster bed and restful pink-and-green decor. One of the prettiest is the room across the hall (king or twin-bedded) sparkling in fresh blue and white with handsome furnishings, fireplace, and private bath. The back bedroom overlooking the fields has unique, wreathlike stencils designed to match the Laura Ashley linens on the striking double brass bed. The larger double across the hall is serene in ivory and cream. The downstairs

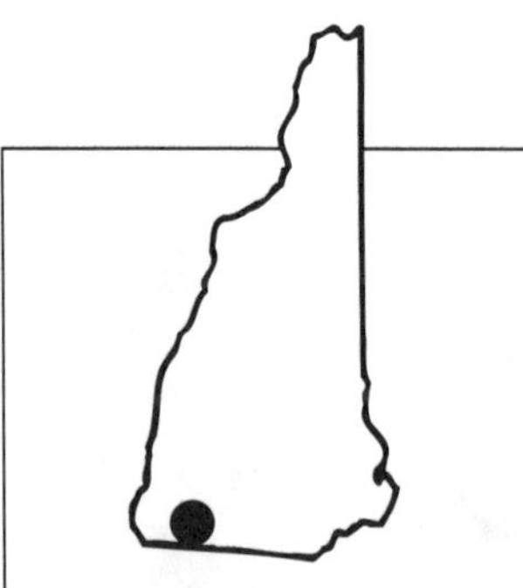

Amos A. Parker House
Route 119
Fitzwilliam, 03447
603-585-6540

Cash or personal check only
Open year-round
$50–$75

suite is a wonderful hideaway; it is spacious and has a working fireplace, a modern bath, a private deck, a kitchen, and its own entrance.

Amos A. Parker House is a wonderful place to visit. As soon as you leave the elegantly landscaped front entrance, you'll be planning your next visit.

Directions: From I-91, take exit 28A at Northfield, Massachusetts. Follow Route 10 north about 10 miles to Route 119 west. Follow Route 119 east about 15 miles to Fitzwilliam. The inn is on the left.

This innkeeper puts enthusiasm and appeal into everything she does, and you'll feel perfectly at home keeping up with her good-natured conversation.

Fitzwilliam • Hannah Davis House

WITH THE ADDITION OF this beautiful inn to its neighbor down the street, the Amos A. Parker House, Fitzwilliam is definitely a destination, not merely a stopping-off place. Kaye and Mike Terpstra have rebuilt their house from the inside out to create a wonderful country inn. It's clear they are not only talented in masonry, but in decorating as well. Kaye explains that she and her husband consider themselves homebodies of sorts: they love to cook, and they love people. They certainly selected the right business—they're naturals at innkeeping.

The five-bedroom inn is a work in progress. Kay will be happy to take you on a tour to show you how the inn has evolved. It's enough to cause inexperienced, but enthusiastic, potential innkeepers to reconsider. This refurbishing project has been a tremendous amount of work, but the results are stunning. The Terpstras have done everything first-class: the bathrooms are luxurious in their country way, the rooms are beautiful, the linens are elegant, and the decorative touches are kept to a minimum.

One of the prettiest bedrooms in New England is Chauncey's Room. Its bold red floral wallpaper is unique and inspirational. Red accents on the bed and in the bath make this room truly special. No less attractive is the Hannah Room. Although more snug, its beautiful blue-tone quilt and embroidered linens contrast with its pink-striped walls. The Canopy Room has a huge bathroom, a luxury for old houses. The bathtub is set at an angle, floating in a sea of floral walls, which gives a decorator's touch to this memorable bathroom. The armoire is a memory from the Terpstras' past careers as shopkeepers; they sold beautiful ribbons by the yard from this piece. The Popover Room over the garage is connected to the house by a wraparound walkway. More contemporary in feeling, it is quite spacious. It has a sitting area and can sleep four comfortably. The half-moon window echoes the Federal fanwork over the attic windows in the front of the house. The Loft Room has exposed beams, a loft bed, and is every bit as beautifully done as the other rooms.

The screened-in back porch is a pleasant place to eat breakfast or relax. The eat-in kitchen, also appealing, has a large hearth keeping things warm in the winter. Kaye serves freshly squeezed orange juice and a fruit course, followed by homemade granola and applesauce and homebaked breads such as pop-

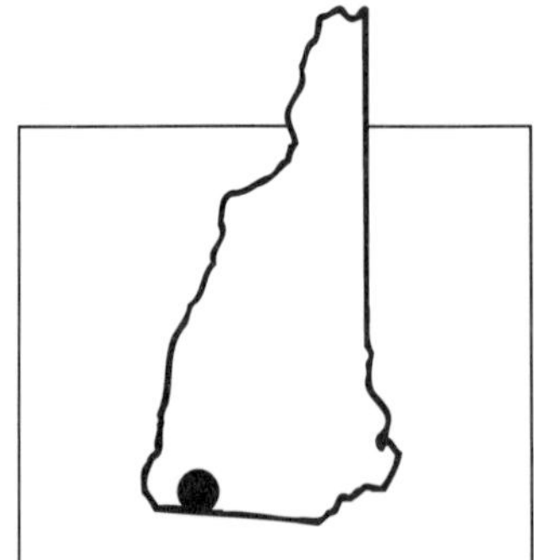

Hannah Davis House
Route 119
Fitzwilliam, 03447
603-585-3344

Cash or personal check only
Open year-round
$60–$65

THE HANNAH DAVIS HOUSE IS ONE OF THE MOST CHARMING IN NEW HAMPSHIRE.

pyseed sour cream, blueberry, and cinnamon-raisin. Entrées are delicious with an omelet stuffed with potatoes, onion, parsley, bacon, and cream cheese, served with tomato aspic for color; or French toast stuffed with country ham and Monterey Jack cheese laced with mustard sauce and served with scrambled eggs and green peas for accent.

The Terpstras have a marvelous mentor in Freda Houpt (her inn, the Parker House, is several doors away). They have been good students, and the Hannah Davis House is exceptional. Whether you stay with Kay and Mike or with Freda (they house each other's overflows), you will no doubt be lured back to Fitzwilliam often for a dose of innkeeping at its best.

Directions: From I-91, take exit 28A at Northfield, Massachusetts. Follow Route 10 north about 10 miles to Route 119. Follow Route 119 east about 15 miles to Fitzwilliam. The inn is on the left before you reach the town green.

Intervale • The Forest

WARMTH AND PLEASANT ACCOMMODATIONS ARE ALWAYS OFFERED BY THE FOREST'S OWNERS.

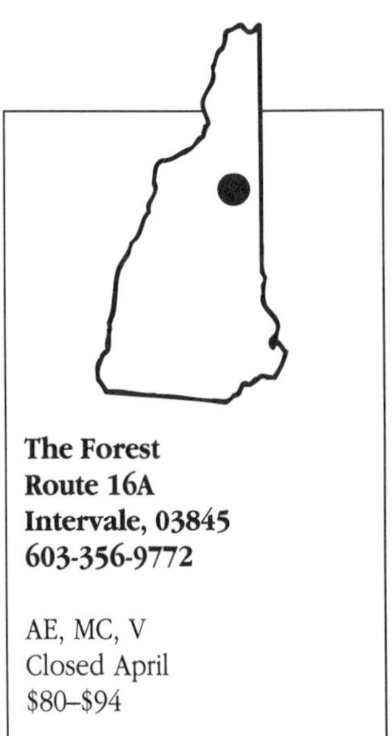

The Forest
Route 16A
Intervale, 03845
603-356-9772

AE, MC, V
Closed April
$80–$94

IF THE OVERDEVELOPMENT of North Conway has finally frazzled your nerves, take the side road to Intervale to visit the Forest and leave the traffic and bargain hunters behind. Rae and Ken Wyman provide peace and quiet in their large 1890 inn. The eleven rooms are country in flavor, and the inn is a calming example of cleanliness and order. Antiques, the Wymans' quilt collection, cheerful wallpaper prints, and simple decor make the Forest a pleasant respite. One of the more charming rooms is Four with its pink-and-green color scheme and Rae's grandmother's circle quilt. Eight is equally pretty in beige and peach with an oversize headboard and an oversize Victorian tub in its private bathroom. There are plenty of twin beds and king-size beds to fit all sleeping demands. Six of the eleven rooms share baths, and many of these can be connected into two-room suites with their own private bathrooms.

For the ultimate in privacy, the Brothers Grimm stone cottage is a perfect hideaway. Cozy in the winter with a fireplace, and cool in the summer, this little guest house offers two different rooms for people who want something even further from the maddening crowd.

The Victorian sitting rooms in the main house are spacious and provide an opportunity to chat with other guests and to compete with each other in one of the Wymans' many board games. The airy dining room is cheery and bright, and Rae serves a generous breakfast. Her specialties have slightly exotic flavors: Amaretto French toast, rum-raisin-spice French toast, piña colada pancakes, and Belgian waffles. She also serves homemade breads and muffins.

The outdoor solar-heated pool is welcome in spring and summer. The inn's twenty-five acres offer ample opportunity to hike and explore. And there is easy access to the cross-country ski trails and the area's downhill runs. For those who like to work hard in the winter, the Forest participates in a local program through which you can cross-country ski from inn to inn, certainly an admirable way to visit many of the inns in the White Mountains area.

When you're ready to venture back into town, there is one shop that is a must for serious antique collectors. **Richard Plusch** (Route 16, 603-356-3333) has a superb selection of high-quality collectibles with temptations such as antique jewelry and silver, porcelains, Federal-period furniture, clocks, splint-wood boxes, and more country-rustic tools. It's worth a visit, and Richard is worth knowing. A longtime resident of Conway, he is New Hampshire at its civilized best.

Directions: From Boston, take I-95 north to Spaulding Turnpike. Proceed north on Route 16 through North Conway. At Intervale, go north on Route 16A. The inn is on the right.

SIMPLE TASTES AND HOMEY COMFORT ARE THE TRADEMARKS HERE.

Intervale • **Riverside Country Inn**

THE COOKING OF FORMER RESTAURANT OWNER ANNE COTTER IS A MAJOR ATTRACTION AT RIVERSIDE COUNTRY INN.

AFTER A VISIT TO Riverside, you might so enjoy the place that you, like one of the Cotters' devoted guests, return here for fall and winter weekends for the next seven years. That's how alluring this little inn can be. Situated on the east branch of the Saco River, Geoff Cotter's ancestral summer house (built in 1906) today offers seven guest rooms and his wife Anne's fabulous cuisine. A former restaurant owner, she concentrates her energies at Riverside in the charming pink-and-green dining room.

The entire house is steeped in family history—so much so that the bedrooms are named after relatives (except for the ones named after the Cotter family's governess and chauffeur). In addition, Uncle Charlie's wonderful winter landscape mural livens up the pantry, and Auntie's Bar graces the wraparound side porch. The front porch is a favorite gathering place for guests, the perfect spot to relax in wicker, read the paper, and watch the traffic drift by. Upstairs, the bedrooms are spacious and simple, decorated with summer furnishings in keeping with the personality of the house.

Anne's cuisine is a major attraction. She loves to express her creativity through food, and breakfasts here give new meaning to the bed and breakfast concept. You'll be treated to a luscious meal of apple or rhubarb sauce, baked custard, corned beef hash, eggs Benedict (with meat or salmon), chicken shortcake, Welsh rarebit, quiche, pork pie, fruit pancakes, or salmon scrambled eggs. The breakfasts alone will necessitate a return engagement, and you won't be disappointed by the Cotters' hospitality, the Saco River's calming pace, and meeting other guests who are as content as you in this little hideaway. When you spot the yellow frame house with green trim, the Cotters' purebred German shepherds in the back yard, and the sparkling water of the Saco, turn in for a delightful respite from the rest of your life.

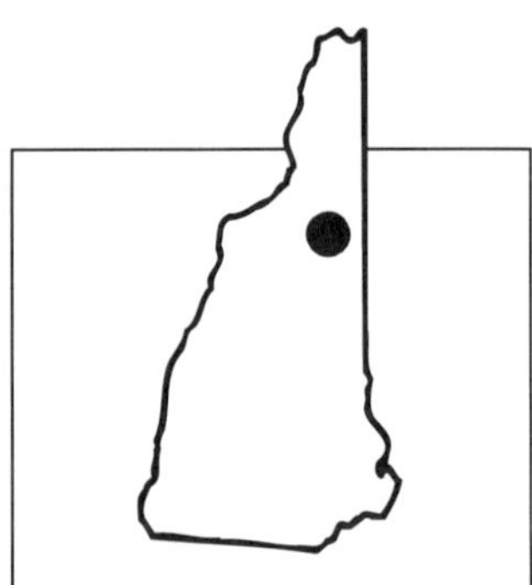

Riverside Country Inn
Route 16A
Intervale, 03845
603-356-9060

All major credit cards
Open year-round
$55–$95

Directions: From I-93 north, take exit 23 onto Route 104 east. In Meredith, turn onto Route 25 east. Follow to Route 16 north, then turn right onto Route 16A. The inn is 1½ miles along on Route 16A. From I-93 south, take Route 302 east until it joins with Route 16 south. Turn left onto Route 16A. The inn is 1 mile along on Route 16A.

Ellis River House • *Jackson Village*

IF YOUR IDEA OF heaven is spending a snowy afternoon immersed in a Jacuzzi, sipping hot spiced cider, and watching cross-country skiers struggle up a hill on the other side of a river, check into the Ellis River House for this singular experience. This rustic country inn offers the Jacuzzi experience on its rugged stone-walled back porch—a recuperative asset for outdoor enthusiasts and an indulgence for the rest of the world.

FARMHOUSE CHARM MAKES THIS INN SO APPEALING.

Barry and Barbara Lubao's inn has six rooms, each with a distinctly country-simple design theme. Calicos, heart-shaped rugs, old-fashioned print spreads, antique beds, and painted wood floors add to the charm of this 1890s farmhouse. Lots of rural crafts detailing (those often-seen oversize straw hats with floral trims, handmade wreaths, and pieced works) gives a cozy feeling to the place. Five of the rooms share two baths, and the upstairs duplex has its own private bathing quarters.

The Lubaos provide 4-H bonuses at Ellis River House. A working farm, their chickens lay the eggs for breakfast. Barry is also a prizewinner for his prowess in growing vegetables, some of which end up in the dinners he cooks by special request for guests. His breakfast dishes are abundant with home-

COUNTRY DECOR AND AN HONEST STYLE ADD THE CHARM.

made muffins and breads, hot applesauce, French toast, pancakes, and sausage and bacon from their own livestock.

Guests who have visited Ellis River House often find themselves front-page news. The Lubaos publish a chatty newsletter three times a year sharing the latest about guests and updating everyone on recent events at the inn. It's a great way to keep in touch with people you've met over breakfast.

Directions: From Boston, take I-95 north to Spaulding Turnpike. Continue north on Route 16 to Jackson. Take a left at the gas station in Jackson. The inn is 300 feet in from Route 16 on the left.

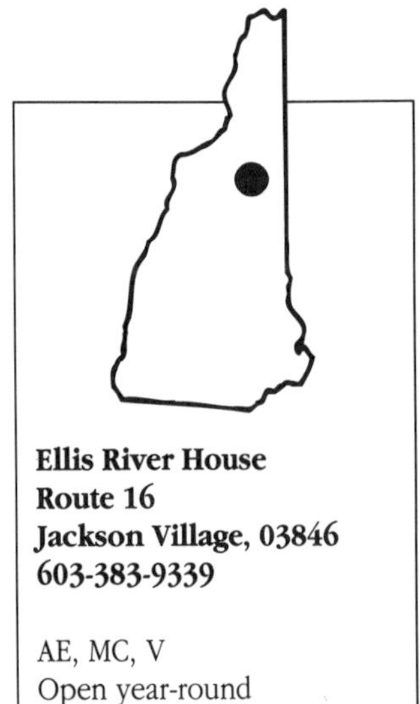

Ellis River House
Route 16
Jackson Village, 03846
603-383-9339

AE, MC, V
Open year-round
$50–$120

Nestlenook Inn • *Jackson Village*

IF YOU REMEMBER Nestlenook Inn from its recent past, a charming, but slightly fading farmhouse, you're in for a big surprise. Approaching Nestlenook on a snowy night is something like chancing on Disneyland of the North. The arched bridges, Victorian gazebos, and farmhouse, all professionally lit, make Nestlenook look slightly like a bed and breakfast theme park. Owners Robert and Nancy Cyr would be flattered to hear this. A professional in the beauty business, Robert specializes in makeovers. And Nestlenook is one of his grand success stories.

The Cyrs overhauled this stunning piece of property and completely redid the inn. No matter what the season, you notice the landscape immediately: there are those gazebos, summer houses, a chapel, arched bridges, a lovely pond stocked with trout, moonlight sleigh rides with Austrian bells making the experience even more festive, miles of cross-country ski trails, resident reindeer, a beautiful swimming pool, and acres of countryside to explore. In winter you can ice skate; in summer you can relax in turn-of-the-century boats.

Innkeeper Roger Bintliff greets you with genuine pleasure and will go to all ends to please. If you want to get married in the inn's outdoor trellised chapel, no problem. Roger is a justice of the peace. If you want to have a highly social evening, you can gather in the game room and participate in a hoote-

NESTLENOOK IS ONE OF THE MOST UNIQUE INNS IN NEW ENGLAND.

The Cyrs overhauled this stunning piece of property and completely redid the inn. . . . No detail has been left to chance.

nanny. And if you want to relax in an oversize Jacuzzi with its superb view of the decorative property, Nestlenook is the place for you.

Robert invested considerable sums in bringing Nestlenook to its new heights. The farmhouse has been painstakingly refurbished; the original section of the house is intact with its exposed beams and farmhouse charm. The rest of the structure has a completely new look with pronounced Victorian overtones. No detail has been left to chance. The woodwork is finely carved, the stained glass beautifully designed, the tin ceilings perfectly restored, the steam radiators given amazing paints jobs, and the bedrooms handsomely redecorated. The Cyrs kept local craftspeople gainfully employed for months with projects around the inn. The results are belle époque in the Continental-American grand manner.

The seven rooms are luxurious and irresistable. Each is named after a White Mountains artist, with a sample of his work on display in the room. Possibly the prettiest is William Paskell, lush in apricot and green with a Count Rumford fireplace, tall-post canopy bed, and lovely decor. Equally attractive is Horace Burdick, soothing in rose with oak furnishings and a Victorian daybed if you are traveling with your mother or child over twelve. Myke Morgan, in the original part of the house, has the exposed beams and is slightly more rustic in feeling. The third-floor C. C. Murdoch is perfect for those honeymooning couples Roger marries or for any couple restoring their relationship. The Jacuzzi with its endless view from arched windows is seductive for everyone. All of the other rooms have ultra-modern private baths with smaller Jacuzzis.

Breakfast is served family style at one sitting in the handsome dining room. Guests are treated to Belgian waffles, eggs, fresh fruits, and breakfast meats. The dining room is open to the public in the evening. The Ansonia is where some highly innovative and very sophisticated cuisine is served by Hoke and Claudia Wilson.

Nestlenook is worth the visit, even if it may be a bit of a stretch on the pocketbook. It is truly unique, definitely outstanding, and memorable in every way.

Nestlenook Inn
Dinsmore Road (off Route 16)
Jackson Village, 03846
603-383-9443

All major credit cards
Open year-round
$144–$196

Directions: From I-93 north, take exit 23 onto Route 104 east. In Meredith turn onto Route 25 east. Follow to Route 16 north, which takes you into Jackson Village. Go through the covered bridge and take the first right onto Dinsmore Road. The inn is at the bottom of the hill.

HONEST, UNPRETENTIOUS LODGING AND GOOD FOOD AWAIT YOU AT THE WILDCAT INN.

Wildcat Inn • *Jackson Village*

WILDCAT INN IS NOT your typical bed and breakfast experience. It looks more rough-and-tumble than Laura-Ashley-sweet . . . and it is. A popular place for skiers, it is a truly useful place for families and tourists who prefer a really rustic approach. There are plenty of bunk beds, functional decor, no-frills furnishings, and basic amenities to make the Wildcat a true bargain. Of the sixteen rooms, some have private baths, all are clean and neat, and each offers a quiet place to sleep.

What you may be unprepared for at the Wildcat is owner/chef Marty Sweeney's talented hand in the kitchen. The attractive dining room is usually sold out during the season, and for good reason. The food here is excellent, with Marty's interpretative cuisine and ample portions to keep any traveler happy. And if you are traveling with children, there's a box of vintage toy trucks and cars to keep them occupied between courses.

Breakfasts are as delicious as dinner with fruit pancakes, waffles, French toast, eggs Benedict, and freshly baked muffins and coffee cakes to prepare you for an invigorating day in the foothills of the White Mountains. Jackson Village is particularly quaint with large, old homes, a picturesque covered bridge, and the Ellis River.

The Wildcat is a great find as it doesn't pretend to be anything it's not.

Directions: From Boston, take I-95 north to Spaulding Turnpike. Continue north on Route 16 to Jackson. Turn right on Route 16A and continue through the covered bridge. Inn is on right.

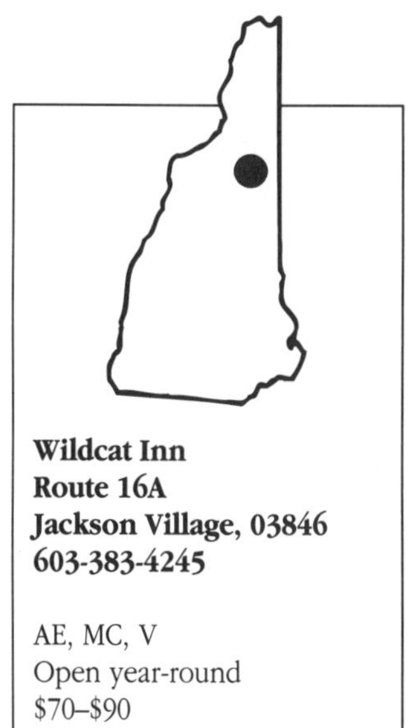

Wildcat Inn
Route 16A
Jackson Village, 03846
603-383-4245

AE, MC, V
Open year-round
$70–$90

Jaffrey • Benjamin Prescott Inn

THE BENJAMIN PRESCOTT Inn is in good hands with new owners Jan and Barry Miller. It should be. After nearly three decades in the hotel business, Barry decided it was time to open his own place, and the results prove that experience pays off. This comfortable inn offers Jan's gourmet cooking, the Millers' warm hospitality, country decor, and Barry's handiwork. When you're not nestled into your sleeping room, you can wander around the inn admiring Barry's handmade wooden ship models and wood carvings—impressive projects that he managed to do in his spare time. You may also find yourself a contributing member of Barry's grandfather's unusual collection of soils and sands, innovatively displayed in small test tubes, each labeled with its point of origin. The Millers' guests have been known to drop off samples of their part of the world to add to this collection dating from the late 1920s.

Homemade decorative details add to the family feeling here.

The ten rooms, all with private baths, are attractive, with understated decor. Many of them have fresh, new looks with Jan's stenciling and amazing needlepoint landscapes. If you are traveling en masse, the back apartment, the Vannevar-Bush Suite, is perfect. With its own entrance and sitting room, it is the ultimate in privacy. There are plenty of large beds and handsome, family antiques sprinkled throughout the other rooms. Phones are available in each room, an accommodation for business travelers and guests who need to keep in touch. But the true charm of the Benjamin Prescott Inn is the third-floor suite, John Adams's Attic. Its pretty sitting room overlooks a nonstop view of the surrounding countryside and is a restorative place to relax in any season. The large bedroom and four sleeping alcoves make this upstairs hideaway perfect for families traveling together, or, as is often the case, ideal for bridal parties.

The Millers are purists. For example, they pick all their own berries for the variety of fruit breads and jams they make for guests. Jan certainly doesn't skimp on her breakfasts. In addition to the fruit breads, she is likely to serve Scotch eggs, Prescott rarebit, eggs Benedict, Dutch-apple pancakes, cinnamon-sourdough French toast in the shape of maple leaves, or fresh-fruit puff-pancakes as light as soufflés.

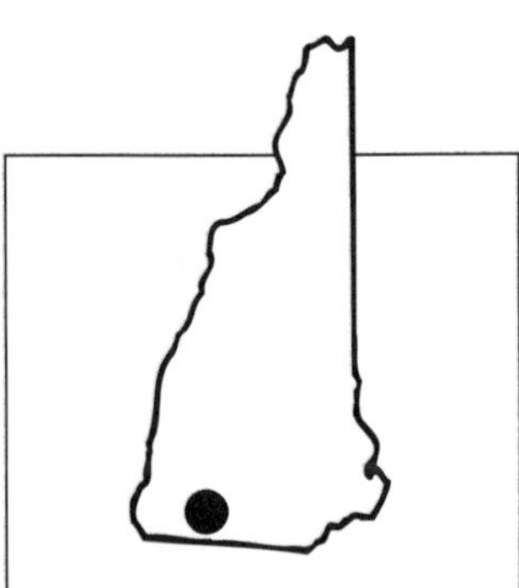

Benjamin Prescott Inn
Route 124 East
Jaffrey, 03452
603-532-6637

MC, V
Open year-round
$60–$120

A visit to this 1853 historic inn is a must. You will be sure to return frequently once you discover that Jan's homemade chocolate truffles, goodnight treats thoughtfully placed on your pillow, are nothing short of addictive.

THE BENJAMIN PRESCOTT OFFERS SIMPLE CHARM AND FABULOUS FOOD.

Directions: From I-91, take exit 3 in Brattleboro, Vermont, onto Route 9 east toward Keene, New Hampshire. Continue on Route 9 east to Route 101 east. Follow to Route 124 east. The inn is about 2 miles beyond the village of Jaffrey, on the left. Or continue on Route 101 to Peterborough and turn right onto Route 202 south to Jaffrey. Turn left onto Route 124 east. The inn is about 2 miles along.

FROM ITS HILLTOP PERCH, GOULD FARM ENJOYS A VIEW OF NEARBY MOUNT MONADNOCK.

Jaffrey • **Gould Farm**

THERE IS SOMETHING very reassuring about staying at Gould Farm, in the same house where innkeeper Margaret Gould visited her Aunt Sally as a child. This handsome farmhouse has been passed down through five generations of Goulds, and Margaret retired several years ago from her teaching career to open her home to overnight guests. The setting is stunning. Perched on a hilltop with a view of Mount Monadnock that is interrupted only by fields and pine trees, it is the perfect place to escape for a weekend. There's hiking in the surrounding fields for an up-close and personal view of the countryside.

The farmhouse itself is cozy, comfortable, and filled with family history. Margaret is a relaxed hostess who will immediately put you at ease, sharing her love for the Monadnock area and stories of her travels. The house is dotted with souvenirs from her visits to her brother, for years based in Bolivia. Her home also contains generations of family treasures, all of which make the farm an appealing place to visit. The living room is bright and sunny, as are the three bedrooms at the top of the maple- and cherry-planked steps. Two are twin-bedded, one is a double, and each has floral-print walls and homemade family quilts that most collectors would die for. All three share a sizable modern bathroom.

Breakfast is served on the front porch in the summer and in the beautiful dining room or in the living room (near the large window overlooking the majestic scenery) the rest of the year. Margaret is a great cook (she and her brother used to run a catering business out of the farm's two huge kitchens), and she is apt to serve up scrambled eggs with chives and

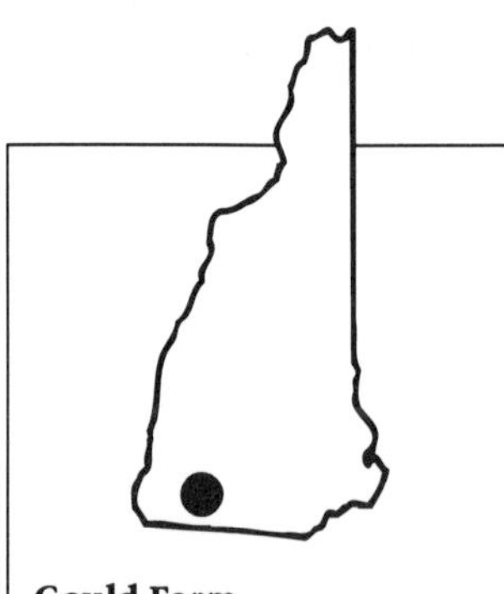

Gould Farm
40 Prescott Road (off Route 124)
Jaffrey, 03452
603-532-6996

Cash or personal check only
Open year-round
$50

cream; broiled herbed tomatoes; homemade muffins; and coffee cake.

When you're ready to explore the area, she'll give you good ideas for day trips. One of her favorites is **Old Town Farm Antiques** (Old Town Farm Road, off Route 202, Peterborough, 603-924-3523), an enormous barn filled with American primitives and an extensive collection of estate carpets. Gould Farm provides easy directions to the renowned **Sharon Arts Center** (Route 123, Sharon, 603-924-7256), where you can view the latest gallery exhibit or take a course in pottery, or sculpture. You also can visit the center's crafts shop, filled with creations by members of the League of New Hampshire Craftsmen; you'll be tempted by wreaths, ceramics, woodworking, weaving, ironwork, glass art, silver jewelry, and other gifts and necessities. Off Route 31, in nearby Mason, is **Pickity Place** (Nutting Hill Road, Mason, 603-878-1151), a two-hundred-year-old farm that specializes in herbs. You can find everything from tansy ant repellent, fragrant wreaths, and herbal teas to bouquets garnis for cooking, herbs to freshen your vacuum cleaner bags, and even herbal moth repellents.

Of course, the biggest (literally) attraction in the area is Mount Monadnock itself. This impressive peak, tallest in southern New Hampshire, has trails for hikers and climbers of various abilities and is said to be the second most climbed mountain in the world after Mount Fuji in Japan. It is part of a New Hampshire state park and is located about three miles west of Jaffrey Village on Route 124.

Directions: From I-91, take exit 3 in Brattleboro, Vermont, onto Route 9 east toward Keene, New Hampshire. Continue onto Route 101 east to Route 124 east. Go 14 miles and turn right onto Prescott Road. The inn is ½ mile down the road on the left. Look for the Gould sign on the barn.

GENERATIONS OF FAMILY TREASURES ADORN GOULD FARM'S INTERIOR.

Jefferson • Stag Hollow Inn

JUST WHEN YOU THINK you have seen it all in bed and breakfast land, you realize you have only begun. Which is another way of saying the best bed and breakfast inn is always your next. Do yourself a favor and book a room at this unbelievably charming place. And second the favor by arriving at dusk when the sun is gently setting behind the fields, the geese are settling in for the evening, the horses are finishing their last meal of the day, the dog and cats are curling up for a nap, and the llamas are serenading you along with the large nature chorus at Stag Hollow. Visiting this unique inn is one way guaranteed to relax and restore you. Surrounded by five acres of farmland and eight hundred thousand acres of national forest, the snow-capped mountains on the horizon, you cannot hope to find a more serene location in New England to put your spirit into balance.

Nor can you find a more self-reliant, resourceful, bright, and energetic innkeeper. Joanna Fyon has an active life, is filled with ideas, and communicates a deep reverence for life and the environment. You, too, will share her perspective when you arrange your own day-long llama trek into the White Mountains. And don't expect to rough it beyond the hiking: those llamas are carrying your superb gourmet lunch with tasteful tabletop accessories to match. Whatever Joanna does, she does with great finesse, good taste, and style.

FARMHOUSE SIMPLICITY WITH SUPERB DECOR MAKE STAG HOLLOW A REMARKABLE EXPERIENCE.

Her four-bedroom inn offers the best a turn-of-the-century farmhouse has. The bedrooms are beautiful with their country-fresh floral wallpapers, lovely antique beds, and comfortable decor. Joanna has restored this pretty house herself, and the results are more than impressive. The house retains an old-fashioned feel, and the detail work is perfect. Her grandmother's furniture and many pieces from Joanna's Canadian childhood furnish the inn. You will no doubt fall in love with the antique Oriental deco rugs, spindle beds, iron headboards, cottage-painted suites, handturned ceramic washbasins, hydrangea wreaths, and Joanna's own handloomed runners. Everything here looks at home in this simple farmhouse, and everything has been chosen with a sophisticated eye and artistic design sense. Three of the rooms share a bath, a room decorated in just as gentle a style as the rest of the house. Peaceful music fills the bathroom in the morning, the perfect time for a leisurely bath in the claw-foot tub with its Colonial-green talons.

NO DETAIL IS OVERLOOKED IN THIS APPEALING, WELCOMING INN.

Breakfast is served in the homey kitchen with Joanna's homebaked nut and fruit breads, French toast, pancakes, or omelets. The unexpected touch here is that the goose laid your breakfast eggs.

Joanna conducts the llama hiking-treks during summer and fall. In winter she coordinates ski treks for expert Double Black Diamond skiers up Mount Washington, practically outside of her front door. This may be New England's answer to helicopter skiing in the Rockies and Tetons. The llamas carry the skis and equipment to Tuckerman's Ravine, where thrill seekers find challenging, spirited skiing at its best. Joanna is an experienced skier (and instructor) herself, as well as a licensed Emergency Medical Technician, on the off chance that anyone may need emergency medical attention.

It is well worth your time to plan a trip to this northern outpost in New Hampshire. It is breathtaking, peaceful, simple, honest, and stylish—all at the same time. Joanna has a special sense of humor which you may appreciate when introduced to her llamas. Dhali is particularly arresting with his compelling face and soulful eyes.

Directions: Take I-93 north to exit 35. Take Route 3 north. Continue north on Route 115. The inn is about 7 miles up on the right.

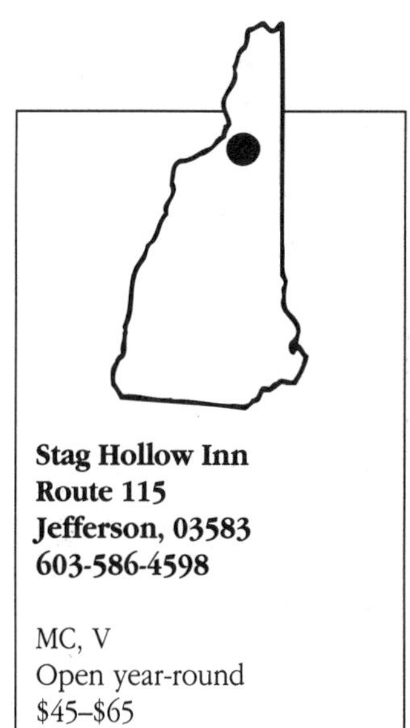

Stag Hollow Inn
Route 115
Jefferson, 03583
603-586-4598

MC, V
Open year-round
$45–$65

NOT EVEN THE ATTRACTION OF NEARBY WINNISQUAM LAKE CAN LURE SOME GUESTS AWAY FROM FERRY POINT HOUSE.

Laconia • Ferry Point House

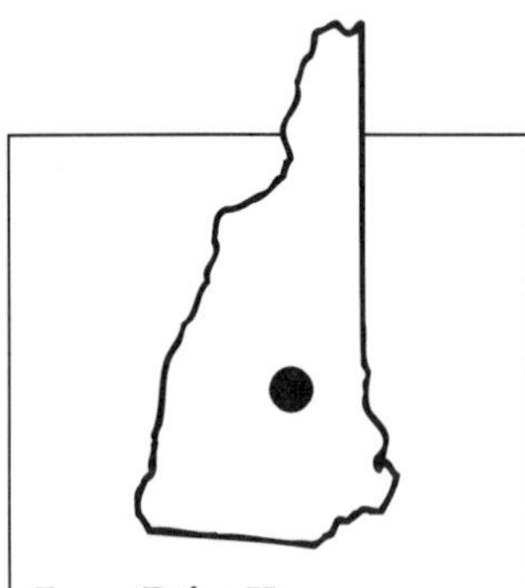

Ferry Point House
Lower Bay Road
Laconia, 03246
603-524-0087

Cash or personal checks only
Closed November through Memorial Day
$55–$65

WINNISQUAM LAKE IS crowded with waterskiers, sailors, and boaters during the summer. It is also seasonal home to innkeepers Joe and Diane Damato and their children, Eric and Danielle, who often can be found boating off to the store on an errand for their mother or showing guests around this beautiful fifteen-mile-long lake. From the water it's easy to spot Ferry Point House, an imposing, deep red, 150-year-old house set on a small rise above the old ferry landing. Its commanding presence is made even more so by its bright white gingerbread-trimmed front porch and the stately pine tree marking the dock and boat mooring.

This handsome inn is a wonderful place to visit during the summer and is even more stunning during foliage season, when the lake is surrounded by a symphony of warm colors. Some guests choose to make the gazebo their rest and relaxation headquarters; it's the perfect place to enjoy the lake with an uninterrupted view. This is one bed and breakfast inn that is truly an escape from city living. In fact, when you awake to see the mists rising off the lake in the early-morning light, you might think you have discovered Shangri-la once and for all.

Ferry Point House offers five rooms (three have private baths, two share), each with a terrific view of the lake. Diane's decorating style is understated, cheerful, light, and airy. She pays attention to the little extras that make this place so attractive: delicate dried-flower nosegays on bureaus, pretty lace-beribboned wreaths, beautiful brass door hardware, lovely bed linens (all air-dried and hand-ironed, a labor-intensive act of love on Diane's part), balloon curtains, and a collection of lace-trimmed linen runners to complement the Victorian-era furnishings. In fact, Diane's decorative touches are so popular, she has a small shop offering dried floral arrangements, wreaths, and other pretty souvenirs of the inn. What makes these souvenirs special is that Diane makes them all herself.

Despite the appeal of the lake, some guests prefer to stay in the house, admiring the stunning living room with its oversize antiques and extraordinary hearth. Constructed from native New Hampshire rock and crystal, the hearth's mica, granite, quartz, and tourmaline sparkle in the firelight and mantel candlelight. This memorable fireplace makes a visit to Ferry Point in the fall almost mandatory.

The dining room is just as attractive as the living room (although the fireplace here is more modest), decorated in the same deep red that is pervasive throughout the house. The long, lace-topped table is a comfortable gathering spot for guests to get to know each other, encouraged by Joe and Diane's warm hospitality and their expertise as hosts. Conversation always gets off to a quick start with a discussion of how fabulous a cook Diane is. She has published the *Ferry Point House Cookbook*, so you can duplicate her specialties back home. Guests may be treated to a full breakfast of baked applies filled with cheese, pineapple-bran muffins, upside-down corn muffins bursting with jam, or French toast stuffed with cream cheese and nuts and served with bananas and marmalade syrup—all of which will spoil even the most confirmed non-breakfast eater. During this delicious meal, guests are joined by the two Damato children and Diane's mother, Mémère. Tiger and Finnegan, the family cats, put in cameo appearances.

When you awake to see the mists rising off the lake in the early-morning light, you might think you have discovered Shangri-la.

Ferry Point House is a wonderful place to visit. The Damatos are perfect hosts; they love people and are interesting conversationalists, fluent in just about any subject. You won't be disappointed by a visit here, and you'll no doubt become a loyal return guest after your first stay.

Directions: From I-93, follow Routes 3 and 11 north approximately 4½ miles. Turn left onto Bay Road at the light. Turn right onto Lower Bay Road (large white sign with names of residents on it). The inn is the eighth house on the left, the second large red Victorian with white trim. The inn's sign is on the house.

Lyme • Lyme Inn

THE THREE-STORY LYME INN RETAINS THE INTIMACY OF A PRIVATE HOME.

LYME INN IS A great place to stay when visiting Dartmouth or when you're in the mood to immerse yourself in a beautiful New Hampshire village drenched in history. This appealing 1809 inn retains the flavor of its original age. Fred and Judy Siemons, who have been sheltering and feeding travelers since the mid-seventies, have kept the intimacy of a private home in their three-story inn.

The fourteen rooms are beautiful, and each has a unique decor; several have Count Rumford fireplaces. Room Eight is particularly appealing, with its lilac wallpaper, canopy bed, and corner location. Nine is one of the more popular, with an impressive suite of handpainted furniture; it is perfect for families traveling with children (as long as the children are over eight years old). Six is sunny and cheerful, with an exposed-brick fireplace; Seven is soothing in green and rose; and Eighteen has unusual black wicker furniture and lush fruit-print wallpaper. The third-floor suites are just as attractive. You'd have to try every room in the house to experience fully the heritage look and feel of the inn.

Fred and Judy are thoughtful hosts. They offer hot mulled cider, hot chocolate, and hot buttered rum to ward off winter's chill, and they cool down summer's heat with wine coolers and iced tea. All of this is offered in the appealing Tavern Room, a tap room decorated just as it might have been in 1809. The old-fashioned ambiance is also reflected in the three beam-ceilinged dining rooms, decorated with antique baskets and samplers. The complete dinners are robust and tasty. Fred, who was trained at the Culinary Institute, gets into the kitchen at breakfast, and he's a terrific short-order cook, serving up delicious eggs, French toast, and muffins.

After you explore the inn (there's a craft boutique on the second floor with a tempting selection of handknit sweaters, quilts, pine-cone wreaths, and other artisan treats), you can take off to explore the area—on bike or by auto—walk along the river, or settle into the inn's large screened-in porch to watch the sleepy town of Lyme move through another tranquil day.

Lyme Inn
Route 10
Lyme, 03768
603-795-2222

AE, MC, V
Closed two weeks in April and three weeks in December
Incl. dinner, $116–$150

Directions: From I-91, take exit 14 to Route 113 east. Turn right onto Route 5, then immediately take the first left, which leads over the bridge into Lyme. Pass a big white church. The inn is at the east end of the town common on Route 10.

Thatcher Hill Inn • *Marlborough*

CAL GAGE'S TWO MAIDEN cousins defied the conventions and in 1948 headed east from Illinois to New Hampshire. Here they practiced the art of self-reliance as Yankee farmers at Thatcher Hill Farm. They worked the land, raised livestock, and settled into a rural lifestyle that kept them going well into their seventies. Today, Cal and Marge Gage have moved east from Illinois themselves to spend their retirement on the family homestead.

The barn is impressive, the fields are for hiking, not tilling, and there is still a gentle, farmlike feeling to the place. The Gages decided bed and breakfasting was to their liking, and they certainly have good instincts, as Thatcher Hill is one of the loveliest inns in New England. Former advertising executives at Leo Burnett in Chicago, they practice their former firm's philosophy of quality and "first-class all the way." They explain their approach to innkeeping as the distillation of the experiences as worldwide business travelers. "We want what we appreciate and what makes us feel comfortable. We want our home to be very special, and we've created an inn with a homelike feeling and first-class accommodations. It's a place we would want to visit ourselves."

The look of the inn is the product of Marge's perfectionism and her personal joy in creating stunningly simple rooms.

They have no trouble finding other people with similar tastes. Guests love Thatcher Hill for its mix of originality and 1794 farmstead authenticity. They also appreciate the amenities of this handsome inn: the towel racks are heated, the prices are reasonable, the bed linens are beautiful, the rooms are superbly decorated, and the Victorian tubs have European showers to preserve the old-fashioned feeling of the spacious, private bathrooms.

The look of the inn is the product of Marge's perfectionism and her personal joy in creating stunningly simple rooms filled with antiques, beautiful wallpaper, decorative detailing, handmade rag rugs, and handsewn quilts. The footed tubs are color-coordinated to the rooms, so you might bathe in a blue, green, red, or blue Victorian tub, depending on the room you choose. The front room, Three, is especially pretty, with a strawberry motif wall covering, fabulous twig furniture, and an enormously high green iron bed. Equally pretty are Six, decorated in crisp blue and white; Seven in red, white, and blue, with a stunning quilted wall hanging; and Five, with its own tiny terrace and a view of the beautiful barn (you can

Thatcher Hill Inn
Thatcher Hill Road (off Route 124)
Marlborough, 03455
603-876-3361

MC, V
Open year-round
$55–$75

AT THATCHER HILL INN, THE APPROACH IS "FIRST-CLASS ALL THE WAY."

climb to the top of the cupola for a spectacular long-distance view of Marlborough).

The Honeymoon Suite, with its four-poster bed, is more city-elegant—a sea of green with fireplace and sitting room. And the wheelchair access room downstairs is a delight in blue, with a fully equipped bathroom for disabled guests. The parlor is lovely in rose and mauve, and the more casual sitting room has comfortable seating and a blazing fire in the winter.

You might be fortunate enough to wake up in the morning to the rich sounds of one of Cal's many music boxes. It is a divine experience to hear the lovely music fill the house, directing you to the downstairs country dining room for a buffet breakfast of fresh fruit and yogurt, homemade fruit breads and muffins, and copious amounts of hot coffee and tea.

This engaging couple brings the best of all worlds to innkeeping. They are true professionals concerned with quality and comfort, delightful conversationalists, and genuinely interested in their guests. It's a wonderful place to visit when in the Monadnock area, slightly out of the way on a back road but close to all the antique stores (one of the best is **Woodward's Antiques**, 166 Main Street, 603-876-3360). The inn also plays host to horse shows, an entertaining bonus for guests.

Directions: From I-91, take exit 3 in Brattleboro, Vermont, onto Route 9 east toward Keene, New Hampshire. Continue onto Route 101 east to Route 124 east. Go 2 miles and turn right onto Thatcher Hill Road. The inn is on the right.

Tolman Pond Farmhouse • *Nelson*

THE TOLMANS HAVE been pond-side in Nelson since the 1700s. With those deep roots, you would expect the area to be ripe with the legend and lore of this interesting family. And it is!

Karen Tolman, innkeeper of her husband's family home, is more than willing to fill you in on the details. It's a fascinating family story, and you'll enjoy meeting all generations of the Tolmans through this entertaining lady. You'll learn, for example, that Uncle Newt designed and built one of the first pair of wooden, double-ended stunt skis, then went on to write the popular book *North of Monadnock.* Father Fran was an artist, and samples of his work are scattered around the house. Mother Floppy, who lives next door, published an entertaining collection of short stories about the early days of the inn, *More Spit Than Polish,* for her debut as an author at the never-too-late age of eighty-seven.

The house has been in the family for seven generations, and the most recent generation of children is always in and out of the inn. The pastoral personality of the already bucolic Tolman Pond is enhanced by the chickens and the occasional pig and sheep.

The inn itself is housed in a converted barn and shed, lending a predictably rustic quality to the decor. The three rooms are modest and comfortable in their simple way. There's a full kitchen and large living room upstairs. The entire place is virtually indestructible, a welcome promise for parents who travel with their children.

There is so much to do here that a visit to Tolman Pond Farmhouse during the summer is spent largely

THERE'S SO MUCH TO DO HERE THAT A SUMMER VISIT TO TOLMAN POND FARMHOUSE IS SPENT LARGELY OUTDOORS.

The place is virtually indestructible, a welcome promise for parents who travel with their children.

THE INN IS LOCATED IN A CONVERTED BARN AND SHED.

outdoors—in a rowboat, sailing, swimming, fly-fishing, canoeing, hiking through the two hundred acres, and playing tennis on the clay court. You can't ask for a more peaceful ending to an active day than sitting outside, sipping a summer drink, watching evening come over Tolman Pond. During the winter there's ample opportunity for cross-country skiing, snowshoeing, and warming up in front of the fire in the ski room, where Uncle Newt's wooden ski furniture is on display. Karen prepares breakfast for guests, serving fresh fruit and loads of homebaked breads. She also has a touch of poetry in her, and you may be the happy recipient of a copy of her ode to the inn, a colorful time capsule that will serve as a reminder of the charms of this special place when you get home.

Tolman Pond Farmhouse is a nonsmoking inn, so be prepared to step outside to admire the peacocks, chickens, and lambs while taking a smoke. All guests love to visit this rustic inn, where the Tolman waters still run deep.

Directions: From I-91, take exit 3 in Brattleboro, Vermont. Follow Route 9 east. About 15 minutes beyond Keene, New Hampshire, look for the Nelson-Harrisville sign and turn right. Follow the paved road through the center of Nelson Village. After Nelson Village take the second left onto Tolman Pond Road. Tolman Pond is on the right; the inn is on the left.

Tolman Pond Farmhouse
Tolman Pond Road
Marlborough, 03455
603-827-3226

Cash or personal check only
Closed March through April
$35–$55

Maple Hill Farm • *New London*

VISITING MAPLE HILL Farm is a little like "bringing it all back home." There's a Big Chill feeling here, from the California-collective decor details to the relaxed pace of innkeeper Dennis Aufranc. If you remember fondly the sixties and flower child political activist life, you'll have lots to reminisce about with Dennis. If you missed that era (or couldn't have cared less), no problem. Dennis had a successful career as an executive with AT&T before becoming an innkeeper, and there's always lots to discuss about business, marketing and management. Of if you want to be left alone, that's easily arranged as well in this no-frills farmhouse near Little Lake Sunapee.

Dennis, a low-key, articulate host, has found innkeeping fulfillment far from the West Coast he left behind. He is quite an accomplished cook, and you'll be the satisfied recipient of a wonderful homecooked dinner when you arrive (if you choose that option) and a fabulous breakfast when you wake up the next morning. This is one place where you can put your feet up and relax. The three-story 1824 farmhouse has an honest homestead feel, unpretentious decor (a combination of California family antiques and period furnishings), and a life of its own. You'll meet Dennis's wife, Roberta, their new toddler, Hélène, Dennis's son, Charlie, and the Aufrancs' dogs and cats during your visit. It's hard to wrest yourself away from the rustic kitchen with its oversize countertop, which makes casual conversation with Dennis a natural as he prepares your meal. The barn-sided dining room, with subtle wood mosaics, has been known to

The pretty blue-and-white frame house, protected by pine trees, is just off Interstate 89 — a welcome sight after a long drive on Friday night.

MAPLE HILL FARM DATES TO 1824 AND HAS "AN HONEST HOMESTEAD FEEL" ABOUT IT.

THE INN'S TWO SITTING ROOMS ARE DESIGNED TO HELP GUESTS ESCAPE ALL THOUGHTS OF THEIR WEEKDAY LIVES.

double as a dance floor when guests get in the mood.

If you choose the dinner option on a given evening, you might be served Dennis's six-cheese chicken scaloppine, paella, beef stew with dumplings, grilled steak, thick-crust pizza, or rack of lamb. Poached pears with chocolate sauce or the best apple pie you'll ever taste will finish off the feast. After a dinner fit for kings and queens, you can sleep peacefully, dreaming about breakfast. To sample Dennis's featherweight pancakes, hearty oatmeal with dried fruits, baked apples, homemade breads and muffins, and egg dishes is to book a return visit immediately.

Dennis has intentionally created an inn with an ambiance designed to help any traveler decompress from the rigors of weekday life. The two sitting rooms are casual, and each of the ten bedrooms, with a certain masculine decor, is streamlined and functional. Dennis feels that this simple, unadorned look is the perfect approach to preserving Maple Hill's authenticity as a farmhouse. The newly renovated barn is home to wedding receptions and private parties.

One of the best aspects of this welcoming inn is its location. There's no risk of getting lost on yet another back road or in an out-of-the-way country village. The pretty blue-and-white frame house, protected by pine trees and Dennis's colorful gardens, is just off Interstate 89—a welcome sight after a long drive on a Friday night.

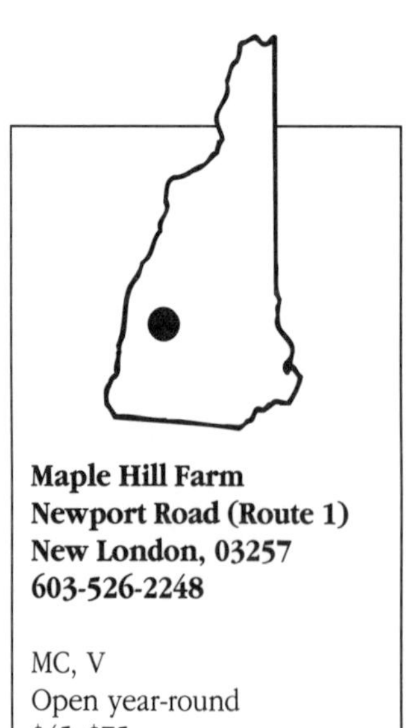

Maple Hill Farm
Newport Road (Route 1)
New London, 03257
603-526-2248

MC, V
Open year-round
$45–$75

Directions: From I-89 north, take exit 12. Turn right at the end of the exit ramp. From I-89 south, take exit 12. Turn left at the end of the ramp. The inn is the first house on the left.

Inn at Coit Mountain • *Newport*

THE FORMER CORBIN/Champollion home, rooted in the local history of upper-echelon Victorian society, certainly is a handsome summer plaything. Built to shelter the privileged family during the warm-weather months, this Georgian home has a grandeur that evokes life as it was for people who had an unlimited income and a lifestyle to match.

Today, this attractive white house is home to Judi and Dick Tatem, who moved their family here from Connecticut to live out their innkeeping dream. There's a certain distinction to the library, with its fifteen-foot ceiling and granite fireplace, so massive that even Falstaff would feel at ease here. The French decor, with lovely oak paneling, is softened by Judi's agile decorating touch, blending prints and more contemporary furniture into this imposing space, giving country charm to an otherwise majestic room. Dick is an avid hunter, and his lovely snow goose trophy occupies one corner. Judi also participates in the sporting life, taking scenic shots with her camera, and her award-winning prints are on display.

The five bedrooms have a homey touch. The master bedroom suite is lovely, large, and decorated with pastel floral wallpaper. Its fireplace is a welcome sight during the winter. The four other rooms are smaller, two share bathrooms and are perfectly comfortable.

Judi is an accomplished chef and caters private parties with her creative cuisine. Breakfasts at Coit Mountain are delicious offerings of an English classic (including fried mushrooms and grilled tomatoes as partners to eggs and sausage) or a house specialty, such as bourbon pancakes, French toast with peaches, or cheese-and-caper crêpes. Whatever your choice, you'll be in breakfast paradise in the inn's small, semiformal dining room.

The Tatems give winter sleigh rides, courtesy of Judi's two horses and pony, and their frame shop adjacent to the house also has a gallery. Bring your prints with you on a weekend getaway for a custom frame job while you're relaxing in this beautiful home with its outstanding hosts.

Directions: From I-89, take exit 13 onto Route 10 south. The inn is 8 miles along on the left. From I-91, take exit 8 onto Route 103 east. In Newport turn left onto Route 10 north. The inn is 2 miles along on the right.

INN AT COIT MOUNTAIN OFFERS FIVE SIMPLE BUT SATISFYING ROOMS.

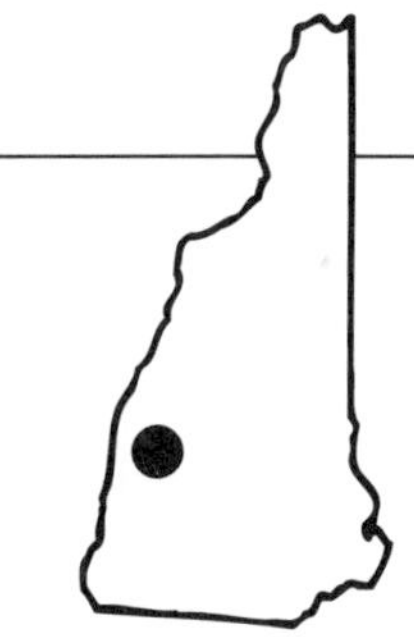

Inn at Coit Mountain
Route 10
Newport, 03773
603-863-3583; 1-800-367-2364 (outside New Hampshire)

MC, V
Open year-round
Double, $85–$115; single, $70–$100; suite $135–$150

A POND, A SMALL FLOCK OF SHEEP, AND EIGHT ACRES ALL ADD TO WHITE GOOSE INN'S APPEAL.

Orford • White Goose Inn

WHITE GOOSE REGULARS say they love this inn, according to owner Karin Wolf, because "it's just like coming home." Everyone should be so lucky to have such a beautiful home. The White Goose is one of the prettiest inns in New England, thanks to Karin's decorating aesthetics. Guests who love the country-crafts feeling of this place will appreciate the fact that Karin and her husband, Manfred, have sixteen rooms, each more attractive than the last. Located on eight acres, with a stream, pond, a small flock of sheep, and the Wolfs' family of schnauzers, the nineteenth-century brick house is made all the more distinctive by the elm tree trunk emerging through its wraparound porch.

Book ahead to guarantee staying in one of the gorgeous rooms, each decorated with Karin's gift eye for design. Six is particularly impressive. A suite in tones of apricot, its mauve and pink bathroom is large enough to double as a sitting room. Three is equally lovely. Handmade house-and-flower stencils grace the walls in a pink-based decor. Five, with its highboy bed, is just as enticing as Two, the brass bed afloat in a sea of pale green and surrounded by Karin's pineapple stencils. Every room is winsome and filled with personal touches—baskets filled with towels, lacy curtains, the occasional shell mirror, bamboo furnishings, and a goose motif.

Karin's hobby is creating irresistible country crafts. Guests have become so demanding that Karin says she barely has time to keep up with the orders. After one visit here, you'll no doubt become an enthusiastic fan yourself. Her pierced lamp shades, quilts,

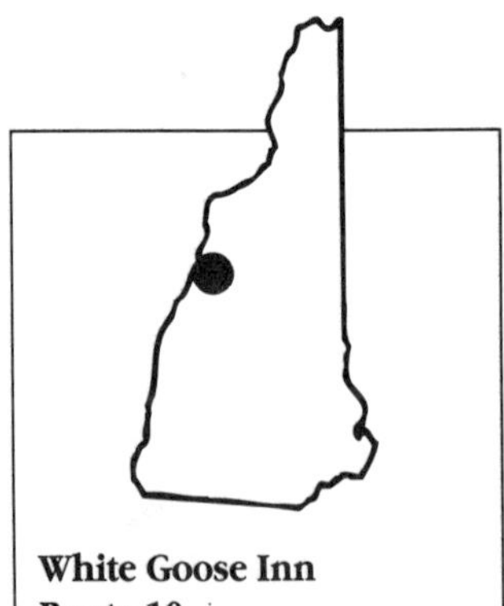

White Goose Inn
Route 10
Orford, 03777
603-353-4812

MC, V
Closed for two weeks in March
$75–$125

pillows, wreaths, geese, and stencils are fabulous. She offers them for sale in a snug passageway between the beautifully appointed parlor and the welcoming dining room.

The nineteenth-century brick house is made all the more distinctive by the elm tree trunk emerging through its wrap-around porch.

Guests feast on Karin's hearty breakfast by candlelight to the strains of Rampal and other classicists. The inlaid pine table and ladder-back chairs are partners to a most impressive mantel, which surrounds a cheerful fire during the winter. Karin's touch is always in evidence, and she creates special displays for each season. Easter-egg trees, valentines and ribbons, Halloween jack-o-lanterns, and Christmas trees, wreaths, and candles liven up the inn. She is as deft in the kitchen as she is at the crafts table; breakfasts are delicious, with her homemade raisin-bran muffins, Dutch baby pancakes (served as individual soufflés), French toast, cranberry bread, and sour cream cake. Afternoon tea also spoils guests.

You'll never be disappointed by a visit to the White Goose. The hospitality is warm, the environment comforting, the food great, and the scenery just what the get-away-from-it-all doctor ordered.

Directions: From I-91, take exit 15 to Route 5 north. Cross the bridge and turn right onto Route 10 south. The inn is 1 mile along on the left.

BREAKFAST BY CANDLELIGHT IS A REGULAR TREAT AT WHITE GOOSE INN.

Shelburne • Philbrook Farm Inn

You might have the impression that you've hit Brigadoon during one of its one-hundred-year appearances.

A CHILD'S FRAMED DRAWING on display at Philbrook Farm says that you have to be a fifth-generation guest to be able to stay at this inn. Not quite. But many of the guests who return to this farmhouse sanctuary are from families who have visited the farm since it first started as an inn in 1861. Some of the rooms are even named after these loyal extended-family members. Five generations later, the Philbrooks are still running the place, which gives this inn an unchallenged authenticity.

You might have the impression that you've hit Brigadoon during one of its one-hundred-year appearances. That's how untarnished and original Philbrook is. Located on nearly a thousand acres, the inn is surrounded by forests, streams, fields, and a World War II veteran's memorial birch grove that is unbelievably beautiful during the autumn. The nineteen-room house rambles through three floors and is filled with family antiques (beautiful maple country pieces). The entire effect is comfortable, simple, and homey. The property also has five summer cottages (not unlike adult dollhouses), attractive to couples or families who want to get even further away from it all. Scattered on the hillside, these cabins have the added attraction of accommodating children and the family pet.

The Victorian parlor has a collection of scrapbooks recalling Philbrook's history. The game room in the basement is the perfect place for kids. And the front porch has a superb view of the mountains, the fields, and Connie Philbrook Leger's flower gardens. Overnight guests are served a simple homestyle dinner (a good thing, since Philbrook is literally in the middle of nowhere). Baked beans and ham, Sunday roast chicken, and pot roast are a few of the down-home offerings. Breakfasts are equally hearty, with eggs, breakfast meats, and homemade donuts. On Sundays guests also have the choice of the Philbrook family's traditional fish balls and corn bread.

The farm is so self-contained that you could stay here for weeks (some do!). A map of the area will keep outdoor enthusiasts busy for days. There are miles of hiking paths (walking sticks and snowshoes are provided, seasonally), swimming holes in the hills, a new swimming pool, cross-country ski trails, and throughout it all, the luminescence of the birches. Located at the edge of the White Mountains,

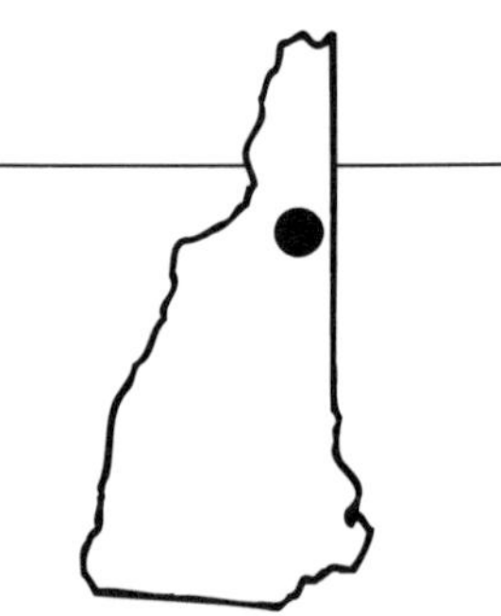

Philbrook Farm Inn
North Road (off Route 2)
Shelburne, 03581
603-466-3831

Cash or personal check only
Closed October 31 to December 26 and all of April
$90–$110; cottages, $400 per week

SOME PHILBROOK FARM INN GUESTS ARE FROM FAMILIES THAT HAVE BEEN VISITING THE INN SINCE 1861.

Philbrook is one of the most appealing places in New Hampshire. It just might convert you into a fifth-generation guest overnight.

Directions: From the Maine Turnpike (I-95), exit at Gray onto Route 26 north to Bethel. Then take Route 2 west to Shelburne. In Shelburne turn right onto Meadow Road. Follow for 1 mile, then turn right onto North Road. The inn is the second house. From I-93, take Route 3 north to Route 115 north. Turn onto Route 2 east. Turn left onto Meadow Road and follow the above directions.

Sugar Hill • The Homestead

THE HOMESTEAD'S OCTOGENARIAN INNKEEPER ESSIE SERAFINI KNOWS EVERY NOOK AND CRANNY OF THIS OLD HOME.

IT YOU WERE TO CREATE your ideal grandmother—a lady who is wise, funny, filled with stories, on the eccentric side, strong-willed, tender, and understanding—Essie Serafini could be her. This lively octogenarian great-grandmother has followed in her grandmother's and mother's footsteps, keeping the Homestead alive and active as its third-generation innkeeper. You know you're in the right place when the owner has slept in every bed in the house. She grew up here and knows every nook and cranny, along with every historical detail of this wonderful home. Essie's grandsons, Paul and Robbie, are keeping the tradition alive as they help her run the inn.

The inn is steeped in family lore, and you might be lucky enough to get Essie's personalized tour, during which she points out each piece of furniture she refinished herself; which blanket chest her grandfather made; which headboards and lamps she made; and what arrived on the ox cart in the late 1700s when her great-great-grandparents built the house. She will also show you her grandmother's linen collection and share her own favorite memories. Essie's tour is a sentimental journey, threaded with stories about growing up in this comfortable, rambling house. What's so special about the Homestead is the feeling that time here stopped a century ago. Everything in the house is beautifully restored, which makes your stay even more of a treat. But you won't be consumed by the past. Essie definitely lives in the present and has a tenacious curiosity about everything life has to offer, which makes her an attentive listener as well as an entertaining raconteur.

The Homestead has a special spirit. Everyone likes to be a part of this lilac-shaded home. Stray dogs and cats adopt Essie. Visitors come and stay thirty years. (The gardener and former pastry chef are two such examples; they loved the Homestead so much that they moved in and made their careers here helping Essie.) And people have been coming back here for generations—because the Homestead is more like home than home. The ten bedrooms in the main house are filled with beautiful country antiques — family treasures. The corner rooms, with bay windows, are particularly appealing, but all the rooms are comfortable and welcoming. (If you can't decide on a favorite, there are nine more with similar furnishings across the street in Essie's great-uncle's house.) The living room features Essie's organ, a gift

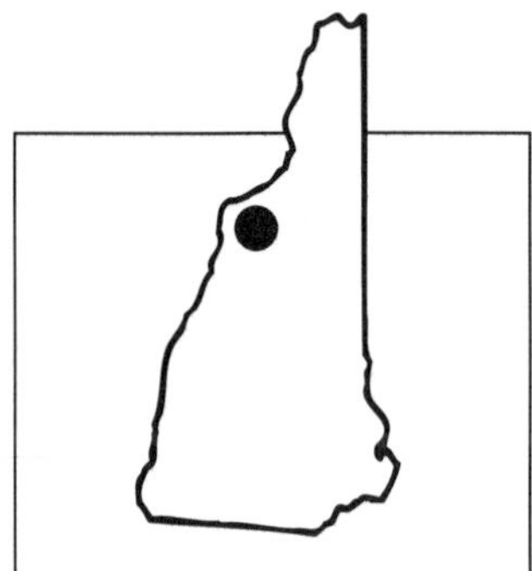

The Homestead
Route 117
Sugar Hill, 03585
603-823-5564

MC, V
Closed April, May, and November through Christmas Eve.
$70–$80

from the town of Sugar Hill on the inn's one hundredth birthday. A former music teacher, Essie loves to play the organ. The parlor has a collection of samplers, along with more of the family's history—books, furnishings, memorabilia. And the dining room is a real gem. It's filled with Essie's collection of cut glass, china, and wedding gifts. The centerpiece is her family of handpainted plates. She painted and fired each one, and the collection tells stories about the Homestead and its life over the past fifty years.

People have been coming back here for generations—because the Homestead is more like home than home.

Essie admits she is starting to slow down slightly. She no longer cooks her famous dinners, and guests miss her well-known soup specialties ("I'm an old soup queen," she confesses) and her authentic New England boiled dinners ("Never an onion near this dish," she admonishes). But she still serves a delicious country breakfast that will keep you more than satisfied.

This sprightly innkeeper has an endless supply of interests. If you can't find her one evening, she is no doubt adding to her thirteen-thousand-mile travel experience, following the New Black Eagle Jazz Band boys through New England. A visit to the Homestead is a wonderful sentimental journey, and you'll remember Essie always.

Directions: From I-93, take exit 38 onto Franconia Village. Turn onto Route 117 west. The inn is 3 miles along on the left, at the top of the hill.

THE DINING ROOM IS FILLED WITH ESSIE'S COLLECTION OF CUT GLASS, CHINA, AND WEDDING GIFTS.

Sunapee • Seven Hearths Inn

SEVEN HEARTHS INN OFFERS TWENTY-FIVE ACRES OF PATHWAYS AND TRAILS FOR GUESTS' DAILY CONSTITUTIONALS.

WHEN MARIANNE CALLAHAN turned forty, her husband, Miguel Ramirez, celebrated her birthday with a private black-tie party with her closest friends at Seven Hearths. It was their first visit to the inn, and a week later they bought it and became its new keepers. They continue to do things with style and finesse, making this elegant little inn a special place for a special clientele.

The couple integrated their own collection of beautiful antiques (Marianne's tall-case clock in the living room is a stunner) and personal touches (you'll no doubt notice Miguel's collection of Mexican art) with the charm of this already charming inn. There's none of the clutter you generally associate with country inns in these sophisticated rooms. Here the look is refined, elegant, and subtle.

The ten bedrooms, all with private baths, are large and airy, most with Count Rumford fireplaces. The back rooms have a view of the inn's pool, a dark, bottomless lagoon of black granite. Especially pretty are Three and the two downstairs corner rooms (One and Two), which share a porch. Five rooms have beam ceilings, all have rag and dhurrie rugs, and all are filled with fresh flowers and plants. The restful living room echoes with classical music, the voices of guests entertaining each other, and the occasional strains of the grand piano. The enormous fieldstone fireplace in this lovely room frequently is guarded by Max, the resident cat.

There are twenty-five acres of pathways and trails for guests' daily constitutionals. The inn has a striking location, well protected from the road, on top of a small hill; it exudes privacy.

Breakfasts are Marianne's specialty, and she treats guests to freshly baked muffins, homemade banana bread, apple pancakes, French toast, and eggs. Everyone who visits enjoys Marianne's bubbling personality, Miguel's warmth, and the comfortable, low-key ambiance of Seven Hearths.

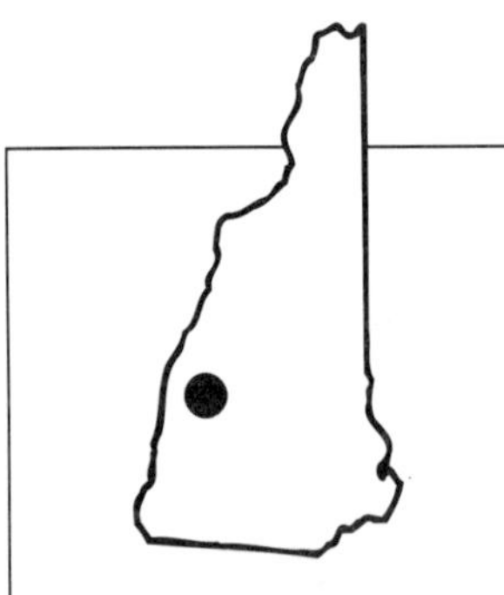

Seven Hearths Inn
26 Seven Hearths Lane
Sunapee, 03782
603-763-5657

MC, V
Closed April and two weeks in November
$73–$138

Directions: From I-89 north, take exit 12 to Route 11 west. The inn is 4 miles along on the right. From I-89 south, take exit 12A and turn right. At the blinking light on Sunapee turn right. The inn is 2 miles along on the right. From I-91 north, take exit 8 onto Route 103 east to Claremont. Then follow Route 11 to Sunapee. The inn is on the left.

GILMAN TAVERN SERVES AS AN OUTLET FOR ITS KEEPERS' HUGE COLLECTION OF EARLY AMERICAN PRIMITIVES.

Gilman Tavern • *Tamworth Village*

IF YOU FIND THAT YOU'VE reached the point where your house is exploding with early American primitives and you don't really have the inclination to open a folk art museum with your own personal inventory, you might take a tip from Sue and Bill McCarthy and do the next best thing. Opening a bed and breakfast inn has been a great way for this successful couple to share their love for country antiques, create a decorative home for guests, and showcase their incredible collection.

These two are serious collectors and have a fine eye for spotting early Americana treasures. Gilman Tavern is overflowing with Shaker rockers, antique baskets, yellowware, Pennsylvania Dutch furniture, quilts, decorative hatboxes, clipper-ship models, earthenware pottery, Shaker boxes, high-poster beds, antiques clothes, and a symphony of stencils. If you love this sort of thing, you'll be in naïf nirvana here. You'll share the sofa with a needlework menagerie or settle into a wing chair surrounded by a seemingly endless supply of unexpected discoveries. Sue has even gone so far as to paint her own naïf wall mural along the stairwell, illustrating the town of Tamworth. Amidst it all, the McCarthy cats perch leisurely on the stairs, peering out through the balusters and posing in cupboards, looking something akine to feline primitives themselves.

The McCarthys come to innkeeping with a proven past. Former owners of the Tamworth Inn (just down the street), they traded in their keys for something

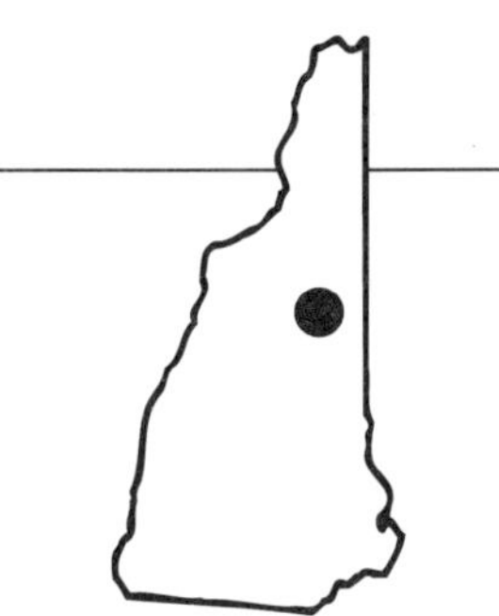

Gilman Tavern
Main Street
Tamworth Village, 03886
603-323-8940

Cash or personal check only
Closed April and May
$60–$85

more intimate. They also run two popular restaurants in the area, **Chequers Villa** (Route 113, Tamworth, 603-323-8686) and **Chequers Harbour** (Route 28, Center Harbor, 603-293-8613), perfect for travelers craving pasta in the New England countryside.

The bedrooms, each named for its view, are studies in Americana decorating prowess. The Village Room has a beautiful canopy bed, stunning pickled-wood floors with heritage stencils, a three-bears dollhouse (looking something like the tavern in miniature), and a view of Tamworth Village. The Swift River Room is the Village Room's counterpart across the hall with its own private bath. The Herb Garden Room evokes an early American child's room, with toys, clothes, and furnishings that give you an idea of what life was like for Colonial youngsters. And the Mountain View Room has eye-catching jacquard coverlets on high maple twin beds. Even the two modern bathrooms have a country feeling, keeping them in tune with this masterpiece of a home.

Gilman Tavern is overflowing with Shaker rockers, antique baskets, yellowware . . . high-poster beds, antique clothes, and a symphony of stencils.

The enormous and welcoming kitchen is the perfect place to settle in and chat with the McCarthys. Breakfast is served, however, in the dining room, on antique plates and crystal. Sue's specialties of home-made muffins and breads, French toast, and egg dishes are as satisfying as the decorative profusion surrounding you. When you manage to pull yourself away from this captivating house, you can wander down the street to take in any of the plays offered by the **Barnstormers Theater** summer stock season (Main Street, Tamworth, 603-323-8500).

Gilman Tavern is one inn you'll always remember. It might even inspire you to begin collecting primitive chairs, wooden bowls, oversize baskets, and a fleet of miniature ships of your own.

Directions: From I-95, take the Spaulding Turnpike north to Route 16 north to Route 25 west. Follow the signs to Tamworth Village and continue on Old Route 25 west. Take a right onto Route 113 north, then a left onto Main Street at the four-way intersection at the monument. Cross the bridge into the village. The inn is on the right. From I-93, turn onto Route 104 east, then take Route 3 north to Route 25 east. Turn onto Route 113 north. Follow the above directions.

Birchwood Inn • *Temple*

IF YOU'RE A RUFUS PORTER fan and follow his distinctive wall murals throughout New England, Birchwood Inn is an essential stop. And if you've never heard of Rufus Porter, that's all the more reason to drop in here, to see his restored 1830s panoramic paintings. You'll relive some fascinating inn history, all brought to life by Bill and Judy Wolfe in this two-hundred-year-old roadhouse.

Located at the picture-postcard crossroads in the tiny hamlet of Temple, this inn has retained the integrity and authenticity of its eighteenth-century origins. The architecture is rambling Colonial, the birch grove is pleasing, and simple, old-world atmosphere indoors is comfortable, thanks to the Wolfes. This cheerful couple believes in the personal approach, and they do everything themselves (often with the help of their three children). Judy is a serious cook—a dietician in pre-inn life—and she runs the inn's small restaurant, serving homecooked dinners from her own repertoire of recipes.

The Country Store Room downstairs has its own bath, and there are seven rooms upstairs, five with private baths. Each room has a theme related to the special interests and hobbies of the Wolfe family. As Bill offers, "We cleaned out the attic and came up with our room decor!" Particularly charming is the Seashore Room, bathed in deep marine blue and floral-striped walls. Equally appealing is the Music Room, filled with musical instruments—including the working ancient organ from the Congregational church down the street. You can also choose from the Editorial, Train, Library, and School rooms.

The common room downstairs is homey and comfortable, with a television to keep you in touch with the outside world. Breakfast is served in any of the three dining rooms, with a full selection of eggs, breakfast meats, and toast.

Come here to taste life from the history books and to meet a delightful couple who have found innkeeping fulfillment far from the New Jersey life they left behind.

Directions: From Route 3 north, take exit 7W in Nashua onto Route 101A west. After 8 miles, turn left onto Route 101 west. Turn left onto Route 45. The inn is 1½ miles along on the left. From I-91, take Route 9 east, which becomes Route 101 east. Turn right onto Route 45 and follow the above directions.

BIRCHWOOD INN'S RUFUS PORTER WALL MURAL IS, BY ITSELF, WORTH THE TRIP TO THE INN.

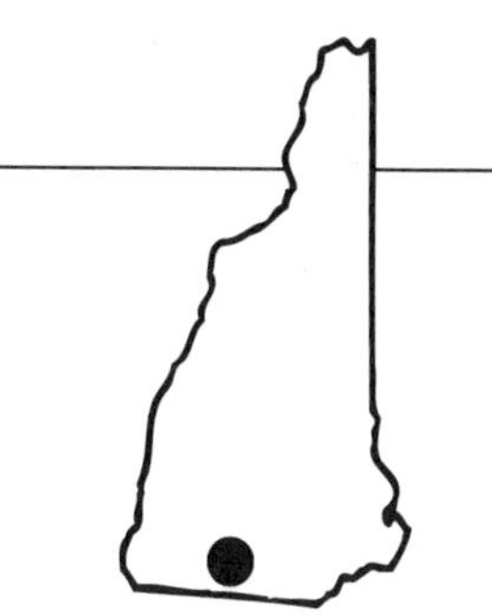

Birchwood Inn
Route 45
Temple, 03084
603-878-3285

Cash or personal check only
Closed two weeks in April and one week in November
Private bath, $70; shared bath, $60

AN IMPRESSIVE SIZE AND REMARKABLE ARCHITECTURAL DETAILING GIVE THE BLACK SWAN ITS SPECIAL LOOK.

The Black Swan Inn • *Tilton*

IF YOU ACCEPT THE fact that as an innkeeper your architecture is your destiny, you, too, would have snapped up this 1880 house that has become the Black Swan Inn. And if you are a smart businessperson, you would also have seen the potential in this piece of property on the edge of the New Hampshire lakes district. Bob and Janet Foster had just such good judgment. After thirty years with IBM, Bob was ready for a change of pace. There is no less work or energy required in the Fosters' new career, but they are fulfilled with the payback. You will be fulfilled, as well, when you visit this memorable inn and get to know the delightful Fosters.

The great thing about country inns is the unexpected. There are lots of surprises at the Black Swan. First is the set of incredible Tiffany-era stained glass windows. And then there's the impressive woodwork. Or the original tinwork and dramatic staircase. Or the fact that Bob is clearly the master carver of Tilton. He made many of the pieces of furniture in the inn and spends his spare time creating extraordinary hand-carved carousel horses. You may find it impossible to resist one of his full-size handpainted horses. The $2,000 pricetag seems like a steal considering the quality of the workmanship. There are enchanting miniature versions for a more affordable $525. He also makes wonderful rocking horses for children of all ages.

The Black Swan has a unique personality. The stained glass windows in the living room and the upstairs bedroom (a similar set of windows brightens the room in their own bay alcove) are stunning. So is the dining room with its wood paneling, enormous fireplace, and lead-glass-windowed built-in cabinet. The six bedrooms are spacious, each painted a different color, each with comfortable furnishings. Three have private baths, three share. Each room is named after one of the Fosters' children or grandchildren. Victoria is truly romantic with its upstairs Tiffany-era windows, oversize brass-and-iron bed, and botanical prints creatively displayed with oversize ribbon trim. It's no surprise that this room is nicknamed the "bridal suite." Valerie is also attractive in deep green with white wicker furnishings; Jennifer is cheerful in azure blue; Brandon has an antique chicken-coop cage that serves as a luggage stand. There are plenty of family pictures scattered throughout the inn to give you a sense of the Fosters' deep family ties.

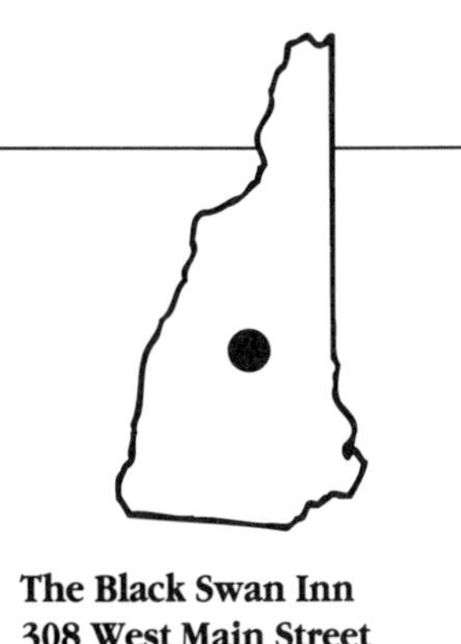

The Black Swan Inn
308 West Main Street
Tilton, 03276
603-286-4524

All major credit cards
Closed March
$55–$65

There are lots of surprises at the Black Swan.

Breakfast is served in one of the most handsome dining rooms in New England. With the antler trophy over the hearth, the room has the feeling of the Vanderbilt's hunting-lodge breakfast room. Janet serves a full breakfast of such traditional fare as waffles and sausage, scrambled eggs with ham and cheese, pancakes, eggs Benedict, and baked apples.

There is a formal garden for relaxing, a screened-in porch for more relaxing, and the Fosters for stimulation. The Black Swan is worth a visit, in any season.

Directions: From I-93 north, take exit 19. Turn left at stop sign onto Route 132. Go 1 mile to the traffic light. Turn left onto Routes 3 and 11 south. The inn is 1½ blocks along on the left on West Main Street.

VERMONT

BACK TO THE LAND

Vermont bed and breakfast inns are particularly popular with cyclists, skiers, leaf peepers, and city people escaping for the weekend. The picturesque back roads and quaint villages offer a wide selection of inns, both for upscale travelers and for those more economy-minded. Although there are many more full-service inns than bed and breakfasts in Vermont (travelers come to this state to stay put over the weekend), the bed and breakfast inns included in this chapter are exceptional. From the Northeast Kingdom all the way south to historic Manchester, these inns offer country charm in historic homes. These inns, most of which are tucked away in the countryside, will tempt you into visiting each and every one, only to discover another new favorite whenever you're on the road again.

VERMONT'S MANY INN HIDEAWAYS MAKE JOURNEYS ALONG THE BACK ROADS ESPECIALLY REWARDING. ABOVE: FOUR COLUMNS INN, REVIEWED ON PAGE 113.

Craftsbury • Craftsbury Inn

THE LONG DRIVE TO CRAFTSBURY INN IS A JOY IN ITSELF, AND WELL WORTH THE TIME.

JUST WHEN YOU'RE convinced you must be within sight of the Canadian border, you are ready to roll into Craftsbury. This northern outpost is one of the prettiest villages in Vermont. Newcomers be forewarned: It takes a certain degree of perseverance and optimism to drive to what seems to be the ends of the earth for a weekend getaway. But first-timers will soon discover that the drive to Craftsbury is almost as beautiful as the town itself. The Northeast Kingdom is clearly God's country.

Rebecca and Blake Gleason run this distinctive, white 1850 inn with its four-column facade and spacious, simply furnished common room, a relief for guests weary of cluttered country-inn living rooms. The high tin ceiling, expansive wood-plank floor, and clean-line decor give an airy feeling to this pleasant gathering room. For the active guests the property includes a trout stream, walking paths, and plenty of space for cross-country skiing.

The ten bedrooms are pleasantly simple; six have private baths, and all provide tranquility and restful sleep. Blake is a professional chef, so you can be sure that his full breakfasts of egg dishes, French toast, wheat-raspberry pancakes, and home fries are satisfying. Dinners are impressive, with entrées such as pheasant with Frangelica sauce, poached salmon with cucumber-dill sauce, baked partridge with Grand Marnier sauce, and veal medallions with wild mushrooms.

If you're looking for a small-town, country experience, visit the inn during the local Banjo Contest and Old Home Day. The Craftsbury Chamber Players also perform during the summer, a nice touch that completes a perfect bed and breakfast experience.

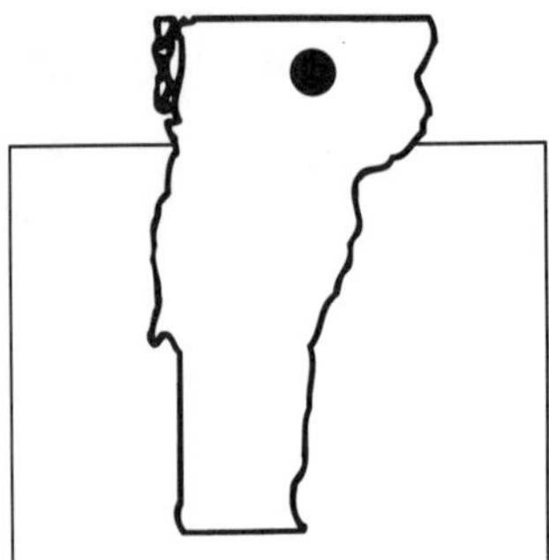

Craftsbury Inn
Main Street
Craftsbury, 05826
802-586-2848

MC, V
Closed November
$55–$95; incl. dinner, $95–$150

Directions: From I-91, take exit 21 at St. Johnsbury. Follow Route 2 west to Route 15 west and continue to Hardwick. Take Route 14 north for 8 miles. Follow the sign to Craftsbury. Take a right onto Main Street and continue up the long, winding road. The inn is about 2 miles along on the right.

Inn on the Common • *Craftsbury Common*

LOYAL GUESTS WHO HAVE discovered Inn on the Common are very protective of this gem. Rightfully so, as this inn offers an unparalleled tranquil, countrified experience. Standing on the inn's gentle precipice overlooking the mountainous vista to admire another perfect summer sunset will cause even the most cynical individual to consider the possibilities of having located nirvana, New England-style. Penny and Michael Schmitt, proud owners of this wonderful refuge, have created something very special. The main house is charming, and its Federal-style exterior fits perfectly into the storybook town of Craftsbury. The eighteen rooms in the main house, as well as the inn's two other houses, are filled with antiques, country details, handmade quilts, Proton alarm clocks (high-tech in Colonial surroundings), fluffy robes, attractive artwork, and a sense of privacy. All have private baths, some also have beam ceilings, and most have extraordinary views.

"We take kids, cats, cockatiels, cocker spaniels — everyone!"

There is plenty to do at the inn. The Schmitts have a collection of videotapes for film buffs, the gardens are beautiful, the croquet court is tempting, the swimming pool (it looks somewhat like a pond banked with river rocks) is refreshing, and the clay tennis court, with its breathtaking location and view, is generally available. There is also the town of Craftsbury. Nice people live here, and they have preserved the best traditions of small-town life. A visit here will introduce you to the joys of living life in the slow lane. The town has a collection of handsome houses to tour, and the cemetery across the street from the inn is steeped in local history. Old Home Day in August is the town's festival celebrating everyone who ever lived in Craftsbury (the type of celebration with a Main Street parade), and there is plenty of space in the area for nature walks.

The inn is good news for families. Penny cheerfully invites the whole family to Craftsbury. "We take kids, cats, cockatiels, cocker spaniels—everyone!"

The inn has a well-deserved reputation for its cuisine. Guests can dine in the beautiful dining room, with its view of the rose gardens. It's not hard to strike up new friendships with other guests over five-course dinners starting with specialties such as fresh artichokes or sweetbreads, followed by a tasty light soup. Entrées are equally delicious, with perfectly prepared homemade wine, locally raised pheasant, partridge, or rabbit, as well as traditional meat

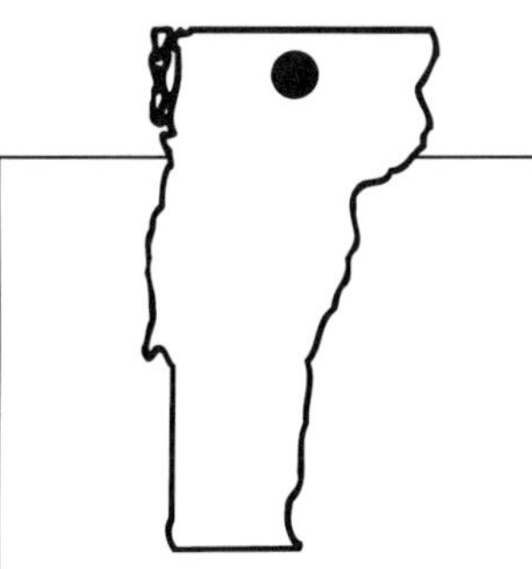

Inn on the Common
Off Route 14
Craftsbury Common, 05827
802-586-9619; 1-800-521-2233

MC, V
Open year-round
$160–$210; including dinner, $190–$240

TRAVELERS WHO HAVE DISCOVERED INN ON THE COMMON ARE EAGER TO KEEP IT A SECRET.

courses. Desserts are varied and imaginative. The salads are always fresh, the service professional, and the company eclectic.

Breakfasts are as hearty as the dinners. Fresh fruits and juices are followed by breakfast breads, homemade cereals, a garden variety of omelets, eggs as you like them, smoked bacon, Vermont sausage, and Canadian bacon. The inn offers such a pleasant experience that you will agree with the coterie of fiercely loyal regulars who believe that it is worth every penny and all the effort it takes to get here.

Directions: From I-89 north, take exit 7 onto Route 2 east. Continue to Route 14 north, then turn right (marked) 8 miles after Hardwick and follow for 3 miles to the inn. From I-91, take exit 26 onto Route 58 west to Irasburg. Then take Route 14 south for 12 miles to marked left turn. The inn is about 3 miles along on the left.

Quail's Nest Inn • *Danby*

WHEN YOU'RE IN THE village visiting the **Danby Antiques Center** (Main Street, 802-293-5484), taking stock of the latest inventory of fine-quality country furniture, rag rugs, Shaker boxes, splint-weave baskets, table-top linens, quilts, and any of the other can't-live-without-it treasures, make plans to stay at Quail's Nest Inn just across the street. The convenient location is perfect for compulsive shoppers who want just one last look before moving on. Chip and Anharad Edson opened this little bed and breakfast because they decided that country living was to their liking and a small country town was the perfect place to raise their daughters Chelsea and Aubrey.

AT QUAIL'S NEST INN, THE DECOR IS SIMPLE AND THE HOUSE IS STREWN WITH ARTWORK.

Their six-bedroom inn offers a cheerful place to stay, surrounded by decor reflecting Anharad's penchant for pastels. The living room is light in pink and ivory, and very pretty floral-print sofas and a warm fire in the winter. Upstairs, one room is lavender, another light blue, a third pink, and the other two are wallpapered in deeper colors. An antique quilt covers each bed. The suite in the carriage house out back is equally soothing in pastels. The decor throughout the inn is simple, and the house is strewn with artwork created by both sets of parents. Chip's handiwork is on display as well. One of his several woodworking creations, a country chandelier, dominates the stairwell.

Anharad makes a satisfying country breakfast, served in the country dining room. Quiche, cheese-baked eggs, French toast, fresh fruit, and homebaked breads and muffins get everyone off to an energetic start. There's plenty to do in the area for outdoor enthusiasts: the Appalachian Trail cuts through Danby, the Mount Tabor National Forest is a wonderful place to hike or drive through, and then there's the antique center across the street for those more domestically inclined.

Come to this blue house with white trim to meet an attractive young couple who have made a peaceful transition from the food-service world in Philadelphia to the guest-service world in this unpretentious and charming country inn.

Directions: From I-91 north, exit at Brattleboro onto Route 9 west. Follow to Bennington, then take Route 7 north. In about 12 miles, turn left onto Main Street in Danby. The inn is in the center of the village. From I-89 south, take Route 7 south. About 18 miles south of Rutland turn right onto Main Street in Danby.

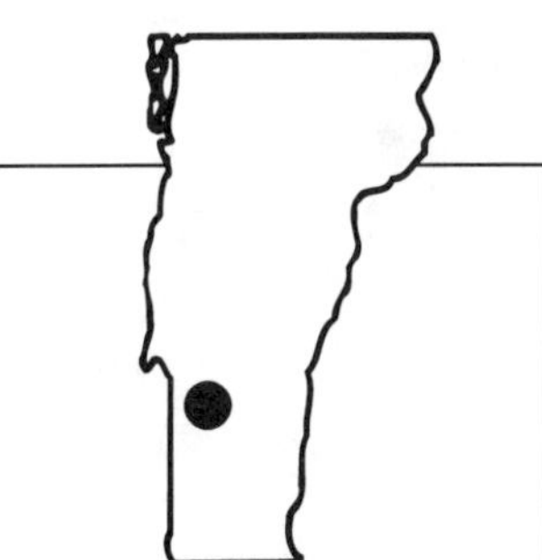

Quail's Nest Inn
221 Main Street
Danby, 05739
802-293-5099

MC, V
Closed two weeks in April
$50–$65

Dorset • Cornucopia of Dorset

YOU CANNOT HOPE TO FIND a more attractive and comfortable inn than Cornucopia. The name is as fitting as the rooms are spacious, the breakfasts ample, and the hospitality thoughtful and generous. You may be greeted with a champagne toast, and you can always expect genuine friendliness from Linda and Bill Ley.

The four large bedrooms and one private cottage are decorated with a fine eye and give you a great sense of privacy. The Scallop Room is beautiful with its lace-canopy bed, fireplace, and rust-and-green color scheme. Green Peak, also with its own fireplace, has a tall-post bed and a pleasant view out back. Dorset Hill has an enormous bed and is soft in lavender and mauve tones; Mother Myrick is soothing in beige; and Owl's Head, the back cottage, is a true getaway. Its exposed-beam ceiling, kitchen, sitting area with fireplace, and sleeping loft make this private retreat a great place to settle in for the season. The common rooms in the main house are quite comfortable, whether it be the more contemporary solarium or the more country-style study and sitting room.

GRACIOUS HOSPITALITY AND AN IMPRESSIVE BREAKFAST PROVE THIS INN'S NAMESAKE.

The Leys take all aspects of the business seriously, and Linda's breakfasts are triumphs. Seated family style at the large dining room table, you may be for-

NOTHING IS SPARED TO MAKE YOUR STAY HERE RESTFUL AND COMFORTING.

tunate enough to be served chilled minted melon soup; fruit puff pancakes; pecan, sausage, and apple crêpes; baked croissants with crème fraîche; bread pudding with warm berry sauce; chilled peach soup; or spiced fruit compote.

The Cornucopia is an exceptional inn. It is contemporary, yet old-fashioned and comfortable in feeling. It is also in the quaint village of Dorset, tranquil in comparison with nearby discount-store headquarters, Manchester. The inn is located across the way from **Peltier's Market** (Church Street, 802-867-4400), a fabulous find offering all the country classics you'd expect and some very chic gourmet fare and good California wines, which you wouldn't expect. But most people visit Dorset for the summer-season **Dorset Playhouse** (Colony House on Church Street, 802-867-2223), a legitimate summer-stock house specializing in lighthearted works and very popular with the Brooks Brothers/Talbot-attired set.

Directions: From Route 7 north, turn north on Route 30. Go 6 miles to Dorset. The inn is located on the right. If you have reached Dorset Village Green, turn back.

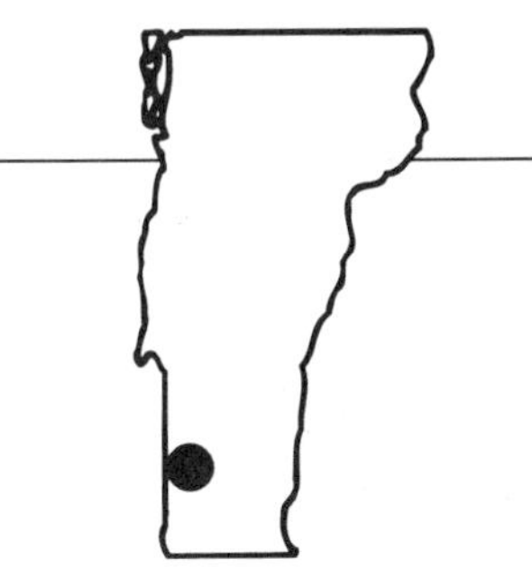

Cornucopia of Dorset
Route 30
Dorset, 05251
802-867-5751

MC, V
Open year-round
$75–$150

EAGLE TAVERN ONCE HOUSED MEETINGS OF ETHAN ALLEN AND HIS GREEN MOUNTAIN BOYS.

East Poultney • **Eagle Tavern**

THERE'S A GOOD CHANCE Eagle Tavern's twelve columns, outlined in bright white to contrast with the canary-yellow house, will lure you into visiting this historical inn. One-time meeting place of Ethan Allen and his Green Mountain Boys (the biblical reference painted onto a ceiling beam, "The gods of the hills are not the gods of the valleys," is apparent testimony to Allen's approach to life), as well as the former home of Horace Greeley, this unusual bed and breakfast has a genuine historical feeling.

Owners Bill and Gertrude Horridge are delighted with their find. They wanted a home large enough to house their antique collection, and this six-room inn fits the bill. Opening the Tavern also gave Bill the opportunity to bring his wife back home; Gertrude was born and raised in nearby Dorset.

The cheerful Horridges will be delighted to take you on a tour of their 1785 home. The Tap Room in the Cellar is just as it was: whole log beams, brick fireplace, and an austerity in keeping with Colonial times. Upstairs, the sitting room is decorated in a simple style, perfect to showcase the Horridges' early American furniture collection. The dining room is a stunner. Original Hitchcock chairs, an elongated table, an antique carpet, and fresh blue walls make this handsome room the perfect place to enjoy Gertrude's breakfasts of muffins (maple, bran, or blueberry), Irish soda bread, waffles, special cheesecake, yogurt, tea breads, Vermont cheeses, and charcuterie meats.

But nothing in this tasteful inn can prepare you for the experience of staying in the upstairs ballroom bedroom, with its twenty-six-foot bowling alley

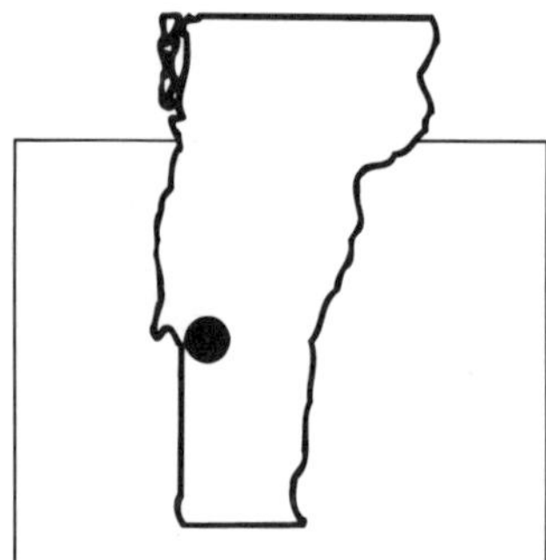

Eagle Tavern
Route 140
East Poultney, 05741
802-287-9498

MC, V
Closed March 15 through April and November through December
Double, \$60–\$75; single, \$45

length and barrel ceiling. Serene in blue, with a trace of echo chamber in the acoustics, this enormous room has its own living room at one end, a suitable place to entertain everyone you've ever met. The scale makes the queen-size canopy bed look like a Lilliputian miniature. The rest of the ballroom has been converted to a separate bedroom, lovely in pink with a barrel ceiling and its own private bath. When the two rooms were still connected during the 1920s, the ballroom was used to construct wooden boats, which were lowered by block and tackle to the ground outside.

In contrast to the gargantuan size of these two rooms, the Horace Greeley room next door is tiny. Its tiger-maple bed is perfect for a traveling single or a child over twelve years old. The remaining three bedrooms are more conventional in size. All four share the spacious bathroom.

Eagle Tavern is a journey into the past. The Horridges are enthusiastic hosts, always looking for additional early American treasures to add to their collection and guests who appreciate the inn for its authenticity and simplicity. Book ahead and be sure to make reservations, as the Tavern is a reservations-only inn. The trustees of nearby Green Mountain College have discovered Eagle Tavern, and these high-powered businesspeople have adopted the inn as their semiannual home away from home.

Directions: From I-91 north, exit at Brattleboro onto Route 9 west. Follow to Bennington, then take Route 7 north. Take Route 11 west to Route 30 north. Turn onto Route 140 east. Inn is 2 miles down the road. From I-89 south, take Route 7 south. Take Route 4A west to Route 30 south. Turn onto Route 140 east.

THE UPSTAIRS BALLROOM BEDROOM MUST BE SEEN TO BE BELIEVED.

Fair Haven • Vermont Marble Inn

IT WOULD HAVE SEEMED unlikely that Bea and Richie Taube and Shirley Stein, firmly entrenched in Long Island life, would cash out and move to Vermont to run a country inn. That, at least, is what their acquaintances thought. Their close friends, on the other hand, advised them to find an exceptional inn in order to be happy. Vermont Marble Inn is not only exceptional, it is run by three exceptional people.

Bea and Shirley, long-time best friends, dreamed of owning a large inn in northern Vermont. When they saw the extraordinary Marble Inn in the southern part of the state, they reconsidered their dreams and traded them in for new possibilities. Although this handsome house, faced in marble, had a widow's walk (no water in sight, however) and Victorian architectural styling, the interior was in dire need of a facelift. Bea and Shirley, coupled with Richie's perseverance, are the can-do team, and they completed restoration of this impressive building in a scant ten weeks.

The 1867 house was built in a spiteful fit of oneupmanship by a descendant of Ethan Allen, more a monument to ego than a home. Original owner Ira C. Allen tried to outdo his former partner in the marble trade, using his partner's impressive marble house across the town green as the model. Allen's result is clearly superior.

MAJESTIC ARCHITECTURE AND UNIQUE HOSTS MAKE MARBLE INN UNIQUELY MEMORABLE.

THE FEMININE DECOR IS PLEASING AND COMFORTABLE.

Today, Marble Inn is a pretty picture of Victoriana. A profusion of pinks and mauves, period furnishings, attractive wall coverings, and comfortable beds contribute to the inn's aesthetic success. Its ambitious owners have also opened the dining room and serve some excellent cuisine here. The professional chef is assisted by baker-Bea, who makes the most delicious breads and pastries. Not to be outdone, Shirley takes over at breakfast with some of her own tempting selections.

The fourteen rooms are filled with large beds and lots of lace and are softened with pastel colors. Each of the bedrooms is named after an English author whom Bea and Shirley admire. The two upstairs front rooms are particularly pretty. The step-up windows in the third-floor rooms are delightful. The back wing is a little like going through a time tunnel; the architecture and decor are Art Deco, with matching furnishings.

Breakfast is served in the lovely dining rooms overlooking the garden. Bea's homemade muffins are partners to Shirley's Grand Marnier French toast, nut waffles, fresh fruit pancakes, and cheese omelets, as light as soufflés. Your hosts here believe firmly that you should indulge yourself . . . an attitude they will happily help you achieve.

Bea, Shirley, and Richie are among the most original New England innkeepers. They are delightful, genuine, and slightly offbeat. A visit to Vermont Marble Inn is a visit you'll remember.

Directions: From New York, take I-87 to exit 20. Take Route 149 east to Route 4 north to exit 2. Follow the signs to Fair Haven to inn.

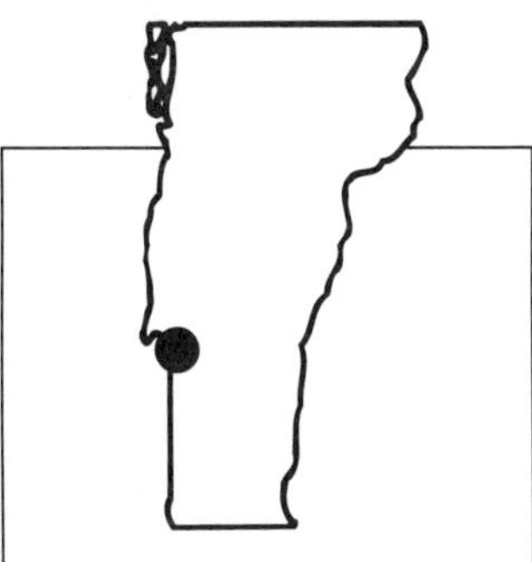

Vermont Marble Inn
West Park Place (on the town green)
Fair Haven, 05743
802-265-8383

AE, MC, V
Open year-round
$80–$110; incl. dinner, $135–$165

FROM THE FOOT OF ROMANCE MOUNTAIN, BLUEBERRY HILL INN BECKONS TO SPORT ENTHUSIASTS.

Goshen • **Blueberry Hill Inn**

WHEN WINTER CROSS-COUNTRY ski addicts are ready to try out their new Fischer Ultra Crowns, or aspiring downhill racers take out their Rossignol 45s for a test run; when hikers are ready to lace up their Asolos boots, and fly fishermen bring out their latest boron rods, they probably are gearing up for a visit to Blueberry Hill, a mecca for serious (and not-so-serious) good sports. Even if you're not a hot-dog skier, you will fall in love with this outpost, located far from everywhere on a deserted back country road (unpaved, so bring your four-wheel-drive winter vehicle), where hospitality is unlimited and the scenery is unbeatable.

Owner Tony Clark has created a fabulous spot, building Blueberry Hill's reputation as a cross-country touring stopover. (This inn participates in winter cross-country ski tours in which skiers trek from one inn to another for a series of overnight visits.) Less-transient individuals can choose to stay put at the inn, with its seventy-five kilometers of nearby trails to challenge all levels of skiers. During the summer the inn provides mountain bikes for cycling the ski trails. No matter what the season, all guests appreciate the stunning location at the foot of Romance Mountain in the Green Mountain National Forest. The inn's spring-fed pond offers swimming to cool guests in the summer; nearby Lake Dunmore is available in any season for its wide range of water sports.

When guests are finally ready to come indoors, the rustic 1813 Blueberry Hill Inn welcomes them with a fire in winter, the fragrance of flowering plants in the solarium throughout the year, and an endless supply of chocolate chip cookies to keep energy levels up. The twelve rooms are simple. Barn siding and country calico are the decor themes here. Clearly the focus at Blueberry Hill is outdoors or in the sporty common room and handsome dining room.

Blueberry Hill also serves a four-course dinner to guests (which is a good thing since the inn is so isolated) and has established quite a reputation for quality, regional cuisine. The food is sophisticated and fresh. During the summer there's a decided blueberry theme, with specialties such as chilled blueberry soup, chicken breasts with a blueberry marinade, blueberry cheesecake, blueberry tarts, and for breakfast, blueberry buttermilk pancakes. Herbs are grown in the garden, and the seasonal produce comes from a local grower. Dinners are celebrations of creative regional dishes such as scallops with tomato-cognac cream sauce, grilled beef with garden herbs (in the summer) or an Irish whiskey-mushroom sauce (in the winter), grilled port marinated in honey-soy sauce, rack of baby Vermont lamb with basil butter, and swordfish steaks with black olive purée and a spicy red hollandaise sauce.

The inn's spring-fed pond offers swimming to cool guests in the summer.

Breakfasts are equally inventive, with a four-course meal of fresh juice, fresh fruit kebabs, homebaked muffins and coffee cake, and an entrée. Apple puff pancakes, vegetable frittatas, eggs baked with Brie, French omelets (delicate crêpelike affairs) filled with fresh herbs, and homemade granola—all served with local bacon or lamb sausage—are among the selections.

Come to Blueberry Hill for an active vacation during any season. You'll be spoiled by the surroundings and pampered by the inn's staff. It's clearly the stuff that outdoor dreams are made of.

Directions: From I-89, take exit 3, the Royalton and Bethel exit, onto Route 107 west. Then take Route 100 north to Route 73 west. As you come into Forestdale, a Blueberry Hill Inn sign will provide further directions. If the sign isn't visible, turn right a few miles after the peak of the mountain onto a paved road that quickly turns into a dirt road. At the stop sign at Camp Thorpe, take a right. Turn right again at the intersection of four roads. Inn is 1½ miles along on the right.

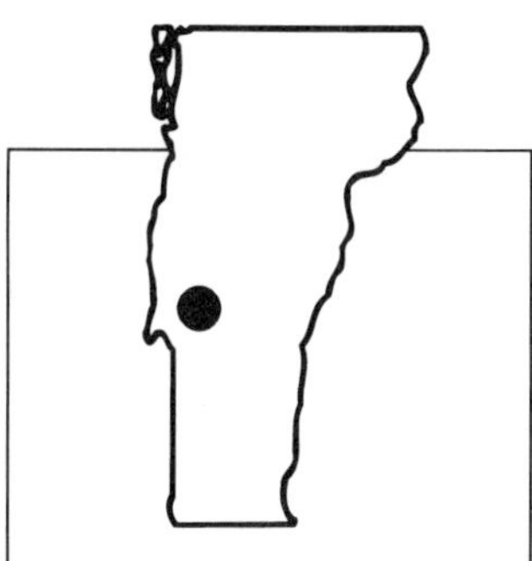

Blueberry Hill Inn
Off Route 73
Goshen, 05733
802-247-6735; 800-448-0707

MC, V
Open year-round
Summer (incl dinner), $150–$200; winter (incl. dinner) $196

Ludlow • Governor's Inn

THE UNUSUAL SLATE FIREPLACES AT GOVERNOR'S INN HAVE LOVELY FAUX FINISHES

CO-OWNER DEEDY MARBLE is Governor's Inn's own best public relations agent. With the lilt of a tour director, she'll guide you through the inn, pointing out its highlights and subtleties; tell you how lovely the house is (it is); explain its history; introduce you to five generations of photographs of her and husband Charlie's families; show you the wall of magazine covers on which the inn has been featured; point out the collection of guidebooks in which the inn is included; and show you the various pieces of heirloom family furniture located throughout the inn. She'll also point out the unusual slate fireplaces painted to look like marble; show you the salt and pepper shaker souvenirs she has collected from her world travels, lead you to the silver tea service and porcelain teacup collection (much of which has been contributed by satisfied guests) she uses when serving tea every afternoon, and present the array of homemade goodies that the inn offers for sale to guests (jams, preserves, chocolates, potpourri, chutney, and Deedy's own cookbook). All of this is done with enthusiastic sincerity. Deedy is proud of their inn. She throws the same energy (which is considerable) into preparing her cuisine, and the inn is well known for its fine dinners.

After enjoying one of Deedy's perfect meals, you'll no doubt float upstairs to sleep in one of the eight handsome bedrooms. A collection of English armoires, family antiques, pretty linens, lacy and crocheted spreads, charming wallpaper, and Victorian furnishings will tide you over until breakfast. The butler's basket in the hallway is a thoughtful touch; it is filled with needed items that the Marbles have forgotten at one time or another during their own travels.

When you awake, you'll be greeted by Charlie's excellent five-course breakfast. A mellow, low-key man, Charlie is the perfect balance to Deedy's high-energy, high-impact personality. He is a master morning chef, offering such delicious choices as strawberry-rhubarb or maple-walnut coffee cake, stone-ground hot cereal, rum-raisin French toast, and the inn's breakfast puffs.

Governor's Inn is a pleasant place to stay, surrounded by well-fed guests and the welcoming, cheerful Marbles.

Directions: From I-91, take exit 6 onto Route 103 west. The inn, located at the intersection of Routes 100 and 103, is 23 miles along on the left.

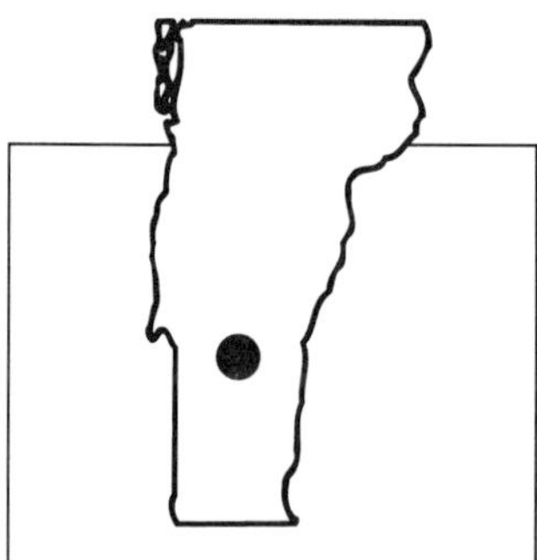

Governor's Inn
86 Main Street (Route 103)
Ludlow, 05149
802-228-8830

AE, MC, V
Closed April and November
$130; incl. dinner,
$170–$180

1811 House • *Manchester*

MARY HIRST'S HOUSE was so overflowing with museum-quality English and American antiques that she felt she had no choice but to follow the British bed and breakfast tradition and open her own inn. She runs 1811 House with husband Jack, son Jeremy, and daughter-in-law Pat.

In this business, architecture (along with your collection of furniture) is your hallmark, and this Federal-style home is clearly the perfect example of a beautiful piece of property enhanced by equally beautiful furnishings. Comfort and quality meet head-on here, making a visit to the inn something like a visit to another country. Perhaps it's the echo of English accents in the hall, the British tea served in the morning, or the perfect little pub that makes 1811 House so refreshingly civilized. In any case, the inn is a treasure trove, far from the madding crowds of Manchester's outlet stores, where everyone energetically fights for the latest marked-down bargain.

AT 1811 HOUSE, "COMFORT AND QUALITY MEET HEAD-ON."

You'll relish the chance to return to the inn after a wearying day of shopping, visiting the **American Museum of Fly Fishing** (Seminary Avenue and Route 74, 802-362-3300), or testing out a new split bamboo fishing rod at the Orvis headquarters down the road. It doesn't take much enticement to settle into the wonderful pub, surrounded by manly thoroughbred prints, pewter tankards, a dart board, and a winter fire. Or you might choose to relax in either of the beautiful sitting rooms, surrounded by elegant touches, tasteful furniture, and peaceful pastel colors. You can immerse yourself in a soft print sofa, admiring the oil paintings and getting to know Bartok the cat on a more personal basis.

Of course, you can always retreat upstairs, following the red Oriental carpeted hallway (1811's refined version of the yellow brick road) to your overnight sanctuary. The fourteen rooms are even better than you could dream up on a good night, offering a unique taste of antique elegance. Each room is named after a local legendary figure, all have private baths, and the choice among them will make your head spin. The consensus is that the Mary Lincoln Isham Room at the top of the stairs qualifies as the pièce de résistance. The stunning pink-and-blue wallpaper is outdone only by the creamy canopy bed and large bathroom with Victorian-era fixtures. Relax in blue wing chairs in front of the fireplace and take in your surroundings; you'll be sure to notice the cat motif here (and throughout the house), a definite sign of feline aficionados.

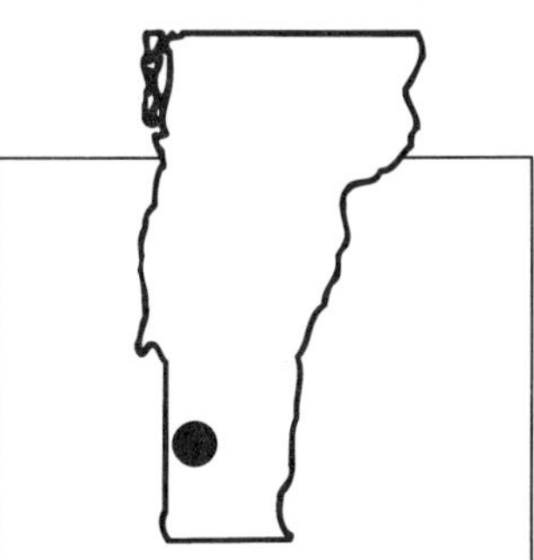

1811 House
Route 7A
Manchester, 05254
802-362-1811

AE, MC, V
Closed Christmas
$100–$170

EACH OF 1811 HOUSE'S FOURTEEN ROOMS IS NAMED AFTER A LOCAL LEGEND.

As beautiful as the Mary Lincoln Isham Room is, you might want to experience the uniqueness of the marble bathroom in the Robinson Room, with its Victorian version of the first shower. The four-poster twin beds are as comfortable as the pencil-post canopy bed in the Grace Hoyt Singer Room, with its lovely patched hooked rug and charming bathroom. The Hidden Room, cozy under the eaves, is as charming as the Franklin Orvis Room, with its seashell-motif rug in keeping with the Orvis marine-life tradition. (Franklin Orvis's company is best known for its high-quality fishing gear.) And then there is always the Jeremiah French Suite downstairs, a spacious hideaway in barn red with a sitting room and high four-poster bed. The three new rooms are even more stunning, each with its own fireplace, collection of antiques, four-poster canopy king bed, orientalia, and superb sense of privacy. No doubt you'll return here as a regular to try out each room. From the largest to the smallest, no detail has been overlooked, and you'll be assured a comfortable stay amidst beautiful surroundings.

The inn is a treasure trove, far from the madding crowds of Manchester's outlet stores.

As befits an inn of this caliber, breakfast is served in the formal dining room (don't worry about dressing to match the decor; life is informal at 1811 House). You are seated on Chippendale chairs, surrounded by subtle stencils, antique chandeliers, an impressive porcelain collection, and an oil painting of a peaceable lamb family living the contented life on the farm. A full English breakfast is served, including the traditional rasher of bacon, eggs, fried bread, sautéed mushrooms and tomatoes, and sliced apples. Eggs Benedict is on the table every Sunday.

You won't be disappointed by this special inn. The view overlooking the Equinox Golf Course is bucolic, there are three acres filled with flower gardens, the Hirst family is a pleasure, and there are plenty of pets to keep life appropriately normal and relaxed.

Directions: From Route 7, take Route 7A south. The inn is 1 mile south of Manchester Center.

Wilburton • *Manchester*

YOU COULD TOUR NEW ENGLAND VISITING THE FORMER HOMES OF TURN-OF-THE-CENTURY CAPTAINS OF INDUSTRY

THERE ARE A HANDFUL OF inns housed in the impressive architecture of the once rich and famous. You can take a swing through New England to visit these summer homes and landed-gentry manors, enjoying the benefits of wealthy family legacies, now passed into the hands of entrepreneurial innkeepers. You will enjoy the illusion of living like the original owners in these palaces, a gift to yourself when you feel like celebrating a special occasion or need an antidote to the rest of civilization.

Wilburton is southern Vermont's entry into the monumental inn cadre. A. M. Gilbert built this handsome house so that he could live nearby his friend Robert Todd Lincoln at Hildene, just down the hill. This oversize brick house welcomes you to the manor-born with large rooms and a taste of nostalgia from the 1890s. The common rooms are enormous, airy, and light, with superb views of the Battenkill Valley. If you plan to stay for dinner at Wilburton, you will dine in high style in the original dining room or wood-paneled billiards room. The latter is particularly attractive during the winter when a roaring fire in the mammoth fireplace keeps you company. The food is quite good, a blend of traditional fare and new American cuisine.

The ten bedrooms are equally large and aristocratic in feeling. All have private baths, complete with large Victorian claw-foot baths.

Breakfast is served in the cheerful terrace dining room, a veritable feast of a country breakfast with blueberry pancakes, eggs any style, sausage and bacon in addition to fresh fruit and homemade muffins.

Wilburton sits on seventeen acres — and includes two full-scale houses with more modest decor in their seven bedrooms, three other villas with an additional eighteen bedrooms, and two tennis courts. Albert and Georgette Levis bought Wilburton after celebrating his fiftieth birthday here. Be careful where you spend your own pivotal birthdays: you may find yourself in the inn business, virtually overnight.

Directions: Take Route 7 north to Route 7A north into Manchester. Turn right at River Road (a large yellow house sits at the corner) and proceed ½ mile to the inn.

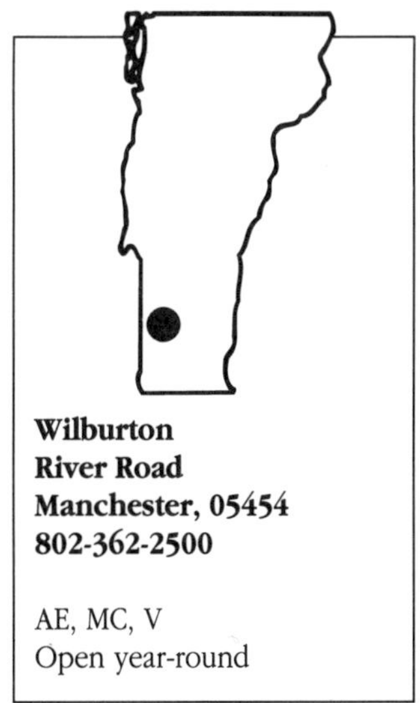

Wilburton
River Road
Manchester, 05454
802-362-2500

AE, MC, V
Open year-round

Middlebury • **Swift House Inn**

PARENTS OF MIDDLEBURY College students love Swift House Inn because it offers the intimacy of a bed and breakfast, Andy Nelson's personalized cuisine, and a decor that makes everyone feel akin to the king of the castle. Andy and her husband, John, have done a sensational restoration job, preserving the integrity of the 1814 Samuel Swift house (Swift was once governor of Vermont), while at the same time providing a comfortable inn that would make any Federal-era aristocratic family proud. The Nelsons pay attention to detail, and each of the twenty rooms is a celebration of good taste and handsome decor. New wallpapers perfectly complement the extraordinary original handblocked papers, creating a harmony of color and design throughout the house. Most of the beds are large, each room has a private bath, and each has a unique spirit.

SAMUEL SWIFT, FOR WHOM SWIFT HOUSE INN IS NAMED, WAS ONCE GOVERNOR OF VERMONT.

The Governor's Room is fresh in blue and white, with a king-size, four-poster bed and a contemporary bath, with a whirlpool and bidet. But it's Jessica Swift's Room that gives spacious-bathroom lovers pause. You can bathe practically alfresco in this charming room. French doors open from the bathroom onto the private second-story terrace, with its view of the beautiful, rolling front lawn and stately trees. The room itself is a replica of the original. To create it, the Nelsons consulted family papers, housed in the **Sheldon Museum** (1 Park Street, 802-388-2117), a historical decorative arts museum designed to preserve the history and legends of the area. The Seymour Room, decorated with vine-motiff walls, has single beds and an enormous bathroom. The Addison

Room is a miniature forest of pink dogwood-print walls and wicker. And the rooms go on and on, each just as wonderful as the last. The five rooms in the Victorian Gatehouse provide a great sense of privacy and getting away from it all. The decor and furnishings are period-appropriate and carry out Andy's attention to decorative detail. There are five additional luxurious rooms in the newly renovated Carriage House offering oversize Jacuzzis, fireplaces, and cable televisions hidden discreetly in armoires.

Breakfast is presented in the formal dining room downstairs, with wood-paneled wainscoting and remarkable purple-and-green grape-cluster wallpaper (the original). The seating is Chippendale and Queen Anne. Andy serves eggs Benedict, French toast, and popovers as centerpieces.

Guests can relax in the entry room on comfortable sofas in front of the fire, in the living room (where the piano helps break the ice among strangers), or on the front porch with its view of the gardens and lawns. Even if you don't have relatives at Middlebury College, there are plenty of reasons to visit. This pretty town offers the **Morgan Horse Farm** (Morgan Horse Farm Road, off Route 23, 802-388-2011) and the **Vermont Crafts Gallery at Frog Hollow** (Mill Street, 802-308-3177), both good reasons to come here for a wonderful weekend in elegant surroundings among newfound friends.

THERE ARE TWENTY DELIGHTFUL ROOMS TO CHOOSE FROM AT SWIFT HOUSE INN.

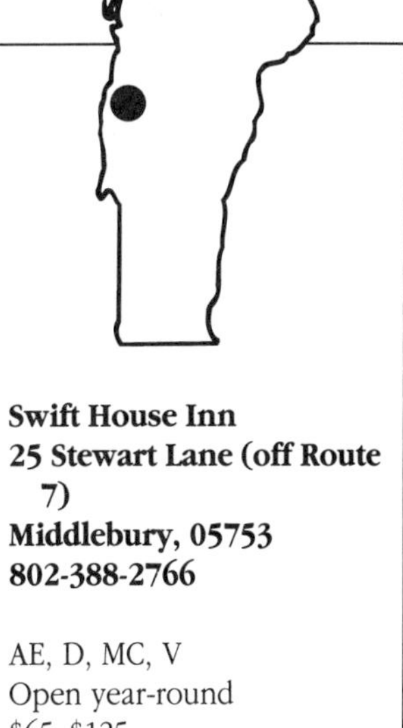

Swift House Inn
25 Stewart Lane (off Route 7)
Middlebury, 05753
802-388-2766

AE, D, MC, V
Open year-round
$65–$125

Directions: From I-89 north, exit at Bethel onto Route 4 west. Take Route 100 north to Route 125 west to Route 7 north. The inn is located on the corner of Route 7 and Stewart Lane, 2 blocks north of the center of town, on the right.

Middletown Springs • **Middletown Springs Inn**

MIDDLETOWN SPRINGS INN IS "DOING ITS BEST TO KEEP THE VICTORIAN ERA ALIVE AND WELL."

WHEN YOU WALK THROUGH the front door at Middletown Springs Inn, you'll enter another era. There's a distinct Victorian feel to this palatial home. The lush foyer wallpaper is simply a preview of the turn-of-the-century decor and environment that make this inn so appealing. Jane and Steve Sax have relocated from Calais, Maine, to this inn, bringing Jane's clock collection, ancestral portraits, and massive Victorian furniture with them. Their collection enhances Middletown Springs Inn's lovely decor—golden print dining room walls, a light pink parlor, and beautiful woodwork and lighting. Life at Middletown Springs Inn is busy. The Saxes provide two Lippett Morgan horses to assist in elegant rides in the inn's Austrian carriage, a royal touch for guests. Their Four Days of Christmas Celebration includes sleigh rides. There are also murder-mystery weekends, and cross-country skiing during the winter.

The ten bedrooms range from mansion size to servants' quarters. Among the most appealing is Four, with its colorful bird-and-flower walls, Jenny Lind spool daybed, and beautiful Victorian double bed with matching dresser. This garden room overlooks the charming town common. Also attractive are One and Six, both large and cheerful.

Steve serves breakfast in the large dining room, which features Jane's glass collection and oversize sideboard furniture. His German apple pancakes, French toast stuffed with cream cheese and marmalade, and a baked egg-and-sausage casserole are as tasty as the dinners, served to guests only. A special Sax picnic lunch is also available to guests who request it the night before.

Jane and Steve had a cottage crafts business headquartered in the inn, where they sell local artisans' creations. Delicate floral wreaths, silk floral arrangements, and Amish dolls are only a few of the temptations available to take home as souvenirs from this lovely inn that is doing its best to keep the Victorian era alive and well in Vermont.

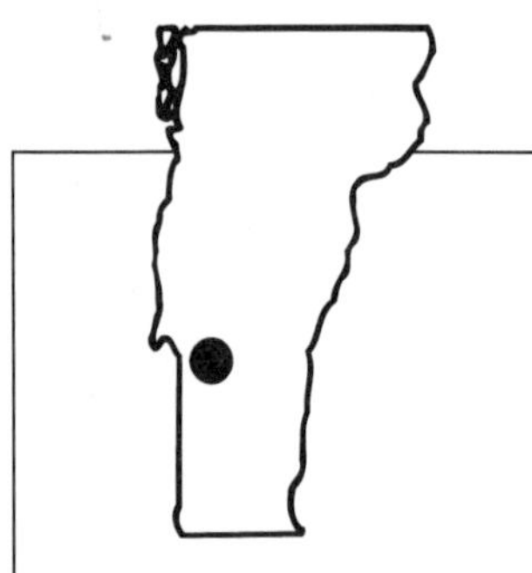

Middletown Springs Inn
Routes 140 and 133
Middletown Springs, 05757
802-235-2198

MC, V
Open year-round
$60–$100; incl. dinner, $100–$140

Directions: From I-91, take Route 4 west to Route 133 south. The inn is on the right, beside the village green in the center of town.

Four Columns Inn • *Newfane*

ASK A CONNECTICUT innkeeper where he or she goes to get away for a weekend, and chances are it will be the Four Columns Inn. Don't assume that the inn's reputation is built on any kind of elitism or snobbishness. Rather, Pam and Jacques Allembert know how to do things very nicely. It's a country-inn experience that innkeepers especially can appreciate, combining a stunning 1830s house (built by Parton Kimbell in the plantation spirit—ionic columns and all—to impress his southern belle wife), an excellent restaurant, lovely gardens, and a light touch in the decorating department. The Allemberts also have a handsome piece of property; their 150 acres reach into the woods and across a stream, and the inn commands a front-and-center position in Newfane's charming town green.

Ask a Connecticut innkeeper where he or she goes to get away for a weekend, and chances are it will be to the Four Columns Inn.

In the spring and summer, you'll find Jacques tending his beautiful gardens, working on the pond, overseeing the swimming pool, or working on the back 146 so that guests have a carefully manicured verdant view. Indoors, whichever room you choose, you'll be assured a pleasant stay surrounded by the Allembert's antique collection, tall-post and canopy beds, private baths, lovely wallpaper, and restrained decorative touches. Room Six is especially pretty, with its garden-print walls in pinks and greens and an impressive canopy bed, handmade by a local woodworker. Seven is Victorian in spirit, with rose-colored walls, deep reds, and turn-of-the-century furnishings. Four has walls of blue bouquets and a handsome iron bed.

The rooms in the annex, above the restaurant, are equally delightful, even if the architecture is slightly less interesting. In Fifteen you'll find the second handmade canopy bed, and Twelve is a yellow suite overlooking the back woods. There are two more rooms in the more contemporary cottage. Mick Jagger celebrated his fortieth birthday in this little hideaway.

The dining room is country-perfect: beam ceiling, chintz decor, antique gadgets, and a view of the English garden through the French doors. An extensive buffet breakfast is served here. Pam offers a delicious health-conscious breakfast with homemade biscuits and muffins, homemade granola, fresh fruits and berries, and local Grafton Cheddar cheese.

In between meals guests can wander on the trails behind the house, sunbathe, swim, relax in the shade, and wander down the street to the **Newfane Country Store** (Route 30, 802-365-7916) to look over

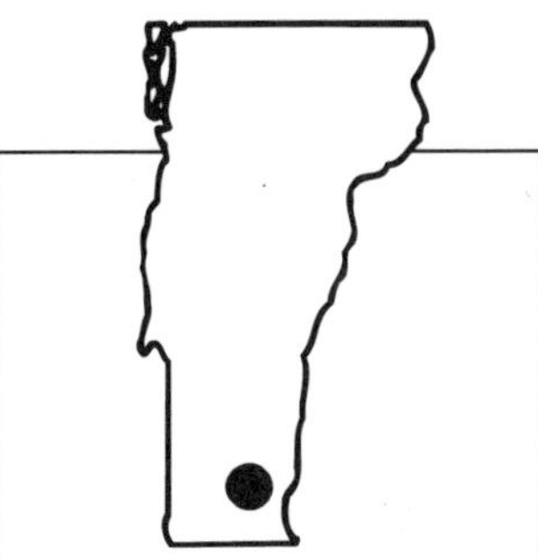

Four Columns Inn
West Street (off Route 30)
Newfane, 05345
802-365-7713

AE, MC, V
Closed April
$95–$135

THE 1830S FOUR COLUMNS INN BOASTS 150 ACRES, IN ADDITION TO ITS INTERIOR CHARMS.

the shop's endless array of country temptations: a hodgepodge of quilts, wooden baby toys, handknit sweaters and caps, candles, soaps, honey, sweets, and so on. But the ambiance of the inn is so peaceful, Pam and Jacques are such gracious hosts, and the entire place is so alluring that you may decide never to leave.

Mick Jagger celebrated his fortieth birthday in this little hideaway.

Directions: From I-91, take exit 2 in Brattleboro to Route 9 east. Continue to Route 30 north. The inn is 11 miles from Brattleboro, 100 yards off Route 30.

Quechee Bed & Breakfast • *Quechee*

IF YOU'RE DRAWN TO the power of waterworks that rival Fourth of July fireworks, make it a point to visit Quechee Gorge. While in the area, plan ahead to stay at the Quechee Bed & Breakfast, a beautiful Colonial home with a spectacular view. You'll be tempted to spend all your time outdoors watching the water rush down the ravine below the inn. Hosts Susan and Ken Kaduboski supply plenty of outdoor chairs so you can settle in for the duration.

The inn has eight rooms, all with private baths, queen-size beds (except two, which offer twin sleigh beds or a king-size bed), and restful colors. The decor here is uncluttered, creating a welcome respite from inns overladen with decorative details.

The Kaduboskis have kept things simple so as not to interfere with the natural surroundings. A lovely country-pine blue room upstairs provides a counterpoint to the more formal four-poster bedrooms sprinkled throughout the inn. The four rooms in the back of the house command the best view, blending their country decor interiors with the hydroelectric flash outside.

The cheery living room is where contemporary prints join forces with a beam ceiling, huge fireplace, and spectacular view. The sunny dining room has separate tables, and the Kaduboskis offer a delicious breakfast of cinnamon-raisin custard, quiches, stuffed French toast, or apple-cinnamon pancakes. Homemade frozen yogurt, apple-cranberry relish, fresh fruits, Vermont cold-smoked bacon, and fabulous steel-cut oatmeal complete the feast.

This country inn combines the best of country living with a superb location. You'll enjoy the company of Susan and Ken (corporate transplants from Boston) as well as exploring the revitalized town of Quechee.

Directions: From I-89, take exit 1 onto Route 4 west. The inn is about 4½ miles along on the right.

QUECHEE BED & BREAKFAST BOASTS SOMETHING "EXTRA" WITH ITS SPECTACULAR VIEW OF A NEARBY RAVINE.

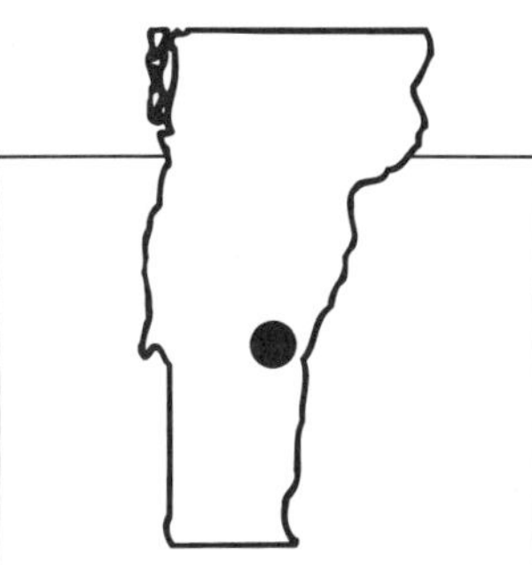

Quechee Bed & Breakfast
Route 4
Quechee, 05059
802-295-1776

MC, V
Open year-round
$85–$125

South Woodstock • **Kedron Valley Inn**

KEDRON VALLEY OFFERS ACTIVITIES TO KEEP YOU ENTERTAINED YEAR-ROUND.

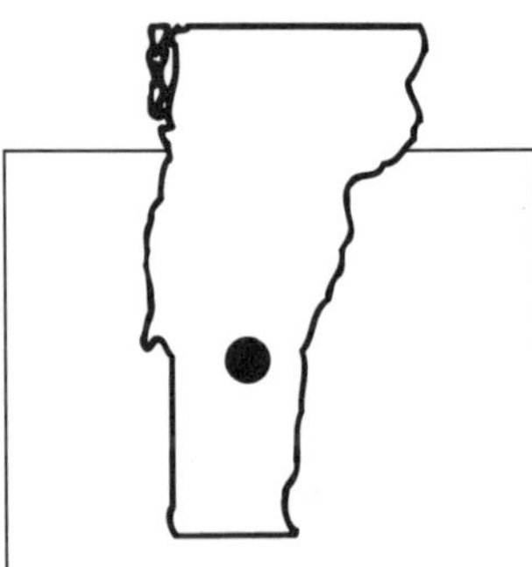

Kedron Valley Inn
Route 106
South Woodstock, 05071
802-457-1473

MC, V
Closed April
Incl. dinner, $138–$199

MAX AND MERRILY Cummins keep themselves practically as busy as they were when they had careers on Wall Street. It appears that it's hard for them to completely slow down the pace. They are active with apple-picking weekends, sleigh rides, and a T-shirt and sweatshirt business as well as maintaining the inn pond with its lifeguard and sandy shoreline, horseback riding, winter cross-country skiing, and redecorating the inn. They are promotionally minded and offer you any number of good excuses to get away to the country.

Kedron Valley Inn has a main house, annex, and more rustic country cabins in the back. It is generally full, as the Cumminses offer a warm welcome and run a professional operation. To add to the charm of the place, Merrily has a quilt and antique clothing collection displayed throughout the inn, complete with homilies on craftsmanship and her family's history.

In the main house, there are fifteen rooms, many of which are quite large; some with fireplaces, and all with private baths. Canopy beds, exposed-beam ceilings, and televisions set the style in most of the rooms. The tavern next door, an 1822 brick house, has seven additional rooms, all attractive and charming. The log lodge out back offers another six rooms with more rustic furnishings and Merrily's hand-drawn stencil work.

Breakfast is served in the peach-tone dining room. Eggs, buttermilk and blueberry pancakes, French toast, and specials such as frittatas, Vermont cob-smoked ham-and-Cheddar omelets, and eggs Florentine prepare you for a day of participating in any of the Cumminses' country activities. At night, excellent cuisine is served here with a sophisticated menu offering local products and a creative approach to country dining. It's always a surprise to find urbane offerings—such as salmon in puff pastry, fresh shellfish with wild mushrooms and Frangelica sauce, and rack of lamb with cabernet-rosemary sauce—in a country inn.

Directions: I-91 north to I-89 north to exit 4 west. Continue to Route 106 south. Inn is 5 miles south of Woodstock Village Green.

HOMESTEAD DECOR CREATES AN AUTHENTIC LOOK TO THE ATTRACTIVE ROOMS.

Vergennes • Strong House Inn

STRONG HOUSE INN, BUILT IN 1834, IS LOCATED IN THE SMALLEST CITY IN THE COUNTRY.

THE NEXT TIME YOU schedule a visit to the fabulous **Shelburne Museum** (802-985-3344, Route 7 Shelburne, open May through November) to reacquaint yourself with its never-ending collection of folk-art masterpieces, reserve a room at Strong House for a taste of country living at its best. Owners Michelle and Rob Bring have used their professional talents and personal charms to make Strong House a delightful experience. This pleasant inn is popular with cyclists, so you may find yourself surrounded by healthy, vigorous guests who appreciate the pastoral setting and the Brings' brand of hospitality. The inn, built in the Federal style in 1834, is located in the smallest city in the country. With only twenty-five hundred residents, Vergennes is exactly the same size as it was in 1820. The population is good news for travelers who enjoy leaving the cities for a gentler country pace.

The seven rooms at Strong House are modest and pretty, with Michelle's fashion-minded decorating taste softening the look. Two of the rooms have working fireplaces, five have private baths, and all have an eclectic collection of antiques. There is a handsome double sleigh bed in the English "Hunt" room, two double four-poster beds in Sheraton—great for traveling families—and a cozy nook under the eaves with one double bed and one single bed.

The downstairs sitting room is comfortable, and the spacious dining room is cheerful. The Brings' delicious breakfasts are served at large tables where guests compare notes on cycle routes and local attractions. The menu of frittatas, eggs Benedict, quiche, French toast, and ham-and-cheese soufflé fuels up guests for a full day in the country. Michelle's homemade granola is always popular, and the fresh fruit brings in a fresh approach in any season.

Strong House is a perfect Vermont interlude, unpretentious, friendly, and private.

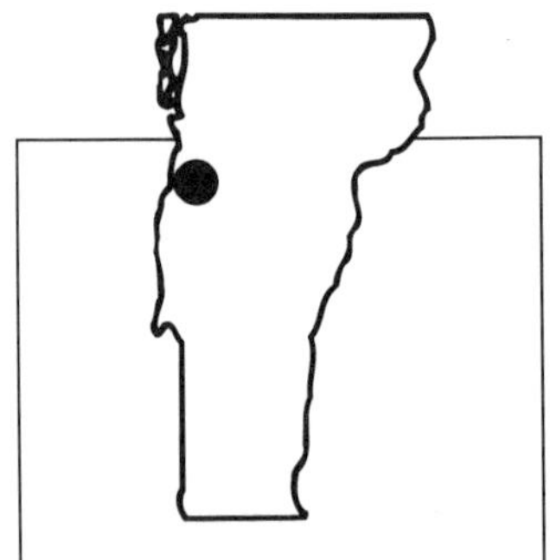

Strong House Inn
Route 22A
Vergennes, 05491
802-877-3337

MC, V
Open year-round
$45–$80

Directions: From I-89 north, take exit 13 to 189 west onto Route 7 south. Then take Route 22A south to Vergennes. Continue through the stoplight, and the inn is ¾ mile along on the right.

West Dover Inn • *West Dover*

WEST DOVER INN'S LOCATION IS CONVENIENT TO A NUMBER OF OUTDOOR AND CULTURAL ACTIVITIES.

WHEN YOU DECIDE TO ski at Stratton, Mount Snow, or Haystack; to kayak the white water of the Deerfield River; to attend the Marlboro Music Weekend Concerts; to go leaf peeping, lake touring, or horseback riding; or simply to do nothing, check into the West Dover Inn for something slightly more refined than what the local ski lodges have to offer. Don and Madeline Mitchell have completely refurbished their 1846 inn with light, cheerful wallpaper, antiques, a handsome collection of beds, private baths, and televisions. The overall effect is country-simple without pretension or fussiness, although the two suites allow visitors to rest their weary bodies in Jacuzzis or in front of fireplaces in their sitting room.

West Dover Inn is a pleasant place to settle for the weekend. The Mitchells' son, Douglas, manages the inn's very good restaurant, Capstone. You can sit and rock on the second-story porch, chat with the ever-candid, no-frills Don and his soft-spoken wife, Madeline, and wander around this charming little Vermont town. You'll know you're in New England on Sunday when the church next door summons you to breakfast with its come-to-meeting bells. Madeline's down-to-earth, all-American breakfasts feature favorites such as pancakes, eggs, French toast, and homebaked breads.

Directions: From I-91 north, take exit 2 to Route 9 west. Continue about 20 miles and turn right at the only traffic light on this route onto Route 100 north. The inn is 6 miles along on the right, exactly 1 mile from the Welcome to West Dover sign.

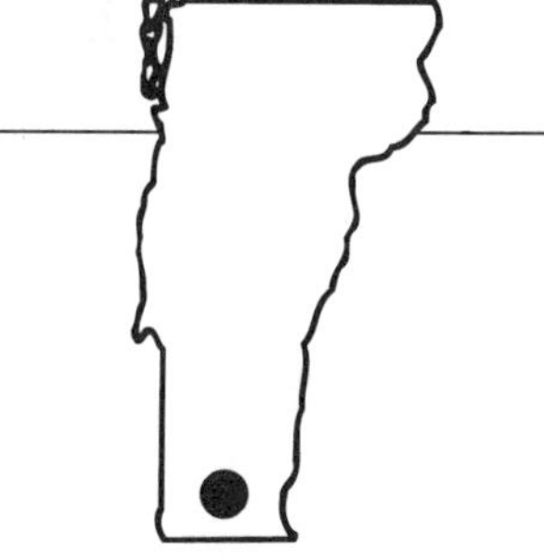

West Dover Inn
Route 100
West Dover, 05356
802-464-5207

AE, MC, V
Open year-round
Off-season, $75–$110; in season, $90–$185 (5 percent surcharge for credit cards)

Weston • 1830 Inn on the Green

THE NAME TELLS YOU EVERYTHING YOU NEED TO KNOW ABOUT WESTON'S 1830 INN ON THE GREEN.

WESTON IS A TOWN SO picture-perfect that you would be disappointed not to find a charming country inn to complete the image. Fortunately, Sandy and Dave Granger have accommodated this need with their very pretty inn, thoughtfully located on the town green, no less. This lovely 1830 home, with its gardens and pond in the back, is a hop and a skip from the summer stock **Weston Playhouse** (On the Green, 802-824-5288) and is a perfect place for theatergoers to stay during the dramatic season.

The 1830 Inn on the Green is just as pretty and romantic under its new ownership as it was in the past. You are greeted by the beautiful spiral staircase, which leads you upstairs to the four bedrooms. All are very appealing in a country way; two have private baths, two share a bath (one of which has its own half-bath); and all are named after women who played strong roles in the history of Weston and beyond. Hetty Green (she was the first female stockbroker, a standard-bearer somewhat before her time) is pretty in pink, with its sweet, old-fashioned wallpaper print. Polly Farrar has an enormous brass bed and lovely floral-print fabrics. Lois Mansur is deep in rose with a panoramic view out back, and Emma Peabody displays a circle quilt pretty enough to inspire your own collection.

The breakfasts are full and tasty, with waffles, pancakes, and French toast popular among guests. The handsome dining room with its rich green color scheme adds to the taste appeal.

In addition to being situated in picturesque Weston, the inn is just up the road from the famous **Vermont Country Store** (Route 100, 802-824-3184). This is one-stop shopping, Vermont-style. If you need rugged wear, children's toys, country crafts, and sensible shoes, this is the place for you. It's everything you can think of, and everything you'll ever need for practical living.

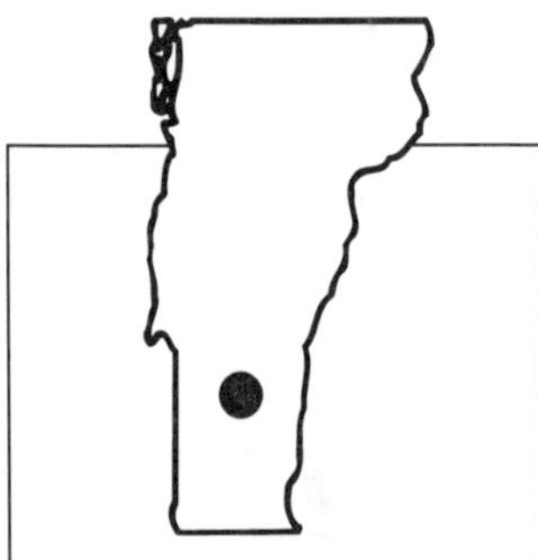

1830 Inn on the Green
Route 100
Weston, 05161
802-824-6789

MC, V
Open year-round
$60–$80

Directions: From I-91, take the Rockingham exit onto Route 103 west to Chester. Take Route 11 west to Route 100 north. The inn is about 6 miles along on the right.

Canterbury House • *Woodstock*

CANTERBURY HOUSE IS THE latest venture of Bill and Barbara Hough, new owners of Charleston House (p. 123), just down the street. This 1880 inn is just as handsome as its sibling, and it is a showcase for Barbara's decorating prowess. The Houghs have refurbished this former boarding house with great style. The antiques were all imported from Denver, and they fit into this comfortable house perfectly. The living room is welcoming in the winter with its blazing fire, warm rose-and-blue color scheme, and impressive period plasterwork. The dining room is also spacious with a large table and formal bamboo Chippendale chairs. The Houghs use beautiful flatware and porcelain, and they serve some fabulous breakfasts. On a given morning, guests may receive puff pancakes, egg-and-artichoke casserole, macadamia nut waffles with strawberries, rice custard, and gingered biscuits. Barbara's gourmet creations are so popular that she published a cookbook, with all proceeds donated to charity.

The seven rooms here are named after its namesake Chaucer classic. Reeve's Tale is a beautiful bouquet of a room, furnished in crisp white wicker—very feminine and romantic. Friar's Tale is light and airy in red and blue. Shipman's Tale has a handsome brass

TASTEFUL DECOR AND A SENSE OF TRANQUILITY MAKE CANTERBURY HOUSE A PLEASANT EXPERIENCE.

EACH OF THE ROOMS IS NAMED FOR A CANTERBURY TALE.

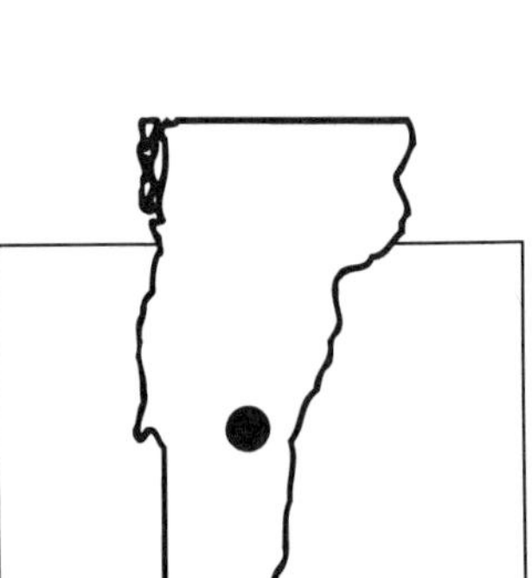

Canterbury House
43 Pleasant Street
Woodstock, 05091
802-457-3077

All major credit cards
Open year-round
$90–$115

bed and part of Barbara's antique linen collection. Squire's Tale has a beautiful tiger-maple spindle bed under its gable roof, and Knight's Tale is masculine and strong, and befits its name. Parson's Tale is one of the prettiest rooms; situated in the front of the house, it is restful in aquamarine. Monk's Tale, in its solitude in the back of the house, has its own fireplace, a huge Victorian bath, and is certainly more luxurious than the cloisters. In any case, it's a suitable place for some quiet reflection and contemplation.

John, the Houghs' son, manages this inn and Charleston House, and does whatever he can to make your visit as pleasant and memorable as possible.

Directions: From I-89, take exit 1 to Route 4 west for 10 miles. The inn is on the left on Pleasant Street.

Charleston House • *Woodstock*

CHARLESTON HOUSE IS IN the capable hands of new owners Barbara and Bill Hough and their charming son John, and they are keeping up the standards set by the inn's former owners. Barbara is a Virginian and offers an inn filled with her good taste, her family's handsome antiques, and a taste of southern hospitality. A considerable amount of this good taste emanates from the kitchen as Barbara's gourmet breakfasts. She has published a collection of her recipes, available to guests with the proceeds donated to charity. Breakfasts are served at an impressive Federal-period dining table, large enough to seat ten. The formality of the style is echoed in the Houghs' collection of Orientalia and their sense of personal style. Charleston House is one of the more attractive inns in New England. It's a lovely place to stay while taking advantage of Woodstock's picturesque qualities and proliferation of stylish boutiques and shops for the upscale tourist trade.

The seven bedrooms are all worth staying in. Gables has Barbara's childhood furniture; Good Friends has her uncle's superb scroll-motif twin beds; Hilary Underwood is cozy in rose and blue with its tall-post bed; Pomfret Hills has an impressive four-post Charleston Rice bed; Henry Hatch is soothing in salmon tones; and Antique Store is lovely in pale peach with its tall-post bed. The Summer Kitchen in the back of the house is a great hideaway with its own entrance and equally beautiful decor.

John manages the inn for his parents, and he can be seen around town and between the family's two inns (see page 121) with his golden retriever, Sander. He is helpful, friendly, and a large part of what makes the Charleston House so special.

Directions: From I-89, take exit 1 to Route 4 west for 10 miles. Inn is on the left on Pleasant street.

THE TRADITIONAL SOUTH AND HERITAGE NEW ENGLAND MEET IN THE 1835 CHARLESTON HOUSE.

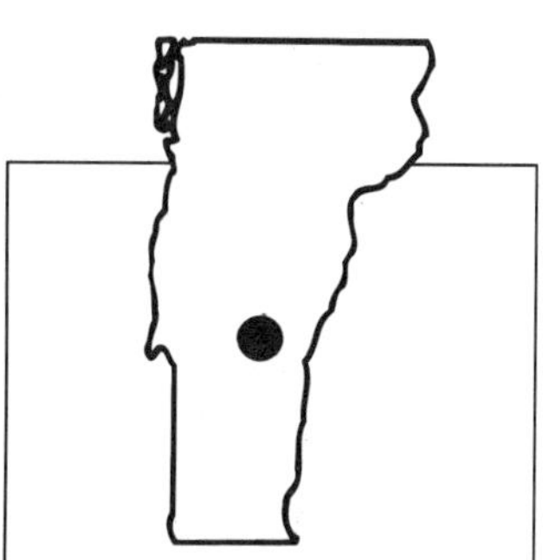

Charleston House
21 Pleasant Street (Route 4)
Woodstock, 05091
802-457-3843

All major credit cards
Open year-round
$100–$125

IT'S EASY TO FORGET YOUR CARES AMIDST THE BEAUTY AND CALM OF JACKSON HOUSE.

Woodstock • **Jackson House**

WHEN YOU ENTER JACKSON House, leave your worldly concerns behind and surrender to the peacefulness and beauty of an inn filled with superb antiques and owned by two engaging hosts. Partners Jack Foster and Bruce McIlveen have created a very refined inn in their large, yellow Victorian house surrounded by three landscaped acres, a brook, and a trout-stocked pond. The house itself is a remarkable monument to original owner Wales Johnson's sawmill business; after all, not everyone's home has curly-maple and cherry-plank floors!

Jack and Bruce have put a lot of energy and thoughtfulness into Jackson House's decor and services. You will be impressed by the 6:00 p.m. hors d'oeuvres buffet, offered to guests every evening. A variety of cheeses, pâté, caviar, and quiche awaits you. A harpist adds to the elegance of the experience on Saturdays.

Not everyone's home has curly-maple and cherry-planked floors!

The beautiful wood floors are covered with Chinese area rugs, soft as cashmere on bare feet, and there is an impressive collection of Oriental porcelain in the upstairs hallway (Jack was formerly cargo director for China Airlines). Each of the ten rooms is decorated in a different style, and each has a private bath and a handsome ceiling fan to take the edge off the summer air.

Before you make a reservation at Jackson House, ask to receive a brochure. It is without a doubt one of the most attractive, best designed brochures in the inn business. It describes each of the rooms and serves as a complete guide to help you preselect your favorite room. In trust, you will want to return here often to experience each room. An even better idea is to have Bruce or Jack take you on a personal tour of the house, revealing the stories behind the room names and furnishings. For antique lovers, this is definitely de rigueur.

Among the more seductive rooms is Thornbirds, with its wonderful bird-print (no surprise) wallpaper in green and mauve, its 110-year-old brass-and-iron bed, and its bamboo furniture. The room was inspired by the King George IV pavilion at Brighton.

On a more American note, Governor Converse has an 1860s cannonball-post bed and patriotic stenciled wall covering, Mary Todd Lincoln is all Victorian, with chrysanthemum-and-stripe walls. Gloria Swanson (she *did* sleep here, in 1948) is golden yellow with a remarkable collection of bird's eye maple furniture. And Josephine (completing the unusual triad of women's rooms) is a pièce de résistance, with an 1860 sleigh-type bed, beautiful gray urn-print wallpaper, and Empire furnishings. Two new suites offer lots of spaciousness, queen-sized sleigh beds, an eclectic blend of antiques, and French doors that open onto a deck overlooking the beautiful grounds.

Come morning, Jack prepares an elaborate breakfast that Bruce serves at a beautiful Queen Anne table with matching chairs in the lovely dining room. Guests are spoiled by his specialties, such as Santa Fe omelets, eggs Grisanti (scrambled with spinach and Parmesan cheese), crab quiche, and eggs harlequin (eggs scrambled with smoked salmon)—all served with rosemary potatoes, homemade scones, and muffins. Breakfast, as is true as the rest of this inn, has a flair for quality and good taste.

Jackson House is an unexpected treasure. Jack and Bruce are wonderful hosts, and only one visit here promises many happy returns.

Directions: From I-89, take exit 1 to Route 4 west for 10 miles to Woodstock Village. Inn is 1½ miles west of the village, on the right.

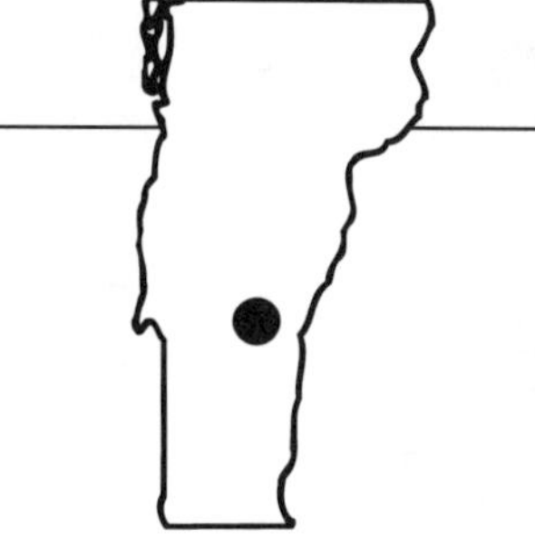

Jackson House
Route 4 West
Woodstock, 05091
802-457-2065

Cash or personal check only
Closed November to mid-December and April to mid-May
$125–$160

31

MASSACHUSETTS

FROM THE MOUNTAINS TO THE ISLANDS

The best bed and breakfast inns in Massachusetts are located as bookends to the center of the state. There are concentrations of inns in the Berkshires (a popular region among New Yorkers because of its easy access and the Tanglewood music festival) and on the Cape and the islands (appealing, traditional summer getaways for Bostonians because of their proximity). You'll find everything in this chapter, from converted summer homes of turn-of-the-century aristocrats in Lenox to Colonial sea captains' homes on Nantucket. There are also a few special places in northcentral and northeastern Massachusetts, popular for their vacation locations. You'll enjoy staying in all these inns any time of the year!

FROM BERKSHIRE HILLS TO ISLAND SHORES, MASSACHUSETTS INNS OFFER A WIDE RANGE OF STYLES AND PLEASURES. ABOVE: CHARLES HINCKLEY HOUSE, REVIEWED ON PAGE 128.

Barnstable Village • **Charles Hinckley House**

The inn is furnished with the great finds Les has made at local auctions, and the selection of antique quilts will make collectors envious.

WHEN YOU ARRIVE AT the Charles Hinckley House, you might meet innkeeper Miya Patrick slightly dusted from baking her twentieth wedding cake of the season. In addition to running this exceedingly attractive inn with her husband, Les, Miya operates a successful catering business. Once you've sampled her breakfast, you'll no doubt want her to cater your every meal.

This talented lady has an equally gifted touch with flowers. The inn's four rooms are decorated with Miya's creative floral arrangements. There are even edible flowers on your breakfast plate, a tasty, decorative touch that does not go unnoticed. The Patricks pay attention to detail, and guests appreciate everything, from the tabard curtains and delicate wreaths to the strategically placed countryside oil paintings and Colonial colors.

The four rooms are as handsome as the 1809 house itself. You won't be able to resist the Summer Kitchen, a study in whitewashed barn siding with a massive brass bed, country furnishings, and a skylight that reveals Cape Cod's crisp blue morning skies. As with the other rooms, there are British toiletries, a basket of fruit, a decanter of sherry, nighttime chocolates, a modern bath, and Miya's ever-present flowers. The three rooms in the main house have tall-post beds, down comforters, working fireplaces and sitting areas. The inn is furnished with the great finds Les has made at local auctions, and the selection of antique quilts will make collectors envious. The Patricks' prowess at restoration is evident in the beautiful job they have done preserving the true feeling of this Federal-era home.

Breakfast is served in the dining room, accompanied by the tranquil notes of New Age music on tape. Whether you choose the French toast, crêpes, or egg dishes, you'll book yourself right back into the Hinckley House as soon as possible to enjoy Miya's excellent cuisine again. The main course is always preceded by fresh fruit, arranged with the aesthetic eye of an experienced artist.

After breakfast you can relax in the lovely living room, filled with flowers, shells, candlesticks, antique dishes, and a miniature village of ceramic houses, lined up on the mantel. Or you can take a stroll down Scudder's Lane past the lovely old homes to

Charles Hinckley House
Old King's Highway (Route 6A)
Barnstable Village, 02630
508-362-9924

Cash or personal check only
Open year-round
$109–$139

EVERY ROOM IN THE 1809 CHARLES HINCKLEY HOUSE IS AS HANDSOME AS THE HOUSE ITSELF.

Hinckley Pond to watch locals and oldtimers launch their dories for a day of sailing and fishing. Those more domestically inclined can walk to the village and check out the latest additions in the **Barnstable Village Antiques Shop** (3267 Main Street, 508-362-8538), a collective filled with some exceptional linens and Oriental pieces, along with everyday items of sentimental value.

Directions: From Route 6 on Cape Cod, take exit 6 to the stop sign at the end of the ramp. Turn left and continue ½ mile to the next stop sign. Turn right onto Route 6A. The inn is 1½ miles along on the left.

Chatham • Captain's House Inn of Chatham

EACH ROOM AT CAPTAIN'S HOUSE INN IS NAMED AFTER ONE OF CAPTAIN HIRAM HARDING'S SHIPS.

YOU COULD EASILY lose your sense of humor trying to find the perfect inn on Cape Cod. It seems there are millions of guest houses, inns, and bed and breakfasts catering to the hordes of summer people who clog the Cape's two main roads. To preserve your weekend sanity and to reduce the clutter of so many choices, drive directly to the charming town of Chatham and book yourself into Captain's House Inn. Owners Cathy and Dave Eakin, super-achievers from corporate life, describe themselves as "selling sleep, comfort, and privacy." Dave adds, "You're only as good as your smallest room," and it can safely be said that this inn's smallest room is as sweet as its other fifteen.

The appealing decor is a tribute to Cathy's decorating prowess; she has successfully created a lovely environment in which you can escape the relative tedium of everyday life. The eight rooms (all with private baths) in the handsome 1839 Greek revival main house offer a stunning collection of antique beds, flattering colors, wonderful hooked rugs (the impressive large run in the downstairs living room was handcrafted by Cathy's father in honor of the inn's opening), early American furnishings, and a noteworthy gallery of paintings and prints.

Each of the rooms is named after one of original owner Captain Hiram Harding's ships. Dauntless has a Sheraton canopy bed, surrounded by a pink-and-blue decor; Challenger offers an ancient harp canopy bed floating in a tiny-floral-print sea; Clarissa sports a splatter-painted floor and handpainted cottage furnishings; Cambridge, on the enclosed sleeping porch, has a beautiful brass-and-iron bed, green decor, and an unusual painted chest. The Garden Room in the back of the house, a lovely little hideaway with fabulous antiques, has its own separate entrance; the Hiram Harding is beautiful in blue; and the Hannah Rebekah has a lacy canopy bed amidst blue floral-striped walls. In addition to having superb decorating instincts, Cathy has done her homework, and the inn is a celebration of good taste and heritage decor.

Every room at the inn is stocked with cut-glass barware, chocolates, English toiletries, and lovely embroidered sheets.

Across the yard from the main house is a charmer of a cottage, built in 1930, with three more rooms. A white picket fence and flower garden give it a storybook quality, and you won't be disappointed by the large wood-paneled bedroom and its enormous fireplace. Across the hall is a second room in bright white, and up the stairs is a suite perfect for guests of petite stature. The newly renovated carriage house offers five large-scale, marvelous rooms, all with exposed beams and Cathy's lovely decor. It's unusual to find such large rooms in a country inn.

The Eakins import a staff of British students every summer on a cultural and educational exchange program. These charming young women are on hand to make your stay absolutely effortless. They'll help you to make dinner reservations in Chatham's many fine restaurants and to plan a day in town. At breakfast, served on the cheery side porch, they replenish the supplies of hot tea and coffee, along with the home-baked muffins, coffee cakes, and pastries.

Chatham is definitely the most charming town on the Cape. It offers lovely old homes, lots of fine restaurants, calming beaches, enough shops to keep the most inveterate shopper satisfied, and a tranquil wildlife sanctuary out on the point. Dave and Cathy also have a thirty-nine-foot sailboat, which they charter to guests, a perfect way to enjoy Chatham's shoreline.

Directions: From Route 6 on Cape Cod, take exit 11. Turn left onto Route 137 south, then take Route 28 south to Chatham Center. Follow Route 28 (Old Harbor Road) through the rotary and out of town, toward Orleans. The inn is ½ mile along on the left.

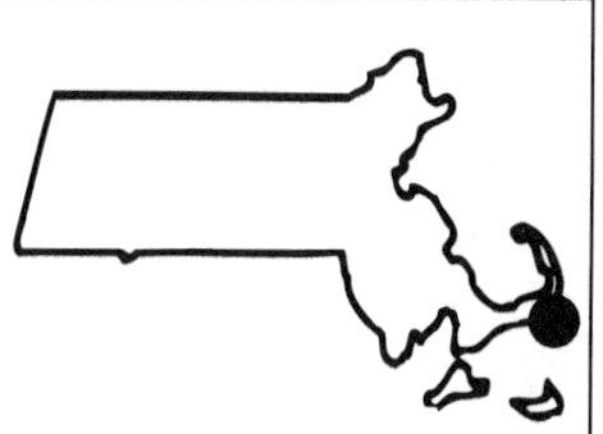

Captain's House Inn of Chatham
371 Old Harbor Road
Chatham, 02633
508-945-0127

AE, MC, V
Closed December-January
$89–$165

THIS ROBUST INN IS GREAT IN ANY SEASON.

Dennis • Isaiah Hall B & B Inn

CAPE COD IN SUMMER is not unlike driving on the San Diego Freeway at rush hour. True, this haven in New England is heaven once you get there. But getting there may be your undoing. A better idea is to experience all of the Cape's pleasures in late spring or late fall and avoid the traffic and hordes of tourists who make this vacation spot such a challenge in high season.

Spring is particularly appealing at the Isaiah Hall Inn when owner Marie Brophy's beautiful garden is in bloom. The blues and lilacs are positively radiant in the clear Cape sunlight. This Greek revival farmhouse offers simple pleasures and a taste of country living. Exuberant Marie is the first to tell you that "I'm the Toyota Camry of bed and breakfasts; I offer good value for the money." Toyota or not, this inn is comfortable, unpretentious, affordable, and appealing in lots of ways.

The inn is a series of houses (main house, little house, carriage house) with an authentic farmhouse feel. Breakfast is served at a huge table in a dining room created from the original breezeway between the two houses. Marie serves a generous Continental buffet breakfast (a local regulation dictates that Dennis inns cannot serve hot breakfasts). You will no doubt enjoy her blueberry-corn muffins, fresh cranberry bread, and other homebaked breads for toasting. A large selection of jams, jellies, and marmalades completes this delicious meal. If you can't live without beach plum jelly, don't worry. You can purchase it and other irresistible jams at the inn.

Isaiah Hall B & B Inn
152 Whig Street
Dennis, 02638
508-385-9928

AE, MC, V
Closed November through mid-March
$44–$85

Guests can choose from any of the eleven rooms, each of which guarantees comfort. Room One is especially pretty with its canopy bed and sweet country decor; the more dramatic Two has a dark splatter-painted floor; Five is snug with country-painted furniture; and any of the more rustic, but spacious, rooms in the carriage house are pleasing and perfect for traveling families (as long as the children are older than seven). Some rooms have tiny decks; all but one have private baths. Antique iron beds and wooden beds are sprinkled throughout the inn, along with lovely hooked rugs and quilts.

The carriage house sitting room is wonderful in winter with its iron stove; the more formal sitting room in the main house is equally pleasant with its own fireplace. Wherever you relax, Marie is always on hand to chat or point you in the right direction for things to see and do. A former personnel professional and high-school guidance counselor, she is a delightful conversationalist, never short on information and opinions.

Directions: From Route 6 on Cape Cod, take exit 8. Go left 1.2 miles to Route 6A, turn right and go 3.4 miles (opposite the cemetery and church). Turn left onto Hope Lane; at the end turn right on Whig Street. The inn is on the left.

THERE IS A COZY QUALITY TO THE APPEALING ROOMS.

Eastham • **The Over Look Inn**

A DISTINCT SCOTTISH FLAVOR IS IN STORE FOR YOU AT OVER LOOK INN.

IF YOU HAVE A YEARNING for the British Isles, but have neither the time nor the resources to pull off a quick trip, try Eastham instead. Unlikely as it may sound, this sleepy town houses a unique inn run by British-born Ian Aitchison and his Scottish wife, Nan. There's a good chance you may feel you've walked into another time and culture when you step into the Over Look Inn. The bagpipes at the entry may give you a clue. Or, the Winston Churchill memorial library in British racing green may tip you off. Not to mention the British and Scottish armies of tin soldiers, tartan plaid tabletops in the dining room, or the fragrant smell of scones baking in the kitchen. The Aitchisons have transported the best of England and Scotland to Cape Cod and offer it to guests, who return often for more of the same.

There's a good chance you may feel you've walked into another time . . . when you step into the Over Look Inn.

The Over Look has much to lure you here; fabulous food, pleasant Victorian-inspired bedrooms, the popular Hemingway Room with its hunting trophies and billiards table (the expected portrait of Papa himself, notwithstanding), or the intriguing short stories son Mark has written and placed in each guest room. You can return here ten times to sample his brand of literature—a separate story for every room. He also publishes an entertaining newsletter, "The Bagpiper," updating guests on local activities and news from the Aitchison family. Son Clive is also an artist. The barn out back is his studio when he's not at the Rhode Island School of Design completing his master's degree. The interpretative Victorian paint job on the house is Clive-inspired. This interesting family makes each visit to the Over Look a surprise.

SIMPLE DECOR AND AN UNPRETENTIOUS AIR MAKE OVER LOOK SPECIAL.

Many guests return here for Nan's hearty breakfasts. She believes that a long-leisurely breakfast is a luxury for today's overworked, overstressed business people. She definitely nurtures guests with some delicious traditional Scottish fare as well as some more exotic dishes. Brittany pie, sausage casserole, kedgeree (an Indian dish of seasoned rice, beans or eggs, and smoked fish), and cheese quiches are supplemented with eggs Havanna, (a Spanish-omelet salute to Hemingway). Afternoon tea offers delicious scones, another recipe from Nan's grandmother.

Other guests return to the inn in an attempt to become an honorary member of Ian's Nauset Point Rangers. This cadre was formed by Colonel Ian and today serves as an elite group of rugged individuals who are able to complete the round-trip trek from the inn to the point at Nauset Inlet. If you're eager for a challenge, here's your chance. A regimental tie is your reward. Resourceful women can always use it as a belt.

Directions: On Cape Cod take Route 6 to the Orleans rotary. Continue on Route 6; the inn is 3 miles up on the left.

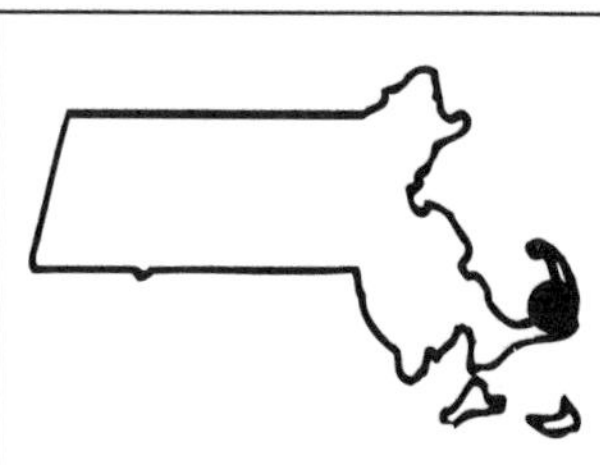

The Over Look Inn
3085 County Road
(Route 6)
Eastham, 02542
508-255-1886

AE, MC, V
Open year-round
$50–$95

Edgartown • **Daggett House**

THE DAGGETT HOUSE IS a venerable institution on Martha's Vineyard, host over the years to generations of guests. Owners John and Jim Chirgwin are keeping the family tradition alive and strong at the inn. The Daggett House has remained much the same through the decades, and the atmosphere of this place is reliable and secure. The new decor is comfortably elegant. The twenty-five rooms are large, filled with antiques or good reproductions, and perfectly charming. All have private baths, and the rooms in the main house (some with harbor views) are just as pleasant as those across the street in the Captain Warren House (named after an Edgartown whaling legend) and those in the garden cottage (originally a schoolhouse).

The original Daggett House was the first tavern on the island, built in 1660. You can get a glimpse of what life might have been like then in the Secret Stairway Room, downstairs in the main house. The room's ancient brick wall and hearth date back to Colonial times. The secret staircase (still in use) is hidden behind a bookshelf, and guests occasionally pop out into the Secret Stairway Room after descending from their bedrooms. A random collection of seafarer paraphernalia is on display in the room—from a blunderbuss over one hearth to a handsome clipper ship weather vane over the other. There is also a mythology that lingers in the room: the house is said

THE ORIGINAL DAGGETT HOUSE, BUILT IN 1660, WAS THE FIRST TAVERN ON MARTHA'S VINEYARD.

TASTEFUL FURNISHINGS AND FIRST-CLASS DECOR ARE SIGNATURES AT THE DAGGETT HOUSE.

to have spirits lurking about. Skeptics need only glance at the photograph taken by an unsuspecting guest years ago to take the stories more seriously. Optical illusion or not, you will see two faces captured forever in the fire's flames.

When you're not considering supernatural possibilities, you'll enjoy the satisfying breakfasts served here. A Continental offering of homemade breads and muffins is provided, and for a surcharge, you can order eggs Benedict, blueberry or banana pancakes, ham-and-cheese omelets, lox and cream cheese, or sour cream coffee cake.

If the Chirgwins are unavailable, engaging innkeeper Sue Cooper-Street is always on hand to make your stay memorable. She is well versed in Daggett House lore and will help you plan a perfect day on the island. Guests can order box luncheons for island alfresco picnics. A recent innovation features overnight laundry services for vacationing families. The inn is situated in the heart of Edgartown, so there's lots of street activity well into the evening. Daggett House offers sanctuary in any season and a dose of island life that hasn't really changed much over the past forty years.

Directions: From the Vineyard Haven ferry or the Oak Bluffs ferry, take Beach Road to Edgartown. In Edgartown turn left off Main Street onto Water Street. The inn is next to the Chappaquiddick ferry landing.

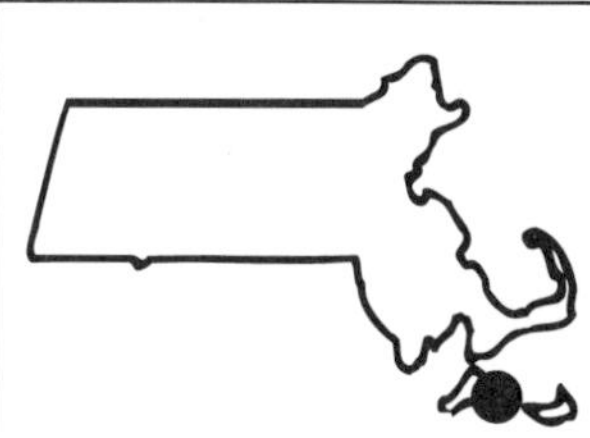

Daggett House
59 North Water Street
Edgartown, 02539
508-627-4600

AE, MC, V
Open year-round
Off-season, \$75–\$95; in season, \$110–\$150.

Edgartown • **Governor Bradford Inn**

THIS 1865 EDGARTOWN guest house makes a perfect sixteen-room bed and breakfast inn. The Victorian house mixes the best of both worlds: country-inn charm with contemporary comfort. King-size beds, ceiling fans, and ultramodern bathrooms make travelers feel that they can enjoy an old-fashioned inn without sacrificing twentieth-century conveniences.

The blend works well. The living rooms are period pieces, decorated with Victorian furnishings and modern-day artwork. The bedrooms have traditional striped walls, a smattering of brass beds, attractive lighting, and thick, muffling carpet. Televisions are available, on request, for guests who can't live without them. The overall appearance is clean, cheerful and pristine. Fresh flowers, complimentary scented soaps, and guides to the Vineyard give each room a special touch. The overall decor is a tribute to innkeepers Kim and Bill Johnson's understanding of how to keep things pretty by keeping them simple.

Guests are well treated by the Johnsons. They are fabulous cooks, and breakfasts at the Governor Bradford are as delicious as they are attractive. The Continental breakfast offers fresh, baked-from-scratch breads. On a given morning, guests are treated to fresh fruit and a variety of tasty muffins, such as peach-cinnamon and lemon-poppyseed.

When guests return from a hard day of sightseeing and beaching, tea is served in the afternoon with an array of temptations: raspberry torte, pecan squares,

THIS REFURBISHED 1865 WHALING CAPTAIN'S HOUSE GIVES GUESTS A CHOICE OF SIXTEEN ROOMS.

LIVING ROOMS AT GOVERNOR BRADFORD INN ARE TRUE PERIOD PIECES.

gingerbread topped with lemon glaze, lemon cookies, or melt-in-your mouth applecake.

Guests receive an information packet upon arrival to review the wide range of activities available on the island. The Johnsons will help you lease a boat or find a bicycle and plan daytrips to out-of-the-way island haunts. The late Henry Beetle Hough, the naturalist, conservationist, and legendary owner and editor of the *Vineyard Gazette*, who rhapsodized about the wildlife sanctuaries, beach walks, hiking trails, and marvelous natural wonders of the island, would be proud of the suggested itineraries.

Directions: From the Vineyard Haven ferry or the Oak Bluffs ferry, take Beach Road to Edgartown. The inn is located on Main Street, on the right, before Edgartown Center.

Governor Bradford Inn
128 Main Street
Edgartown, 02539
508-627-9510

All major credit cards
Open year-round
Off-season $60–$155; in season, $95–$195

TRADITION PLAYS A CENTRAL ROLE AT POINT WAY INN.

Edgartown • **Point Way Inn**

IF YOU HAPPEN TO arrive at Point Way Inn at the right time to catch a glimpse of owner Ben Smith, dressed in proper croquet whites, working out on his regulation court or relaxing in the gazebo with martini shaker in hand as he watches the sun set, you might realize that you've stumbled onto something different. A retired attorney and son of a New Bedford whaling family, Ben embraces the good life. Together with his wife, Linda, he has created a bed and breakfast inn that offers a taste of gentility in unpretentious surroundings.

It's clear that tradition plays a central role here; the hallways are lined with seven generations of family photographs (capturing the privileged life at its best), and three generations of sailing trophies double as flower vases on the breakfast tables. You'll also find subtle traces of private-school and Yale memorabilia scattered about the house. Ben and Linda are living life their way. They hold on to the past but are definitely enjoying their careers as innkeepers, offering a perfectly accessible home to guests.

The hallways are lined with seven generations of family photographs, and three generations of sailing trophies double as flower vases on the breakfast tables.

The fifteen rooms, all with ceiling fans and private baths, are lovely. Canopy beds, pretty wallpaper, and coziness predominate here. Ten working fireplaces make Point Way Inn a marvelous place to visit during the winter. The Smiths themselves are reason enough to check into the inn. Their active lives make for great story-telling. It's not often (if ever) that you run into an innkeeper who travels the nation playing in croquet tournaments. Or a family that decided to make a life change and spent a year on their thirty-eight-foot ketch, sailing the Caribbean. And the saving grace of this sophisticated couple and their inn is that there is no trace of elitism. Everyone is welcome at Point Way Inn, and everyone feels comfortable here.

Breakfast is served in the dining room with its splatter-painted floors. Linda's carrot bread, bran muffins, and sour cream coffee cake are the main attractions. The orange juice is freshly squeezed, and the tea and coffee are served in pretty, bird-print mugs and teacups. Details are taken seriously, from silver flatware to an honor bar to prestamped note cards, thoughtfully placed in each room to encourage you to tell your friends to visit the inn—before the urge passes. The croquet court is open to guests who generally play a less complex, more interpretive game than Ben and the other members of his Edgartown Mallet Club. Oatmeal cookies are in large supply to keep guests' energy level high. The conversation in the evening is lively, and the atmosphere of this lovely inn is seductive enough to make you want to take up croquet full-time.

Directions: From the Vineyard Haven ferry or the Oak Bluffs ferry, take Beach Road to Edgartown. The inn is located on the corner of Main Street and Pease's Point Way, just before Edgartown Center.

Point Way Inn
Upper Main Street
Edgartown, 02539
508-627-8633

AE, MC, V
Open year-round
$60–$200

Falmouth • **Mostly Hall**

IF YOU ARE FOND of the great houses in New Orleans or Natchez but cannot stand southern summer humidity, drive to Falmouth on Cape Cod for a touch of the South with the crisp, clear weather of New England. Mostly Hall was originally built for a southern bride in 1849. The result is evocative of the historic houses in Louisiana and Mississippi: lofty ceilings, very tall windows, spacious rooms, and a cool interior during hot weather. Caroline and Jim Lloyd did their homework before they acquired this handsome inn. They traveled to the South for inspiration in decorating and restoring their impressive house.

Today, Mostly Hall is fresh and appealing, thanks to Caroline's redecorating talent. The six bedrooms, all with private baths, are especially charming with breezy floral wallpapers and queen-size canopy beds. Downstairs, these oversize beds look like miniatures with such tall ceilings. The overall effect is airy, light, and clean.

The spacious living room, Victorian in feeling, has Jim's clock collection as a decorative accent. The newly restored fireplace provides welcome warmth during the winter months. A full breakfast is served at one end of this large room. Caroline's specialties are

MOSTLY HALL OFFERS A GLIMPSE OF PERIOD SOUTHERN GREAT HOUSES.

irresistible. Stuffed French toast, eggs Benedict soufflé, Mexicali eggs, cheese blintz muffins with blueberry sauce, cheese crêpes, puffy apple pancakes, and sunshine eggs (baked eggs with cheeses) will tempt you into visiting Mostly Hall as often as possible to sample her delicious cuisine. As with many innkeepers who know their stuff in the kitchen, Caroline has written her own cookbook, *Mostly Hall Breakfast at Nine*.

Caroline and Jim are cheerful and enthusiastic and will fill you in on all the details of this stately home. They will also help you find the right restaurant for dinner and whatever you need to keep busy in touristy Falmouth. Or, you may choose to settle into the sitting room in the third-floor widow's walk, a tranquil aerie with a terrific view of this historic town.

Your arrival at Mostly Hall will prepare you for a pleasant stay. The gardens and imposing architecture do not disappoint. You might even consider the stress-free way to get to Nantucket and Martha's Vineyard: spend the night here instead of the typical last-minute, mad dash to the ferry at Wood's Hole. If you plan to travel to other parts of the world on a bed and breakfast itinerary, be sure to ask the Lloyds for advice. They spend their own vacation time researching bed and breakfasts from Washington State and California to New Zealand and Australia.

Directions: From Boston, take Route 3 to Sagamore Bridge circle. Exit on Route 6 west to Bourne Bridge circle. Take Route 28 over Bourne Bridge south into Falmouth. The inn is across from the village green.

Mostly Hall
27 Main Street
Falmouth, 02540
508-548-3786

Cash or personal check only
Closed January through mid-February
$55–$95

Great Barrington • **Elling Guest House**

JO AND RAY ELLING ARE OLD HANDS AT INNKEEPING, AND THEIR EXPERIENCE SHOWS AT ELLING GUEST HOUSE.

JO AND RAY ELLING are clearly the innkeepers of record in the Berkshires. After more than twenty years of running a guest house in Great Barrington, raising four sons in the meantime, and helping neighboring innkeepers set up their businesses, this sincere couple already has third-generation guests. Perched on a hilltop, surrounded by stately pine trees and six acres of land, the Ellings' 240-year-old six-room house is absolutely charming. Jo Elling is easygoing and cheerful; Ray is gregarious and helpful. Both seem to be able to keep their sense of humor and their perspective in the face of the ins and outs of innkeeping.

Each room is decorated with lovely, hand-me-down family antiques. Some have handblocked wallpaper, and all are immaculate. The Blue Room is pretty, with wicker furniture and an impressive white iron bed. The Empire Room houses the Ellings' original bridal suite of furniture. The Green Room offers the luxury of a king-size bed. And if you happen to forget your room's color while you're in a shared bathroom, the towels are color-coded as a subtle reminder.

The Guest House is a perfect and reasonably priced place to stay if you're attending the Boston Symphony Orchestra's summer season at **Tanglewood** (Route 183, Lenox, 413-637-1940) or the **Jacob's Pillow Dance Festival** (Route 28, Becket, 413-243-0745). It's also right down the road from several ski slopes.

Jo will get you going in the morning with a healthful Continental breakfast of homemade biscuits, fruit juices, and plenty of coffee and tea. Ray will contribute suggestions for activities and for a place to dine in the evening. These two innkeepers are naturals, without pretentions or affectations. A Brooklyn retiree from the New York Department of Corrections, Ray might, in one of his more reflective moments, muse about his nearly two decades of innkeeping, and he has been overheard to reveal—with a good-natured twinkle in his eye—"You know, taking care of prisoners was really a lot easier."

Elling Guest House
Route 23
Great Barrington, 01230
413-528-4103

Cash or personal check only
Open year-round
June through October, $65–$80; November through May, $55–$65

Directions: From I-90, take exit 2. Follow Route 7 south to Routes 23 and 41 west. The inn is ½ mile along on the right off Route 23.

LITTLEJOHN MANOR IS AN "EMINENTLY CIVILIZED" PLACE TO STAY.

Littlejohn Manor • *Great Barrington*

WHEN YOU SEE THE distinctive newsboy statue, an old-fashioned reminder of the early days of the *New York Daily News*, you know you've arrived at the former summer home of Colonel William Brown, distinguished publisher of the tabloid that is the nation's second-largest daily metropolitan paper. You also know that you've arrived at the charming inn of Herb Littlejohn and his partner, Paul DuFour, who retired here after twenty-year careers managing Harvard University's food-service program.

The 1830s Littlejohn Manor is lovely, made even more so by Paul's herb gardens. Paul lovingly tends these and uses each season's crop as part of his fabulous English breakfasts and tea cakes, as fragrant displays in the dining room, and as a cottage industry that involves concocting herbal vinegars, olive oils, and condiments. You may find it impossible to head home without some of these tempting creations, all reasonably priced. The gardens are marked to initiate newcomers to the personalities of each of the 120 varieties he grows. Paul also writes a popular weekly newspaper column, the "Culinary Herb Scrapbook." He introduces readers to new herbs and suggests ways to use them in cooking and other household applications. And when Paul and Herb aren't gardening, you can find them taking care of their two Maine coon cats, Robin Hood and Marion.

Littlejohn Manor
Newsboy Monument Lane (Route 23)
Great Barrington, 01230
413-528-2882

Cash or personal check only
Open year-round
Off-season, $60–$75; in season, $65–$80

BREAKFAST AT THE LITTLEJOHN HAS A DECIDEDLY BRITISH ACCENT.

The four rooms, all air-conditioned, are simple and attractive. A combination of antiques, favorite personal furnishings, and charming wallpaper prints offer pleasant accommodations. The front room, overlooking the newsboy in stasis, is particularly pretty, with its fireplace and luxurious spaciousness.

Breakfasts provide an opportunity for Paul to show off his considerable cooking skills. A coterie of British-born guests return often for a nostalgic taste of the motherland. English breakfasts at the Manor are bountiful offerings of eggs, potatoes broiled in their jackets, ham and bangers, mushrooms sautéed with crumpets. You'll be served in the formal dining room surrounded by the cut-glass collection, crocheted linens, and pretty china. Breakfast is such a success that guests are anxious to return to the inn after an afternoon filled with local activities to sample Paul's afternoon tea. Homebaked scones, oatcakes, honeycakes, and marigold muffins tide everyone over with style until dinner.

Littlejohn Manor is an eminently civilized place to stay. You'll appreciate the hospitality and the comfortable accommodations. And you'll return as often as possible to be spoiled by Paul's good cooking and Herb's gracious charm.

Directions: From I-90, take exit 2. Take Route 7 south to Great Barrington. Turn onto Route 23 west. The inn is ½ mile west of the town center. From I-87, turn onto Route 23 east, then follow the above directions.

Walker House • *Lenox*

AS YOU ENTER Walker House and see a family of oversize stuffed animals waiting patiently at the dining room table for tea, you're tipped off to the fact that someone here has a sense of humor. The same someone also has six cats. In fact, you might get the feeling that everyone calls Peggy and Dick Houdek whenever a new litter of cats arrives.

It's not hard to tell that the Houdeks are animal lovers. The cat motif pops up all over the house, including Peggy's collection of animal sweaters. Peggy and Dick obviously are having fun as New England innkeepers, three thousand miles from Los Angeles, where they left musical and publishing careers. Peggy still runs out of the house after serving you Sunday breakfast to perform as soloist in a local church. Dick is an opera consultant for the National Endowment for the Arts. Their love for music is evidenced by the names of the inn's rooms, all homages to their favorite composers.

The house is filled with art, musical instruments, and a magazine collection extensive enough to suit anyone's taste.

This 1804 Federal-style house has eight enormous rooms, each with a private bath stocked with British toiletries. Each composer's room has a special look. Handel features formal wallpaper and a joyous Hallelujah Chorus brass bed, which looks like a giant tuba. Portraits and a bust of the composer compete for space with cat prints. Debussy has impressionistic

THREE ACRES OF BEAUTIFUL GARDENS ADD TO THE ALREADY ABUNDANT APPEAL OF WALKER HOUSE.

print wallpaper, Mozart a canopy bed and antique harmonium, Puccini its own private porch, and Verdi a riot of wicker and summer season colors. Peggy also has dreams of an art deco Gershwin room. And who knows what's next?

The house is filled with art, musical instruments, and a magazine collection extensive enough to suit anyone's taste. Associate innkeeper Robert Wallace, another Californian, brings his own appreciation of the arts to Walker House. A carpet and tapestry designer, Robert shares his current projects with enthusiasm. He is also likely to conduct special seminars on Federal furnishings, in counterpoint to the Houdeks' seminars on opera.

Cookies and tea are served in the afternoon, and a Continental breakfast of homebaked muffins (delivered in calico animal warmers) and tea or coffee (served in cat mugs) is dished up in the large dining room. Classical music in the background competes with the Big Ben doorbell chimes.

The engaging and slightly eccentric Houdeks will make your stay memorable. They have an easy openness characteristic of Californians, and their domesticated zoo is sure to provide comic relief. Dick has three acres of beautiful gardens, and Peggy keeps up the energy level with her cheerful conversation. Christmas is a a special time at the inn: guests are invited to trim the tree, and Peggy is happy to perform impromptu concerts, giving a beautiful cadence to this nostalgic holiday experience.

It's only a short walk into Lenox, and the Houdeks have a fleet of bicycles guests can use to tour the area. All in all, Walker House is one of the more entertaining inns in the Berkshires.

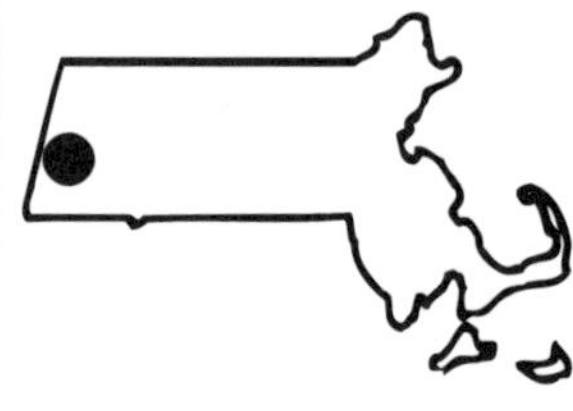

Walker House
74 Walker Street (Route 183)
Lenox, 01240
413-637-1271

Cash or personal checks only
Open year-round
$50–$135

Directions: From I-90 take exit 2. Follow Route 20 west to Route 183 south into Lenox. The inn is 1½ miles from the intersection of Routes 183 and 20, on the left.

Whistler's Inn · *Lenox*

RICHARD AND JOAN Mears are both successful authors and the owners of Whistler's Inn, a bed and breakfast with a personality as eclectic as the Mearses' interests. This creative couple (she is also an artist; he is an enthusiastic photographer) got into the innkeeping business to allow themselves the flexibility to pursue their art. They chose the Lenox location for its (relative) proximity to Europe and Africa, the latter of which captivates their artistic imagination and spirit. Both are particularly found of Zambia, Zimbabwe, and Kenya, and they have been known to vanish for stretches of time to go canoeing down the Zambezi River, getting in touch with a life not much changed from its primordial beginnings.

You might forget you're in twentieth-century New England as you enter the music room, with its gilt chairs and oversize mirror, reflecting the grand piano and all-American fireplace.

You won't find any zebra-striped trophies at Whistler's; the Mearses are strictly conservation-minded. What you will find is a cross between European and American Victorian summer palace decor. You might forget you're in twentieth-century New England as you enter the music room, with its gilt chairs and oversize mirror, reflecting the grand piano and all-American fireplace. The impressive dining room, with its Tudor-style windows, large hearth, and baroque candelabra with putti, is equally arresting. One of the more appealing rooms is the library, with chintz-covered oversize chairs, doors that open onto the inn's grassy terrace (and its seven acres of gardens and grounds), walls of books, and a black marble fireplace.

But the rooms are merely stage sets. The Mearses' real accomplishment is providing a sanctuary for guests to share ideas, to explore the possibilities of life, and to ruminate on how things are or seem to be. If you have the slightest interest in the arts, literature, and the human condition, you might find yourself still going strong with this couple at three in the morning, debating such topics as natural selection and the challenge of living to one's full potential. Whistler's is an energizing place to visit, offering far more than your average bed and breakfast experience.

When you've cashed out on the intellectual debate, you need only to climb the stairs to one of the bedrooms, decorated in Joan's unpretentious and welcoming personal style. Among the prettiest is Five, a comfortable haven in pinks and roses with a Victorian bed, complete with valentine-shaped headboard. Seven sports an enormous bathroom and

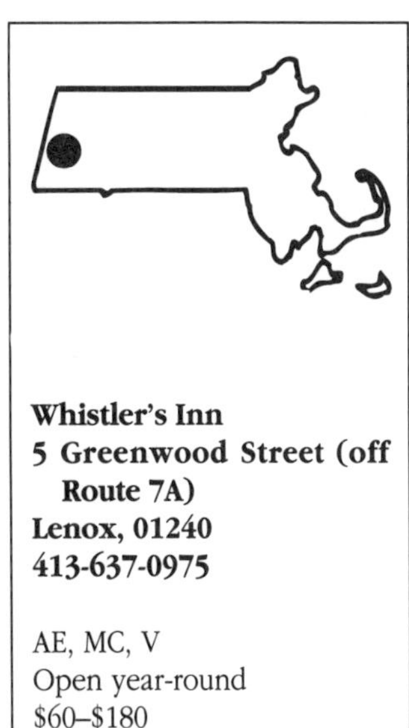

Whistler's Inn
5 Greenwood Street (off Route 7A)
Lenox, 01240
413-637-0975

AE, MC, V
Open year-round
$60–$180

IF YOU LIKE, YOU CAN SIMPLY "DISAPPEAR" INTO THIS DECEPTIVELY LARGE TUDOR HOME.

oversize bed, and Two has a brass bed surrounded by navy calico print. All the rooms have private baths, and most have ceiling fans. The smallest room is as charming as the master suites.

Breakfast is served in the formal dining room in winter and on the sunny side porch in summer, with the Mearses' famous blueberry muffins and pumpkin, pineapple-carrot, apple-nut, or zucchini bread. Either of Joan and Richard's two daughters might be on hand to help serve cheese, fruit, and pastries.

Come to Whistler's to meet this intriguing couple, to engage in a little salon talk, to learn about Richard's and Joan's latest film and book projects—or to simply disappear into this deceptively large Tudor home where privacy is as valued as sharing the finer points of the lively arts. Any way you look at it, Whistler's is a rambling exercise in country comfort, in a house built for the captains of industry in the 1820s.

Directions: From I-90, take exit 2. Follow Route 20 west to Route 183 south into Lenox. Take Route 7A north, then turn left onto Greenwood Street at the top of the hill.

Century House • *Nantucket*

JEAN HERON DESERVES recognition as the most enthusiastic innkeeper in New England. Her optimism, intensity, and sincere interest in making people feel comfortable at Century House are apparent from the moment she greets you. It's easy to conclude that these qualities helped make her a success in her computer software career, pre-Century House. Her high energy level is perfectly matched by husband Gerry Connick's steadiness (although he is not without his own impish ways). Together they run the oldest continuously operating inn on Nantucket. The 1833 home has been completely refurbished after four years of hard labor. Yet the inn is a work in progress, and each return visit reveals more of Jean and Gerry's dedication to making it a delightfully fresh place to stay.

The inn is a work in progress, and each return visit reveals more of Jean and Gerry's dedication to making it a delightfully fresh place to stay.

The overall look is Laura Ashley, without appearing to be a page out of a mail-order catalog. Jean's personal imprint, in colors and mixed prints, and Gerry's carpentry skills blend to create a special look. A collection of antiques, Jackson Pollockseque splatter-painted floors, canopy beds, unusual architectural detailing (the window dormers on the third floor double as triangular half-canopies, covered in shirred fabrics), wicker, plants, and lovely linens all create an ambiance that is unpretentious and comfortable. Each of the fourteen rooms has a private bath and is named after an island flower.

If you've run out of conversation, you can borrow any of Gerry's many magazines. An eclectic reader, he subscribes to everything from Foreign Affairs and Vogue to Hot Rod and Hemmings Motor News. If

EVERY ROOM AT CENTURY HOUSE HAS A PRIVATE BATH AND IS NAMED AFTER AN ISLAND FLOWER.

EVERY ROOM AT CENTURY HOUSE HAS A PRIVATE BATH AND IS NAMED AFTER AN ISLAND FLOWER.

you have an attraction to vintage automobiles, ask him for an introduction to his 1945 Ford pickup truck, a gift from Jean catering to his collector's weakness and giving him a chance to win a prize in the Daffodil Weekend Antique Car Parade, an annual spring tradition in Nantucket.

Jean serves a substantial Continental breakfast buffet at rough-hewn tables in the pine-paneled kitchen. It's an opportunity to meet other guests, such as the architect who returns to Nantucket on business on a weekly basis and has practically made Century House his second home. You also can dine alfresco, transporting your breakfast to the veranda on one-hundred-year-old wooden trays. Afternoon tea is also served on the porch, a pleasant way to unwind after an active day.

Jean and Gerry have introduced a popular program to Century House. Artists who have one-man shows on the island are invited to the inn to host evening receptions: salons Nantucket-style. The inn is sprinkled with these artists' works, visual souvenirs in the inn's ad hoc gallery.

While you wander the streets of Nantucket, you'll feel right at home when you see Jean or Gerry zip by in their jeep with the Century House logo emblazoned on the door or when you bump into one of their staffers sporting logo-printed polo shirts. Come to Century House to meet Jean and Gerry, to relax in simple country surroundings, and to enjoy a touch of history in a place where privacy is as valued as striking up new friendships with other guests. It's a wonderful home away from home.

Century House
10 Cliff Road
Nantucket, 02554
508-228-0530

Cash or personal check only
Open year-round
Off-season, \$65–\$95; in season, \$85–\$145.

Directions: From the ferry landing, take the first right onto South Beach Street, then turn left onto Easton Street. Turn right again onto Cliff Road. The inn is the fourth house on the left.

LEFT: PEARCHED ON A HILL, CLIFF LODGE IS VERY APPEALING. BELOW: THE ROOMS HERE ARE BREEZY AND FRESH—A LOVELY BLEND OF COLORS AND FURNISHINGS.

Cliff Lodge · *Nantucket*

IT IS HARD TO imagine a breezier, more refreshing inn in Nantucket than Cliff Lodge. The color palette here is so light and refreshing that you practically feel you are in a tree house overlooking the harbor. Most of the light wood floors are splatter-painted, many of the rooms are large, there are televisions hidden away in country-pine cupboards, the linens are crisp and lacy, the bathrooms private, and the telephones available for travelers who need to stay in touch with the rest of the world. Located on a hill, it is a perfect aerie for summer visits. The garden patio adds to the charm, as does innkeeper Gerrie Miller.

There are eleven rooms and one apartment for those visitors who plan to stay a while. Among the most stunning rooms, One, downstairs, is a wash of cornflower blue. Upstairs, Four is equally beautiful with its own blue-and-white color scheme. Even the smaller rooms on the fourth floor are irresistible, and you'll be thankful for the air conditioning on particularly hot summer days.

Breakfast is simple, according to Nantucket bed and breakfast regulations, and served outdoors or in the handsome sitting room. Guests enjoy fresh fruit, homemade muffins and breads, granola, apple crisp, and coffee cake.

Directions: From the ferry landing, take first right onto South Beach Street, then turn left onto Easton Street. Turn right again onto Cliff Road. Inn is on right.

Cliff Lodge
9 Cliff Road
Nantucket, 02554
508-228-9480

AE, MC, V
Open year-round
$35–$140; apartment, $105–$190

Nantucket • Corner House

Floors are on a permanent tilt, doorjambs are oddly angled, and the rooms have all the best eccentric architectural charm of the 1700s.

SANDY AND JOHN Knox-Johnston are perfect examples of innkeepers who have been able to put their personal tastes and preferences to work in creating an inn that offers guests historical perspective and plenty of privacy. As soon as you enter Corner House, you realize that you might have passed through a time tunnel instead of the front door. The Colonial feeling of this place is overwhelming. Floors are on a permanent tilt, door-jambs are oddly angled, and the rooms have all the best eccentric architectural charm of the 1700s. And if you admire seafaring dioramas, the Knox-Johnstons have some stunning clipper-ship examples.

Sandy has an international architectural design practice and has taken great care to make the inn reflect its 1723 origins. The furnishings downstairs are lovely, and the kitchen-living room, with its gigantic hearth, is just as it was when the house was built. The gardens are lush and the sixteen bedrooms are sterling examples of Sandy's good taste.

The Knox-Johnstons travel to England each year, so the inn is a combination plate of English and American furnishings, designed to create a comfortable harmony. In the nine bedrooms in the main house, the tall-post beds are impressive, the lighting perfectly suited to reading at night, and the detailing perfect. You're sure to be another satisfied Corner House customer whether you choose the Blueberry with its handpainted, sponged walls and pretty blue-and-apricot chintz (complete with a view of the old Congregational church across the street); the Beach Plum, soft in rose and green, with its enormous bath-

GREAT CARE HAS BEEN TAKEN TO MAKE CORNER HOUSE REFLECT ITS 1723 ORIGINS.

room, paneled walls, and fireplace (complete with a view of the gardens); the Bayberry, with Sandy's signature deep-green lacquered walls and tiger-maple king-size bed; the Cranberry with rose-apricot sponge-painted walls and its own dressing room, complete with a daybed; or any of the snug third-floor rooms, reminiscent of a farmhouse with rough-hewn beams, pine floors, bright-white plastered walls and views of the gardens or harbor.

ENTERING CORNER HOUSE IS LIKE PASSING THROUGH A TIME TUNNEL TO THE EIGHTEENTH CENTURY.

Corner House is so popular, Sandy expanded the operation into two more houses. Swan's Nest is a new house built to fit into the look of historic Nantucket. Here, the interior architecture is more dramatic with barnlike ceilings providing a spaciousness that accommodates queen-size canopy beds. Televisions are available in the four rooms, in consideration of guests who feel the need to see what's happening off-island. There is also a private garden for on-island relaxation. Rose Cottage, Sandy's other decorating masterpiece, has three more rooms. Pale yellow sets the tone in Country Lane, a romantic hideaway complete with a crocheted-lace canopy queen-size bed. Bandbox is more tailored, an exercise in pinstriping, with a crisp lacy-and-white color scheme. The third-floor suite, pleasing in rose and green tones, is very romantic with its harbor view.

Sandy's sister made some of the beautiful rag rugs; the coverlets—perfectly matched to each room—come from Wales; and the sheets are from designer collections. All the pillows and comforters are down-filled. Hot water is abundant (thanks to Sandy's father, who felt guests should be able to take hot showers at any time of the day).

Breakfast is served buffet-style in the sitting room, and the guests enjoy their homebaked muffins and coffee on the screened-in porch. Afternoon tea with fruit breads, cookies, and other temptations (lemonade instead of tea during warm weather) helps revive guests after a busy day of sightseeing or beachcombing.

The Knox-Johnstons are committed to service and will help you to plan the perfect day, give you beach towels, suggest a place for dinner, and offer you an itinerary for a walking tour. Corner House is one of the most attractive inns on the island, and if you appreciate the finer subtleties of Colonial architecture, antiques, and interior design, you'll be in art-and-antique heaven.

Directions: From the ferry landing, go up Broad Street to Centre Street. Turn right, and the inn is four houses along on the right.

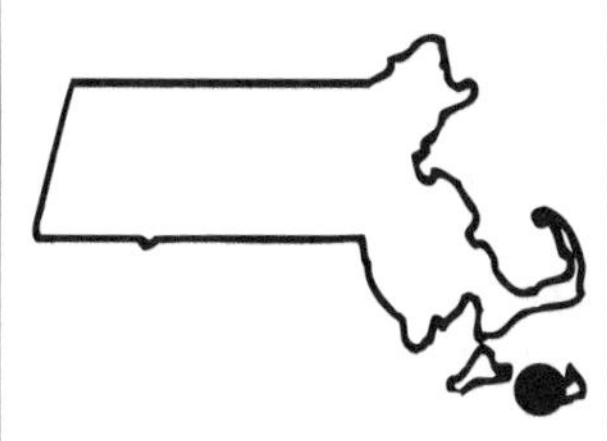

Corner House
49 Centre Street
Nantucket, 02554
508-228-1530

MC, V
Closed January
$65–$130

FAIR GARDENS OFFERS COUNTRY DECOR AND A BEAUTIFUL GARDEN

Nantucket • Fair Gardens

YOU WOULD NEVER expect such a lovely inn behind the unassuming facade and plain-Jane doorway at 27 Fair Street. Lee and Stuart Gaw have taken over this pretty place, and they run it along with Great Harbor Inn. The eight rooms here are cozy, each with its own sun-washed decor. All are named after herbs found in the famous Shakespeare herb garden out back. Among the more attractive is Camomile, pretty in pink with a Victorian iron bed. For more privacy, reserve the Garden House, a separate little cottage. The famous herb garden is outside your doorstep, a pleasure to look at with a bouquet of special fragrances to boot. All the rooms here are sweet: Rosemary is a splash of confetti wallpaper, Sage has wild-strawberry-print walls, and Tarragon has handstenciled walls and a traditional cannonball-post bed.

A generous Continental breakfast is served in the breezy dining room, with its perfect seacoast cottage feel. Or, guests may dine alfresco in season overlooking the garden.

Directions: From the ferry landing, go up Main Street. Turn left onto Fair Street. Inn is on right.

Fair Gardens
27 Fair Street
Nantucket, 02554
508-228-4258, 508-228-6609

MC, V
Closed January-March
$55–$140

Four Chimneys Inn · *Nantucket*

THE FOUR CHIMNEYS is one of the few whaling captain's house inns on Nantucket. A reflection of Betty York's insistence on gracious elegance, it offers something slightly out of the ordinary compared to the Colonial and Federal-style inns so prolific on the island. Betty has successfully created an elegant atmosphere that is not the least bit off-putting. The house itself is imposing from the street. Symmetrical and handsome with its ionic columns and four distinctive chimneys, it gives you an idea of how impressive original owner Captain Frederick Gardner must have appeared to his friends and fellow sea captains. Inside, high ceilings (effective air conditioning on hot summer days, although all the rooms are also air-conditioned, for complete comfort), chinoiserie touches in keeping with a whaling captain's travels, double fireplaces in the double drawing rooms (with ionic columns to match the exterior), and Empire furnishings help to make the inn an exercise in restrained good taste.

ELEGANT DECOR IS THE KEY TO FOUR CHIMNEYS INN'S APPEAL.

Climb the commanding staircase to find the ten rooms, all with private baths. Six are restored as they were in 1835, and one has a private porch. Some are associated with modern-day stories that give them individual personalities. The Gardner Room, for example, is nicknamed the honeymoon suite for the bride whose photograph is permanently on display. Other rooms echo the history of the house. Particularly stunning is the Lindley Room, with its floral-painted hearth, canopy bed, wall of books, and tentlike bathroom.

Breakfast is served to guests either in bed, on a pretty tray with crisp linens and a silver tea service, or downstairs on the back porch, overlooking the small garden. Betty offers a light Continental breakfast in deference to the current-day interest in keeping slim and because she knows most guests come to Nantucket to enjoy the gourmet dinners offered at the island's many excellent restaurants.

Betty is a pro at concierge services. She'll make your dinner reservation, supply you with beach towels, offer suggestions for sightseeing, get you to the right beach, and make you feel at home. A visit to the Four Chimneys is the next best thing to visiting Captain Gardner upon his return from the China Sea in the 1800s.

Directions: From the ferry landing, go up Main Street. Turn left onto Orange Street. The inn is on the left, at the corner of Orange Street and Gorham Court.

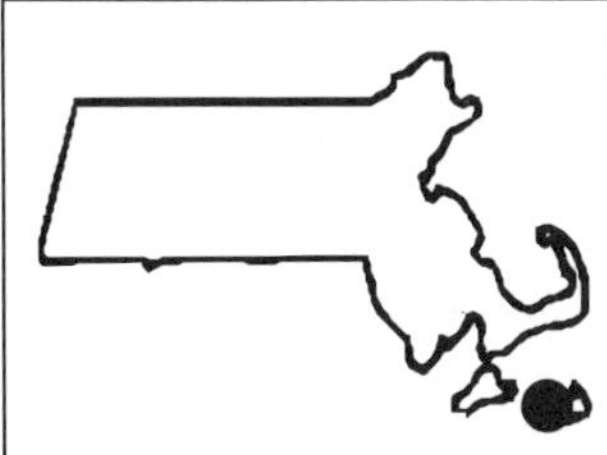

Four Chimneys Inn
38 Orange Street
Nantucket, 02554
508-228-1912

All major credit cards
Closed mid-December through mid-April
$98–$155

Nantucket • Great Harbor House

RIGHT: GREAT HARBOR IS PERFECTLY LOCATED TO ENJOY NANTUCKET'S PLEASURES.

ABOVE: REFINED DECOR IN SIMPLE SETTINGS ADD TO THIS INN'S PERSONALITY

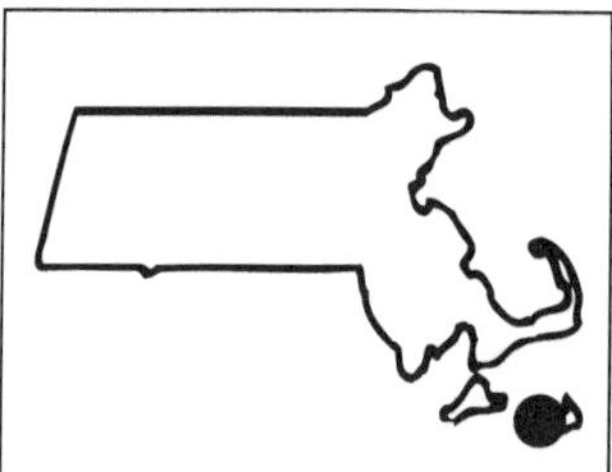

Great Harbor House
31 India Street
Nantucket, 02554
508-228-6609

MC, V
Open year-round
$50–$145

OLD-WORLD COMFORT and a civilized touch await you in this handsome Nantucket inn. Colonial colors and simple decor reflect the personality of this 1790 house. The eight rooms are unpretentious and comfortable, and each is named after a flower found on Nantucket. Columbine is one of the more seductive of the rooms here, a subtle color play in green and cream. Its queen-size canopy bed and pull-out sofa make it ideal for guests with children (of any age). Wood Lily is also lovely with its pale rose decor and ivory-colored canopy bed. All of the rooms have private baths and televisions, which tend to look intrusive in such Colonial surroundings. But guests love them!

A Continental breakfast is served downstairs in the common room or in your room. Many guests prefer their meals in the garden during the summer. Great Harbor House is an experience in combining Colonial authenticity with all the comforts you need and expect on vacation.

Directions: From ferry landing, go up Broad Street and turn left on Centre Street, then right onto India Street. Inn is on right.

Morrill Place • *Newburyport*

NEWBURYPORT HAS A shop for every member of the family. There are toys for the kids, handcrafted jewelry and fashionable clothes for mom, gadgets for dad, quality antiques for everyone—and even a year-round Christmas store for Santa. This town, with its rows of renovated brick buildings, is a favorite with tourists, who enjoy visiting the waterfront and strolling around town and who come here on the way out to Plum Island. Connected to Newburyport by a small bridge, this island is home of the Parker River National Wildlife Refuge, and when you visit, you may glimpse a family of deer or a community of snow geese safe in its sanctuary.

After a day of shopping and sightseeing, spend the night at Morrill Place, a large, handsome white house, squared off in Federal architectural style. The 1806 mansion was built by a whaling captain, and the Morrill family lived here for eighty-three years until Rose Ann Hunter bought the house in 1979. No ordinary innkeeper, Rose Ann always has a million projects going on. You might be a guest at Morrill Place during a mystery weekend or be in residence during one of her fashion show events. There are psychic Saturdays, poetry readings, art shows, and more. And you can always talk Rose Ann into giving you a tour of the new home she is building for herself in the carriage house behind the inn. She is a very busy lady; in addition to full-time innkeeping, she handles real estate for prospective innkeepers and teaches innkeeping classes to give aspiring owners tips on the trade.

You might be a guest at Morrill Place during a mystery weekend or be in residence during one of the fashion show events.

MORRILL PLACE PROVIDES A SATISFYING SANCTUARY AT THE END OF A BUSY DAY IN POPULAR NEWBURYPORT.

Morrill Place is an impressive building. The large rooms are decorated in a variety of styles, a legacy from the inn's role as a show house in 1985. Each room was redecorated by a different interior designer, and the house was on display as a fund-raising effort for a local hospital. Today bits and pieces of Morrill Place's facelift are still in evidence, and there is a fascinating scrapbook chronicling the design exercise. The eleven bedrooms are large, and many have trompe l'oeil detailing (the upstairs front room has an incredible rug painted onto the floor), high-post beds, antiques, and arresting color schemes. You might want to request a room on the second floor, which has been renovated more recently than the third floor.

When it's time for breakfast, you can choose to descend the lovely cantilevered staircase (a popular site for local weddings) or take a short cut down the back staircase to the formal dining room, which is highlighted with designer touches, including a marbleized mantel and "comb-painted" walls. Breakfast is a simple affair. A streamlined Continental meal is served at the long table, or you can sip your coffee or tea in the library across the hall, luxuriating in the red-and-gold decor.

When it's time to leave, do yourself a favor and depart through the front door, to get a closer look at the stunning blue cut-glass entryway. It will serve as a visual reminder of the good taste and careful decor of the Federal era.

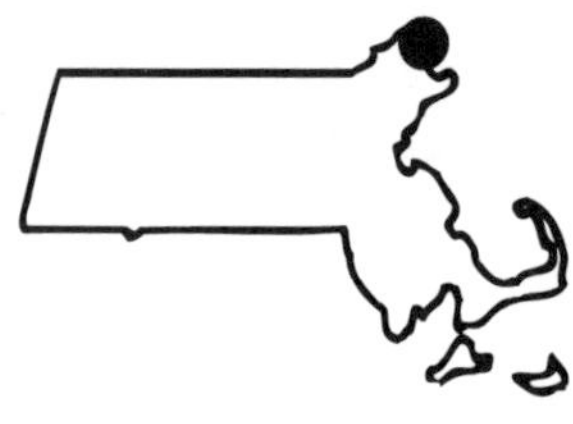

Morrill Place
209 High Street (Route 113)
Newburyport, 01950
508-462-2808

All major credit cards
Open year-round
$60–$90

Directions: From I-95, exit at Route 113 east (historic Newburyport sign). Continue on Route 113 (High Street) for 2 miles toward Newburyport. The inn is on the right, 1 block after the high school, on the corner of High and Johnson streets.

Northfield Country House · *Northfield*

WHEN ANDREA DALE visited Northfield Country House as a guest, she whimsically mentioned to its owners that if they ever planned to sell, they should give her a call. To her amazement, they offered to sell her the place on the spot, and the former credit director of Saks Fifth Avenue in New York City found herself the proud new owner of this sweet inn. A storybook house located on sixteen acres of lovely grounds, with a barn and swimming pool, the inn is seductive in every season. In the spring Andrea's gardens are in full bloom, summer is green and restful, fall is a colorful celebration, and winter makes the Country House look like something out of a Brothers Grimm fairy tale. The house originally was built by a wealthy Bostonian as a retreat where he could be close to the Reverend Dwight L. Moody, the popular late-eighteenth-century New England gospel teacher.

NORTHFIELD COUNTRY HOUSE'S ATTRACTIONS INCLUDE A BARN, A SWIMMING POOL, AND SIXTEEN ACRES.

The cottage is charming, with touches of the good life still in evidence. The dining room has handsome handcarved wood paneling with exceptional handcrafted corner cabinets (Andrea says this room is what tempted her to offer to buy the inn). An enormous fieldstone fireplace in the spacious living room provides the perfect place for guests to congregate.

Upstairs in the seven lovely bedrooms a real country feel characterizes the decor. The bedrooms (all share four pretty bathrooms) have iron beds, bright floral-print walls, comfortable chairs, and lovely linens. Three have stone fireplaces, one has fresh white wicker, and the snug former servants' quarters are just as charming as the larger rooms.

Andrea serves a hearty breakfast in the dining room. Guests sit at small tables with bright blue linens to enjoy fresh fruit, freshly squeezed orange juice, fruit muffins, and a main course of omelets, scrambled eggs, quiche, or French toast.

As soon as you drive up to this shingled and stone house, framed by hydrangea bushes and surrounded by flowers, you no doubt will already be planning your next visit.

Directions: From I-91 north, take exit 28A. Turn onto Route 10 north to Northfield center. At the firehouse turn right onto School Street. Proceed about a mile along School Street, crossing Birnam Road and continuing straight onto a dirt road. The inn is on the right. From I-91 south, take exit 28, then follow the above directions.

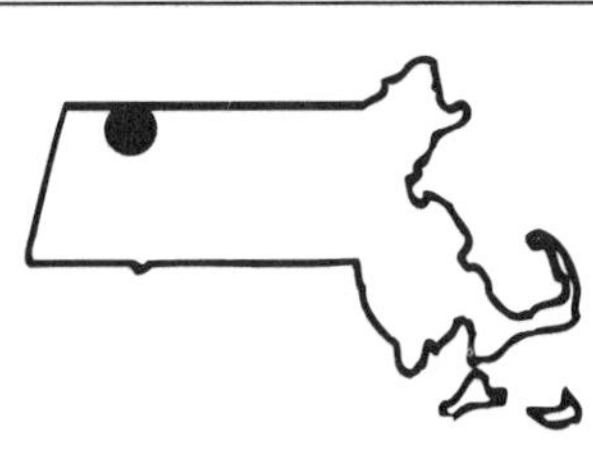

Northfield Country House
School Street
Northfield, 01360
413-498-2692

MC, V
Open year-round
$50–$80

Rockport • Inn on Cove Hill

IF YOU VISIT ROCKPORT on a summer weekend, you may fall in step with the hordes of tourists—children, parents, and grandparents—who fill the narrow streets. Rockport is very popular among out-of-towners for its collection of crafts galleries and gift shops (many houses in former fishermen's shanties), for its lovely harbor, and because of the prospect of returning home with a special souvenir.

There is at least one antique that is as old as the house in each room.

Your best bet may be to visit this quaint little town on a weekday in autumn, when you'll have the place more to yourself and might have the opportunity to talk to residents and learn more about their picturesque town. In any case, plan ahead and make a reservation at Inn on Cove Hill.

This pretty, two-hundred-year-old home is run by Marge and John Pratt, who have made every attempt to keep the spirit and decor of their lovely inn a reflection of Colonial tastes and times. They have restored and renovated every room in the house. There is at least one antique that is as old as the house in each room, and the wallpaper, beds, and furnishings are in keeping with tradition. The cheery bathrooms in nine of the eleven rooms are modern counterparts of the heritage look of the place. Marge has a sweet decorating touch: each room has its own soft color scheme, many have pencil-post canopy beds, all have lovely wallpaper, and a few have wonderful views of the harbor. Braided or Oriental rugs, a television, wreaths, fresh flowers, and attractive

AN AUTUMN VISIT TO INN ON COVE HILL IS AN ESPECIALLY PLEASING EXPERIENCE.

SOME OF COVE HILL'S ROOMS OFFER EXCELLENT VIEWS OF ROCKPORT HARBOR.

linens complete each room. The two bedrooms in the front of the house are at the top of a beautiful spiral staircase, while the other nine are up the steep (very steep), narrow stairs off the sitting room.

In good weather breakfast is served outdoors in the daisy garden. This restful and pretty setting is enhanced by umbrella tables, lawn furniture, and Rockport's warm weather. When there's a chill in the air, breakfast is served in bed. John bakes seven types of muffins, one for each morning: pumpkin, cranberry, blueberry, bran, banana, apple, and ginger. Stay a week and enjoy them all! Delicate floral-patterned English china and blue linens make a pretty breakfast picture—indoors or out.

An autumn visit to Cove Hill is always tempting: burnt-orange chrysanthemums, a display of seasonal pumpkins, and sprigs of bittersweet greet you at the front door. Spring is equally seductive: the front yard and gardens are filled with tulips, and fresh flowers are placed throughout the house. In any season, be sure to drive out on Marmion Way to take in the dramatic seascape and to remove yourself from Rockport's many shops and the urge to go home laden with too many arts, crafts, and gifts.

Directions: From I-93, take exit 27 onto Route 1 north. Continue on Route 1 to Route 128 north. When Route 128 ends, continue on Route 127 into Rockport. Take Route 127A to the center of town; Route 127A becomes Mount Pleasant Street. The inn is 2 blocks along on the left.

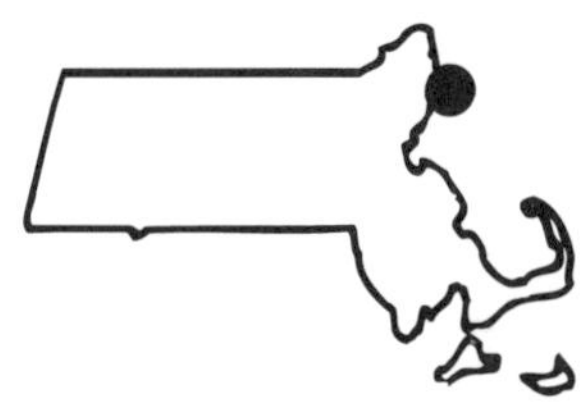

Inn on Cove Hill
37 Mount Pleasant Street
Rockport, 01966
508-546-2701

Cash or personal check only
Closed November through March
$48–$91

THE STATELY ARCHITECTURE HOUSES A HANDSOME INN.

Sheffield • Staveleigh House

WHEN YOU ARE BEST friends and never seem to find enough time together, opening a bed and breakfast inn could change all that. Dorothy Morosy and Marion Whiteman are still best friends, but their lives are pretty busy running this exceedingly attractive inn. A feminine touch is evident throughout the 1821 house, but it is never intrusive. Instead, the soft colors and neat-as-a-pin decor are sure to tempt every couple into many return visits. Sometimes it's a visit just for the girls; Dorothy and Marion often host needlework weekends, inviting outside experts to teach techniques and skills to needlepoint groups and other enthusiastic amateurs. Evidence of their own needlework skills is scattered throughout the inn. Dorothy and Marion do what they do very well.

The five rooms are beautiful. Especially lovely is the wicker room with its crisp navy-and-white color scheme. The room across the upstairs hall is just as pretty in deep pink with vintage chenille spreads and deep blue walls. The antique hooked rugs complete the country decor. The back room upstairs is pretty in banana yellow and blue calico. One of the two downstairs rooms with its own private entrance has a decorative sponge-painted floor. The other private entrance leads to a sparkling yellow-and-white room. Everything here is as fresh and clean as the rest of this attractive inn.

Dorothy and Marion serve a full breakfast as ample as their generosity. Crêpes, puff pancakes, strata, waffles, homemade muffins, fresh fruits, and breakfast meats satisfy healthy appetites. This feast is served in

Staveleigh House
South Main Road
(Route 7)
Sheffield, 01257
413-229-2129

Cash or personal check only
Open year-round
$60–$85

the pastel-tone, blue-and-rose dining room on crocheted tablecloths. The living room is also soothing in pink and mauve tones. Collections of blue glass, saltcellars, and artwork decorate the house in their own personal style.

A visit to Staveleigh House is a pleasant interlude in any season, and a welcome alternative to the throngs that make Lenox fatiguing during Tanglewood season.

Directions: From New York, take the Taconic Parkway north to Route 44 east. Follow Routes 44 and 22 to Route 7 north. The inn is in the heart of the Sheffield business district.

BEAUTIFUL DETAILS GIVE THIS INN ITS IMMENSE APPEAL.

Stockbridge • The Inn at Stockbridge

"CLASSIC" IS THE WORD TO DESCRIBE THE INN AT STOCKBRIDGE.

YOU'LL DISCOVER THIS perfect gem of an inn up a winding drive, protected by stately shade trees, and overlooking an impressive twelve-acre rolling lawn. Even the not-too-distant hum of the Massachusetts Turnpike doesn't affect the serenity that the Inn at Stockbridge offers. The house is a tasteful exercise in architectural symmetry; four pristine pillars are balanced by matching porches flanking the Colonial-red front door. The inn is classic enough that it might easily have had its portrait painted by Norman Rockwell. You can enjoy some of the American master's work by visiting the **Norman Rockwell Museum** (Main Street, 413-298-3822), where guided gallery tours are informative and touching.

Lee and Don Weitz have done a lovely job blending old and new to create an inn with an elegant touch and a personality intended to spoil you. The handsome living room is formal, the sitting room more casual with its floral-splashed seating, and the dining room a dedication to pampered and civilized treatment. Queen Anne seating, a long, formal table, and touches of crystal make breakfasts here more than a humdrum experience. The Weitzes believe that a stay at their inn should represent something special, and breakfast soufflés, French toast with Grand Marnier butter, blueberry pancakes, herbed scrambled eggs, and Sunday eggs Benedict are regulars. There are also heart-healthy breakfast alternatives that are equally delicious.

Each of the eight lovely bedrooms has a distinct personality, melding new furniture with country-inn charm. If you're partial to an Oriental motif, the Chinese Room offers exactly that. There's also North Corner Room, with a country-casual decor; South Corner Room, in flattering pink with beautiful flora-and-bird-print walls; and the Rose Room, in which you are surrounded by cabbage-and-rose-print wallpaper. The new terrace room is ultraluxurious with a king-size bed, its own Jacuzzi, and private deck overlooking the garden and reflecting pool.

When you're not exploring the area, you'll no doubt enjoy relaxing in the swimming pool or on one of the two porches, ensconced in wicker, imagining that you've drifted back into another era when spending the summer in the Berkshires was de rigueur for many fashionable New England families.

The Inn at Stockbridge
Route 7
Stockbridge, 01262
413-298-3337

AE, MC, V
Open year-round
\$80–\$200

Directions: From I-90, take exit 2. Follow Route 102 west into Stockbridge. Take Route 7 north. The inn is about 1¼ miles along on the right, down a long driveway.

Captain Dexter House • *Vineyard Haven*

WHEN YOU'RE READY to give yourself a special treat, come to Captain Dexter House. New owner Roberta Pieczenik has maintained the high standards of the inn, and this lovely 1843 home is a feast for the eye. Its dense decor instantly makes you feel safe and secure. The compact rooms are brimming with beautiful furnishings and a palette of soft colors. Each of the eight rooms is named after a sea captain who lived within two blocks of the house in Vineyard Haven. All have private baths, some have fireplaces, and most have sitting areas.

Perhaps the most impressive quality of the Captain Dexter is that the bedrooms envelop you in tasteful heritage decor. You can sleep under the lace ceiling of a canopy bed and be refreshed by the gentle breeze of a ceiling fan, while immersed in lovely linens and surrounded by early American art and beautiful wallpaper. The rooms are snug and tight as a ship—the perfect place to stay for an entire winter.

Breakfast here is a baker's dream. Innkeeper Alisa Lengel offers homemade apple bread, coffee cake, croissants, apple strudel bread, and strawberry or lemon muffins. Herbal teas and hearty coffee are available in copious quantities.

If you love the look and feel of the Captain Dexter House, you'll be just as happy in the new "down-island" branch of the **Inn in Edgartown** (35 Pease's Point Way, 508-627-7298). The same aesthetics rule this eleven-room 1840s house, and innkeeper Michael Maultz will see to your every need.

CAPTAIN DEXTER HOUSE FEATURES "MUSEUM QUALITY" EIGHTEENTH-CENTURY FURNISHINGS.

Directions: From the Vineyard Haven ferry landing, turn left onto Water Street. At the first intersection turn right. Turn right again onto Main Street. The inn is located between Church Street and Colonial Lane, about 1 block from the ferry landing.

Captain Dexter House
100 Main Street
Vineyard Haven, 02568
508-693-6564

MC, V
Open year-round
$55–$140

Vineyard Haven • **Thorncroft**

THORNCROFT AND ITS SURROUNDINGS ARE A PLEASANT "UP-ISLAND" ALTERNATIVE TO BUSTLING EDGARTOWN.

Thorncroft
278 Main Street
Vineyard Haven, 02568
508-693-3333

AE, MC, V
Open year-round
Off-season, $99–$219; in season, $129–$249

KARL BUDER IS STILL the first to remind everyone that, yes, there is an "up-island" on Martha's Vineyard, and yes, it is very much alive and thriving. Thorncroft is proof positive that Vineyard Haven is a pleasant alternative to the always popular Edgartown and its mushrooming population of bed and breakfast inns. And Karl and his wife, Lynn, are proof positive that innkeeping is a stimulating, creative business. Thorncroft has expanded and improved, offering guests pleasant accommodations with twenty-first-century services. To cater to the growing number of guests who combine work with play, or make no distinction at all between the two, the Buders have installed a state-of-the-art Merlin phone system that even hooks up a laptop computer to its parent mainframe. And all this in a pretty Victorian setting.

This full-service inn includes four buildings, offering nineteen rooms. The original 1918 oversize cottage has Victoriana decor, lots of lace, and an impressive collection of antique wicker. The carriage house has nine rooms, all with oversize Jacuzzis and fireplaces. The two new buildings—turn-of-the-century houses, down the road in town—provide the same attractive decor and amenities.

Guests are greeted each morning with the *Boston Globe*, then treated to a full breakfast. The young chefs-in-residence whip up buttermilk pancakes with blueberry or strawberry honey, almond French toast, bacon-Swiss quiche, croissant breakfast sandwiches, spinach-sausage-cheese pie, or an old-fashioned country breakfast of eggs, sausage, and buttermilk biscuits. The Buders have begun to serve dinner limited only to guests for an additional fee. The fare is equally satisfying with Louisiana roast tuna steak, panfried shrimp with roasted red pepper sauce, and filet of beef with Pommery-rosemary cream just a sampling of the inventive cuisine. Lunch is also available with upscale picnics of pâtés, antipasto salads, cheeses, and luscious desserts. And if you're still hungry, there is a delicious afternoon tea served to guests.

The Buders have lovely taste and have created an inn that is professionally run. Service is a top priority, and the location is terrific. If you decide not to bring a car to the island, you can take a taxi or walk the mile to the inn from the ferry. All of the inn's buildings are accessible to the village of Vineyard Haven and its many shops and restaurants. Come here once and you'll return a convert to "up-island" living.

Service is a top priority, and the location is terrific.

Directions: From the Vineyard Haven ferry landing, turn left onto Water Street. At the first intersection turn right. Turn right again onto Main Street. The inn is 1 mile along on the left.

IT IS WELL WORTH YOUR PERSEVERANCE TO MAKE YOUR WAY DOWN THE LONG, WINDING, SANDY ROAD TO STAY IN THIS INN.

West Tisbury • **Lambert's Cove Inn**

You'll be enveloped by a feral garden of cornflowers, irises . . . lilacs, lady's-slippers, and an ancient wisteria vine, all of which blossom on cue.

IF THE ENERGY LEVEL of Edgartown's street life makes you yearn to get away from it all, drive directly "up-island" to West Tisbury and the Paradise Lost atmosphere of Lambert's Cove Inn. Here in summer you'll be enveloped by a feral garden of cornflowers, irises, lilies of the valley, bridal wreaths, lilacs, lady's-slippers, and an ancient wisteria vine, all of which blossom on cue to make this place a veritable botanical garden. Even resident sparrows are thoughtful enough to lay their perfect little eggs in the centers of the hanging fuchsias. The nearby pine forest is fragrant, the lawns are verdant and cool, the apple orchards are bountiful, and the tennis court is fenced with sweet peas and its trellis laden with Concord grapes.

It is well worth your perseverance to make your way down the long, winding, sandy road to stay at this inn. Some guests never leave during their stay—not even for dinner, since there is a terrific restaurant at the inn, completing the hospitality circle. These people are satisfied relaxing in lawn chairs, surveying their surroundings, and listening to the mourning doves finishing another perfect day.

The 1790 country house is typical of the Vineyard. The large library opens up on the huge deck overlooking the orchard. A smaller, more formal sitting room with a comforting fireplace is cozy in the winter. The fifteen bedrooms vary in decor, but each is fresh, cheerful, and airy. You might prefer to stay in the carriage house or barn out back. In the carriage house the Greenhouse Room has its own solarium sitting room and beautiful pink-and-red-print walls, and the Geranium Room is equally festive in a simple floral print. Every room at the inn has a private bath.

Not to be upstaged by the decor, the restaurant menu changes frequently. Aromatic cioppino with cod, swordfish, and shellfish; rack of lamb; veal cutlet Marsala, and any number of fresh seafood specialties might be listed during your stay. Breakfast is served in the lovely dining room, with an equally delectable range of Continental possibilities: homemade croissants; zucchini, banana, and cranberry breads; and poppyseed muffins.

Owners Libby and Banning Repplier travel quite a bit; in their absence, innkeeper Marie Burnett sees to your every need. Be sure to visit Lambert's Cove. Chances are you'll become an instant devotee, returning here to enjoy the Vineyard during each of its four glorious seasons.

Directions: From the Vineyard Haven ferry, take State Road. Turn right at Lambert's Cove Road. Look for the inn sign 3 miles along on the left. Follow the dirt road ½ mile. From the Oak Bluffs ferry, follow the signs to Vineyard Haven. Take Beach Road to State Road and follow the above directions.

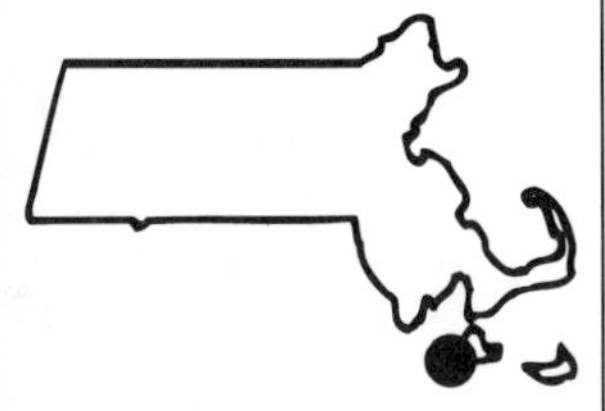

Lambert's Cove Inn
Lambert's Cove Road
West Tisbury, 02568
508-693-2298

All major credit cards
Closed January
$65–$125

Yarmouth Port • **Wedgewood Inn**

A REFINED DECORATING STYLE IS WEDGEWOOD'S SIGNATURE.

WHEN YOU DRIVE BY country inns at night, you may often be impressed by dramatically lit architecture that promises a beautiful interior, pleasant hosts, and a unique inn experience. On Cape Cod, there are dozens of inns that offer this illusion; Wedgewood Inn is one of the handful that actually delivers. Milt and Gerri Graham are as special as their handsome inn. You can be assured of tasteful decor, great food, genuine friendliness, and intelligent conversation from the Grahams. Milt, an innkeeper by way of the FBI and professional football with the Patriots (he's as imposing as the house and brings new meaning to the mythology of Eliot Ness), and Gerri, a former schoolteacher, are warm, sincere, and terrific innkeepers. You will assuredly fall in love with Wedgewood Inn and return here as often as you can.

The six rooms are virtually perfect. Especially handsome is Room Three in deep Wedgwood blue. With its tall-post bed and quality furnishings, it is lush and rich. Two, also in the pervasive blue theme, has its own porch. Room One has a sitting room in its own porch; Five is secreted away in the back of the house and has a daybed; Six on the third floor is another tribute to the Grahams' impressive ability to restore and renovate this Federal-era house. Room Four is lovely in blue and ivory. Four of the rooms have fireplaces, all have private baths, and each one is as beautiful as the next.

The inn sparkles, the style is impeccable, and the warmth is real. . . .

Gerri serves a full breakfast. Belgian waffles, pancakes, French toast, minicroissants with scrambled eggs, ham, and hollandaise, and waffles with whipped cream and strawberries are the popular choices. Fresh fruit and homebaked breads complete the meal which is served by candlelight on lovely botanical plates.

Gerri is meticulous. The inn sparkles, the style is impeccable, and the warmth is real—from both the fireplaces and the hospitality. You can purchase souvenirs of Wedgwood ceramic ware in its distinctive blue. Or, you can sit in the garden and compare notes with Milt about your respective assaults on Mount Kilimanjaro. He has every reason to be proud of the fact that he has made it to the summit twice,

THIS ELEGANT INN OFFERS FIRST-CLASS ACCOMMODATIONS AND FASCINATING HOSTS.

most recently at the in-shape age of fifty-four. The Grahams are always inspiring in surprising ways.

Directions: On Cape Cod take Route 6. Take exit 7 (Willow Street) and turn right. At the stop sign, turn right onto Route 6A. The inn is located 75 yards along on the right.

Wedgewood Inn
83 Main Street (Route 6A)
Yarmouth Port, 02675
508-362-5157

All major credit cards
Open year-round
$95–$145

RHODE ISLAND

ELEGANT MANSIONS, COASTAL CHARM

Most of Rhode Island's bed and breakfast inns are clustered in popular, historic Newport. It's a warm-weather season here (most inns close for the winter), and the town is always filled with visitors who come to get a glimpse of the former summer palaces of turn-of-the-century American industrialists. An equal number of boat people come to enjoy Newport's nautical personality. The inns tend toward the dramatic, as most are homes of former wealthy Newport residents and sea captains. Both the Rhode Island coast—which has surprisingly few inns—and the popular Block Island also are represented in this chapter. Rhode Island's vacation spots are great places for bed and breakfast visits to take in rustic island charm or impressive mansion history.

WHAT RHODE ISLAND INNS LACK IN QUANTITY, THEY MORE THAN MAKE UP FOR IN QUALITY. ABOVE: THE INN AT CASTLE HILL REVIEWED ON PAGE 182.

IN ADDITION TO ITS MAIN HOUSE, BLUE DORY OFFERS THREE COTTAGES OUT BACK.

IMAGINE FALLING ASLEEP to the sound of surf pounding the shore and the plaintive cry of a sea gull. Or awakening to the distinctive fragrance of the ocean and beachgrass. This, and much more, can be yours when you stay at the Blue Dory Inn.

Block Island has many guest houses, and this handsome one-hundred-year-old blue house is one of the nicest. Thanks to new owners Ann and Ed Loedy, the Blue Dory is just as charming as it has always been. This cozy Victorian house has some lovely features; if you want privacy, book yourself into one of the three cottages behind the main house. The Doll House is tiny, pretty, and quiet. The two-room cottage next door is great for two couples or a family. The Tea House is honeymoon-perfect, with its private porch and view of Crescent Bay. All three houses open onto the patio and brightly colored flower gardens.

The main house has ten more bedrooms; many are air-conditioned, all have private baths. The decor leans toward Victorian, with turn-of-the-century furnishings, lacy curtains, brass beds, lace runners, and cheerful wallpaper. One snug room on the third floor has a sky-window that opens onto the beachside of the house, bringing the ocean sounds inside and offering a tranquil view of the surroundings. A new suite is quite plush, and perfect for a family of four. The Blue Dory is one of the few inns that accepts children of all ages.

Innkeeper Vince McAloon is on hand to prepare a delicious breakfast in the bright eat-in kitchen. Small tables with bentwood seating are set with marine-blue linens, and breakfast on a given morning might be a feast of banana-carrot muffins, date-nut bread, croissants filled with apples or raspberries, strudel, cinnamon rolls, and fresh fruit.

The parlor is lovely, with a television for keeping up with the onshore news. And there's all of Block Island to explore. The town is a welcome place to walk; you can rent a bike and ride out to a lighthouse, Payne's Dock, and the beaches; there are plenty of souvenir stores; and lovely hiking paths offer a chance to get further away from it all. Block Island is especially popular in the summer, but autumn is its magical season. The air is crisp, skies are clear, the sun is warm, trees are turning, and the Blue Dory is open, waiting for you.

Blue Dory Inn
Dodge Street
Block Island, 02807
401-466-2254

AE, MC, V
Open year-round
Off-season, $55–$95; in season, $125–$245

Directions: At the ferry landing, turn right onto Water Street. Continue around the bend as Water becomes Dodge Street. The inn is the second house on the right.

Admiral Benbow Inn • *Newport*

THE HIGHLIGHTS IN this 1885 home, originally built by Admiral Augustus Littlefield as a guest house for his sailor friends, are the collection of religiously polished brass beds and the stunning Palladian windows. Room Five is particularly appealing, with its floral-papered walls, fireplace, and glimpse of the admiral's own home just down Pelham Street (this bright white study in dramatic architecture is still impressive amidst its more contemporary neighbors). Room Nine also is a gem, cheerful and romantic in red, with its lace-laden canopy bed. All of the fifteen rooms have private baths.

BRASS BEDS AND PALLADIAN WINDOWS ARE HIGHLIGHTS OF THE 1885 ADMIRAL BENBOW INN.

Innkeeper Linda Christie is carrying on the inn's tradition of offering a tasty breakfast in the country-decor basement breakfast room. Linda's fruit, yogurt, and granola buffet is as popular as her freshly baked peach bread and peanut butter muffins. Every day offers a different bread, muffin, and fresh pastry.

Guests enjoy congregating around the wood-burning stove in winter and appreciate the coolness of this cheerful room in summer. Generally speaking, they already know each other; this inn has a loyal clientele that returns often.

The inn is well situated for a walk to Thames Street and its stretch of shops, nearby restaurants, and cafés. Or you can wander in the opposite direction to admire the "cottages" on Ocean Drive, always a reliable educational diversion.

Directions: From Route 24 south, continue onto Route 114 south. Follow into downtown Newport onto Thames Street. Turn onto Pelham Street. Inn is 2 blocks on the right side. From I-95 north, turn onto Route 138 east. Follow over the Jamestown and Newport bridges onto America's Cup Avenue. Turn onto Thames Street, then Pelham Street. The inn is 2 blocks along on the right.

Admiral Benbow Inn
93 Pelham Street
Newport, 02840
401-846-4256

AE, MC, V
Closed January
Winter, \$45–\$70; summer, \$95–\$110

Newport • Brinley Victorian Inn

WHEN YOU PLAN TO visit Newport and want to stay in a quiet inn not far from the tourist trade and frantic pace of Thames Street, find your way to Brinley Victorian Inn for a restful stay. This lovely old home is turn-of-the-century pretty, with its calm pace. Some guests are content to sit on the porch and relax their way through an entire afternoon.

Some guests are content to sit on the porch and relax their way through an entire afternoon.

Others, who have an appreciation for the arts and Newport's history, might enjoy the Brinley's proximity to **Newport Art Museum** (76 Bellevue Avenue, 401-847-0179). The Tudor cottage that houses the museum was architect Richard Morris Hunt's first Newport commission, a warm-up for his monument, the Breakers. The museum always has an interesting exhibit. Shows, whose subjects range from contemporary glass to Rhode Island classicist painters, change every two or three months.

After a museum visit, wander across the street to the historical sleeper of Newport, the **Redwood Library and Athenaeum** (50 Bellevue Avenue, 401-847-0292). Entering this astonishing place is like walking into the Colonial past. The handsome building is filled with ancient leatherbound books, eighteenth-century portraits (by Gilbert Stuart, among others), leather wing chairs, vintage chandeliers, an impressive tall-case clock, Townsend and Goddard tables, and the wonderful serenity of an old library

BRINLEY VICTORIAN INN'S WELL-CHOSEN FURNISHINGS ARE AUCTION FINDS.

THE INN PROVIDES A QUIET REFUGE, YET IS NOT FAR FROM NEWPORT'S THAMES STREET.

filled with history and memories. The grounds are beautiful, and you might find yourself checking out a tome on Newport's history and steeping yourself in tradition while relaxing in the gardens.

Back at the Brinley, there are seventeen lovely rooms in the main house and the annex next door, all decorated in the Victorian style. Owners Edwina Sebest (a psychologist by training) and Amy Weintraub (a documentary filmmaker and writer) did all the wallpapering themselves when they bought the inn nine years ago. They love the Victorian era and furnished the inn from auctions. The parlor is one of the prettiest rooms in the house. A pale mauve-and-gray color scheme and fairly formal furnishings create a civilized environment for the inn's Continental breakfast. Guests can also take their homebaked muffins and breads to the porch or the garden, with its collection of Victorian wrought-iron furniture.

The Brinley is a pretty place to stay. The setting is quiet and peaceful, and Edwina and Amy do whatever they can to make your stay as pleasant as possible. First-timers generally become regulars. Perhaps you will, too.

Directions: From Route 24 south, continue onto Route 114 south to Broadway. After about 12 blocks turn left onto Everett Street, then turn right onto Kay Street. In 2 blocks turn left onto Brinley Street. Inn is on the left. From I-95 north, turn onto Route 138 east and continue over the Jamestown and Newport bridges. Take the first exit off the Newport Bridge and turn right at the end of the exit. Turn left onto Touro Street, then left onto Kay Street, then right onto Brinley Street. Inn is nearly a block along on the right.

Brinley Victorian Inn
23 Brinley Street
Newport, 02840
401-849-7645

MC, V
Closed two weeks in January
Winter, $55–$70; summer, $80–$125

Newport • **Cliffside Inn**

THIS INN HAS AN eccentric past. In the early 1900s it was owned by Beatrice Turner. This socialite refugee from Main Line Philadelphia fled her family to become a painter, a career then frowned on by polite society. The fledgling artist spent most of her life painting her self-portrait. When her father died, word has it, she propped him up for two weeks to paint her questionable masterpiece *Daddy in Death*. As if this memorial tribute were not enough, she proceeded to paint the entire house black, in mourning.

Today there are no ghosts. Cliffside is light, airy, enchanting, and surrounded by a perfectly normal picket fence. The inn is slightly cluttered, sometimes ruffled, and definitely unique. The decorating approach takes creative liberties: a corner cabinet is hung upside down, antique mahogany kitchen cupboards are covered with wallpaper, a massive antique mantel doubles as a stunning headboard, a sewing machine table is a base for a sink, a forgettable table is painted in trompe l'oeil, antique wicker is recolored in sea-foam green, and a striking vanity is created from a very boring desk.

THIS 1880S HOME WAS ONCE OWNED BY BEATRICE TURNER, SOCIALITE REFUGEE FROM MAIN LINE PHILADELPHIA.

Each of the ten rooms at Cliffside has a distinct personality (and a private bath). The Miss Beatrice Room is large, lovely, and equipped with a huge bathroom. Miss Adele's Room, with the recycled mantel headboard, is romantic and warm. Wicker Room has a handsome brass bed and wicker furniture. And the Turner Suite, with a sitting room that could easily double as a blue gingham nursery, can accommodate a small family or part of a sailing crew. Arbor Room, by the front porch, is cozy and private.

The entire house is filled with pastel-painted ceiling moldings, beautiful furniture, and unexpected touches. The living room, where a delicious homemade breakfast is served, is filled with Victorian seating, a piano, and round tables at which guests become overnight friends. New innkeeper Annette King is a talented breakfast cook and has a repertoire that offers a different breakfast each day of the month. Eggs-and-sausage casserole, pineapple soufflé, mushroom-sausage strudel, baked pears, and curried fruit are some of her specialties. Her southern hospitality sparkles in the kitchen and throughout the inn. As a professional inn consultant, Annette is a fabulous hostess who knows how to make guests feel right at home.

You will be impelled to return to Cliffside often, to sit on the porch (with its beautiful, handpainted, seashell-motif rugs) surrounded by friendly faces, enjoying the sound of the ocean's roar from down the street. Cliffside is perfectly situated at the beginning of Cliff Walk. This scenic pathway, dating back to Colonial times, is the best way to get a personal look at the summer castles dotting Newport's shoreline. The walk can be rather dramatic at times, as you carefully make your way along the ocean through tunnels and overhangs. And as you go, you can eavesdrop on the gardeners helping their employees through their tasks, get a glimpse of Marble House's brilliant red teahouse, and look for famous faces framed by large, awning-shaded windows. It's one of the most pleasant ways to get a private tour of turn-of-the-century mansion life. There is a public access at Bailey's Beach, from which you can return to Cliffside along the road. It's a wonderful walk; take a picnic and sun yourself on the rocks with the other smart Newporters who have made this discovery.

BREAKFAST AT CLIFFSIDE INN IS SERVED IN THE LIVING ROOM.

Directions: From Route 24 south, continue onto Route 114 south. Then take Route 138 west into downtown Newport. Turn onto Route 238 south and follow to Memorial Boulevard. Turn right onto the sixth street (Cliff) and then left onto Seaview. Inn is on the left corner. From I-95, turn onto Route 138 east and follow over the Jamestown and Newport bridges. Take the first exit off the Newport Bridge onto Route 238 south to Memorial Boulevard. Follow the above directions.

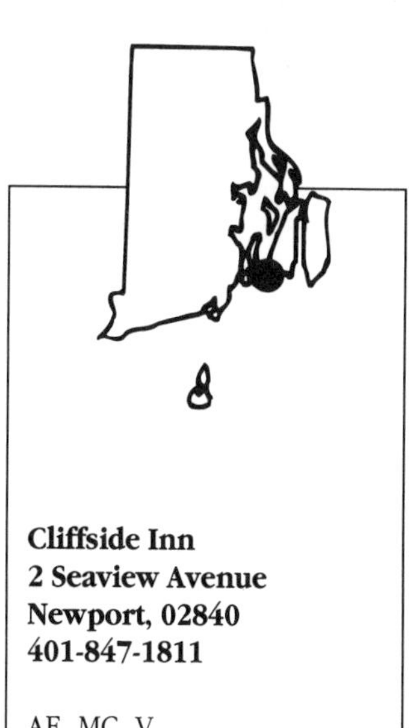

Cliffside Inn
2 Seaview Avenue
Newport, 02840
401-847-1811

AE, MC, V
Open year-round
$75–$175

Newport • The Inn at Castle Hill

ROOMS AT INN AT CASTLE HILL GIVE THE IMPRESSION THAT YOU ARE THE PRIVATE HOUSE GUEST OF A VERY WEALTHY FRIEND.

THERE'S NO URGE TO visit any of Newport's summer palaces if you stay at the Inn at Castle Hill, originally the private home of world traveler Alexander Agassiz. Owner Paul McEnroe has preserved the building's Victorian atmosphere in style. After finding your way through an impressive grove of trees (Newport has more varieties of trees than any other American city, a vestige of the time when the idle wealthy competed against one another with imported trees and designer gardens), you'll approach the inn, perched on a hill, commanding a stunning view of Newport Harbor.

The house, modest by Breakers' standards (the Breakers was the summer home of Cornelius Vanderbilt II), is nonetheless impressive. It became an inn in 1938, as the story goes, after Alexander's daughter-in-law, Mrs. Maximilian Agassiz, was marooned overnight by a flood following a particularly rough sea storm. "Get me out of the house," she commanded, and then left for good.

Today you might be among the fortunate few who have the foresight to book early enough to get a room in this unique inn. If so, you'll get a taste of what life was like for people for whom dedicating oneself to conspicuous comfort was the norm. But don't fret if you can't get into one of the ten rooms; you can always visit the inn's outdoor terrace bar and watch the sunset while sipping a cocktail.

What is so delightful about Castle Hill is that any of the perfectly maintained rooms gives you the illusion of a very wealthy friend. Mr. Agassiz, fascinated by the Orient, filled his home with priceless treasures, many of which are still in situ. Everything—from the subtle, handpainted wall panels, the handcarved panel above the mantel, and the massive, ornately carved furniture in the sitting room, to the more contemporary chinoiserie wallpaper and ginger-jar lamp collection in the bedrooms—evokes an appreciation of the Far East. You also might feel as though you've traveled through a time tunnel to reach this handsome inn; there are no televisions or telephones to disrupt your nostalgic visit.

It's difficult to select a room. Each one, with its own architectural detailing, is so special that you'll have to come here ten times to find your favorite. On the third floor is a lovely suite, complete with fireplace and sitting room large enough to host a small party. Soft lighting, Chinese side tables, and elegant details (as in all the rooms) help to make this room distinctive. Six is one of the most popular and tempting. With a full view of the ocean from its second-story corner outlook, it was originally the best place for a wife to watch for her sea captain husband's return. Peaceful in apricot and blue, the room has an enormous bathroom with a matching, oversize, free-standing tub. Equally seductive is Seven, with its warm, wood-paneled walls, divan for recovering after a day in the sun, and large bathroom with Oriental chrysanthemum-and-songbird print. The most contemporary room is Eight, located under the eaves on the third floor, with white wicker, bright green wallpaper, and a freestanding Victorian tub.

There are no televisions or telephones to disrupt your nostalgic visit.

The Inn at Castle Hill has a well-deserved reputation for fine dining. Breakfast for inn guests is served in the elegant Agassiz Room during the winter. An attentive staff will bring you croissants filled with lemon, fresh fruit, almond, or some other delicacy. As you start the day, seated on velvet-upholstered formal chairs looking seaward, you will appreciate the charm of this inn even more. During the summer, breakfast is served in the Sunset Room, buffet style. You'll be given the difficult decision of choosing from among the hearty offerings of pastries, cheeses, yogurt, fresh berries and cream, bagels, and breakfast meats.

The inn is especially welcoming in the winter when you are greeted by the nearby foghorn and a healthy fire in the hearth. The rates are also much lower. Visit Castle Hill to be your own weekend Jay Gatsby, to retreat from the twentieth century, and to enjoy the good life. Even though it might cost more, the indulgence can easily become addictive.

Directions: From Route 24 south, turn onto Route 138 south. Take Route 138A, which becomes Memorial Boulevard. Follow to the bottom of the hill and turn left at the light onto Thames Street. Turn right onto Wellington and take every right thereafter until you reach Ocean Drive. The inn is around the corner from the Coast Guard station. From I-95, turn onto Route 138 east and follow over the Jamestown and Newport bridges. Take the Newport exit into downtown. Take America's Cup Avenue south to Thames Street. Turn right onto Wellington and follow the above directions.

The Inn at Castle Hill
Ocean Drive
Newport, 02840
401-849-3800

AE, MC, V
Closed Christmas Eve and Christmas Day
$55–$230

Newport • Inntowne

After a fire destroyed the original 1935 boarding house, the building was gutted, and a country inn with a modern feel was created from the inside out.

YOU MIGHT BE FORTUNATE enough to be welcomed to Inntowne by the soothing fragrance of simmering spices, wafting from the kitchen. It's this sort of detail that gives Inntowne its friendly atmosphere. Betty McEnroe is head of this household (her husband, Paul, is king on Newport's Castle Hill, with its own civilized inn), and her feminine touch is as apparent as her concern for a loyal clientele. A former nurse, she is dedicated to making her guests feel comfortable and well cared for.

The seventeen rooms in the main house and the six up the street in the annex, Mary House (20 Mary Street), provide a veritable field day for garden lovers. Each room has a profusion of hothouse floral prints, which can be found almost everywhere in the room: on the curtains, on the upholstered wing chairs, on the canopies and the dust ruffles, on the wastebaskets and the shower curtain . . . not to mention on the wallpaper. But fear not: This sea of flowers is not overwhelming.

Each room is as charming as the next, and all are air-conditioned. The bathrooms are up-to-date, and even the smaller rooms are cozy, not cramped. It if all looks slightly new, it is. Betty started from the ground up with Inntowne. After a fire destroyed the original 1935 boarding house, the building was gutted, and a country inn with a modern feel was created from the inside out. Be forewarned: It's not so modern as to have televisions, telephones, or an elevator; the four flights of stairs might give you an unexpected workout.

Although the rooms lack the random architectural detailing of old inns, they more than make up for the loss with an attractive, integrated design. The furniture is Colonial reproduction and fits perfectly with the heritage decor. Room 202 as its own private balcony and is always in great demand by guests who have discovered this extra bonus. But there is plenty of outdoor space for everyone to gather on the fourth-floor deck, filled with comfortable furniture and potted flowers during the summer—a peaceful place to end the day. The rooms on the Thames Street side tend to be a little noisy, perfect for New Yorkers who are inured to street sounds.

In Mary House, up the street, several of the rooms have efficiency kitchens, for guests who stay longer

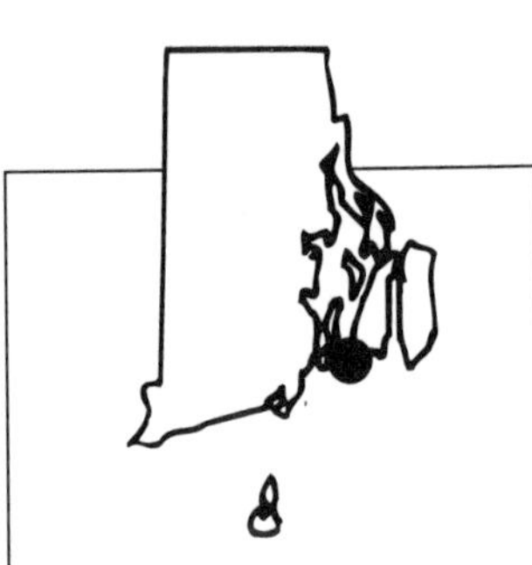

Inntowne
6 Mary Street
Newport, 02840
401-846-9200

AE, MC, V
Closed Christmas Eve and Christmas Day
$80–$140

than a weekend. Here the decor is more contemporary, with stylish wallpaper prints and furnishings. In the basement is a charming, snug, "hobbit" apartment, scaled for guests who are as petite as Betty. This cozy hideaway is equipped with a kitchen larger than you'd find in most condos, a great asset for guests who like to entertain while on the road.

Breakfast is served in what appears to be a minishop for antique tables and chairs—and so it is! You can purchase the chair you sit on, the table you eat at, and the English bone china teacups and saucers your coffee is served in. Freshly squeezed orange juice, piping hot muffins, croissants, and coffee or tea in a silver service are presented by an amiable staff amidst the cultivated English antique decor. At breakfast you might find yourself surrounded by parents visiting their children at local boarding schools, couples weekending with their boat-owner friends, tourists, and a host of guests who have discovered Inntowne and fallen in love with it.

Afternoon tea is popular with guests and a welcome touch during the winter months. As with everything at the inn, it is done with panache and good taste. Inntowne is the perfect location for easy walking to all Newport's shops and restaurants. It is especially pleasant to visit during the off-season, when there is little competition on the streets and when it provides a warm and welcoming haven away from the tedium of winter home life.

INNTOWNE'S ROOMS DISPLAY AN ATTRACTIVE, INTEGRATED DESIGN.

Directions: From Route 24 south, continue onto Route 114 south into downtown Newport. Take Thames Street and turn left after 1 block to the corner of Mary Street. From I-95, turn onto Route 138 east and follow over the Jamestown and Newport bridges. Take the first exit off the Newport Bridge, then turn right at the end of the ramp. Continue straight through 3 traffic lights. Inn is 1 block beyond the third light at the corner of Thames and Mary streets. The entrance is on Mary Street.

Newport • Queen Anne Inn

THE ONLY THING YOU might appreciate about the Queen Anne more than practical owner Peg McCabe is the fact that the inn has a parking lot, an almost unheard-of rarity in space-crammed downtown Newport. Park your car here and check in before you take off to walk the streets of this popular tourist spot in search of souvenirs, good food, and a touch of history.

THE VIEW FROM QUEEN ANNE INN'S FOURTH-FLOOR SERVANTS' QUARTERS ROOMS IS THE BEST IN THE HOUSE.

Peg may suggest that you strike off to visit the **Samuel Whitehorne House** (416 Thames Street, 401-847-2448), where you'll be given a private tour by a well-informed docent. Be sure to call ahead to reserve your tour. Among the tour's highlights is a priceless furniture collection of Goddard and Townsend originals, signed and in perfect condition. (Each room here is a celebration of authentic decor, all made possible by Doris Duke in her campaign to salvage historic eighteenth-century Newport homes and give them perpetual life through her generously endowed trust funds). Or Peg may point you in the opposite direction toward one of Newport's 1748 homes, the **Hunter House** (Washington Street, 401-847-7516). This sea captain's home is slightly more modest, but no less impressive, than the Whitehorne House. It contains a stunning collection of antiques, artwork, and souvenirs of a privileged life and is run by the Newport Preservation Society. Volunteers here are enthusiastic, well educated, and clearly in love with their work of sharing Newport's unique heritage.

After a long day of sightseeing, sunning, and shopping, a return to the Queen Anne offers a welcome respite from the ardors of vacation life.

After a long day of sightseeing, sunning, and shopping, a return to the Queen Anne offers a welcome respite from the ardors of vacation life. The fourteen rooms are pleasing, in various shades of pink and lavender (except for the one room Peg's children refer to as the "male room," which is more subdued in blue and green). A Victorian theme runs rampant throughout the inn; delicate crocheted spreads, period antiques, stained glass, stunning parlor lamps (in the bedrooms), footed bathtubs with pastel color treatments, lovely floral-print sheets, crochet and lace works under glass, and a collection of beautiful beds complete the look. The smaller rooms on the fourth floor offer the best view in the house; it's worth the climb for the privacy these former servants' quarters offer.

Breakfast is served in the living room (pleasing in

PINKS AND LAVENDERS SURROUND THE VICTORIAN FURNISHINGS IN MOST ROOMS.

pink) or outdoors in the garden, overlooking Peg's springtime peonies, poppies, and pansies. Guests are off to a light start with homemade breads, plenty of tea and coffee, and fresh juice. Peg is always on hand to help plan the day's itinerary and to lend advice on the best bets in Newport.

Visiting the Queen Anne is a delightful experience. With characteristic straightforwardness, Peg maintains that "it's the best value in town." As you pass through the front door with its impressive Queen Anne's lace-etched window, you may be inclined to agree.

Directions: From Route 24 south, turn onto Route 114 south and continue onto Broadway Avenue. At Washington Square make a U-turn. The second street on the right is Clarke Street. From I-95, turn onto Route 138 east and continue over the Jamestown and Newport bridges. Take the first right exit and turn right at the end of the ramp. Bear left at the second light. Turn left at the third light. The second street on the right is Clarke Street. The inn is ½ block along on the left.

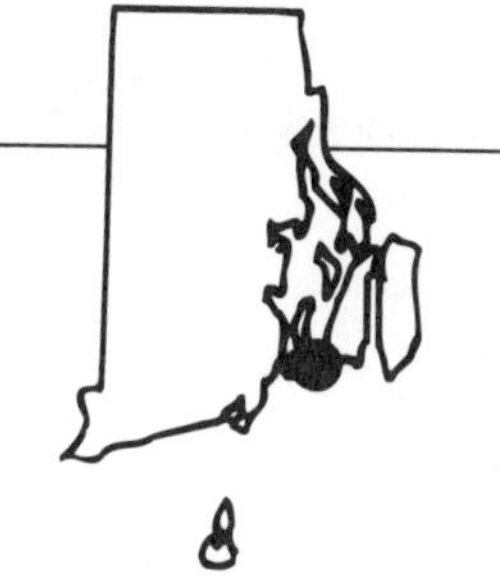

Queen Anne Inn
16 Clarke Street
Newport, 02840
401-845-5676

MC, V
Closed November 1 through March
$50–$75

Westerly • Shelter Harbor Inn

SHELTER HARBOR INN ALSO SERVES AS A RESTAURANT FOR BOTH LOCALS AND GUESTS.

IF YOU'RE A DIE-HARD paddle tennis player, come to Shelter Harbor in the middle of winter and you won't have any problems picking up a game. The two courts here are official home to Westerly's Shelter Harbor Inn Paddle Tennis Club. If none of the members is around, you may be able to catch innkeeper Jim Dey between projects (among his recent efforts is the creation of a professional croquet course) for a quick game. Along with his wife, Debbye, Jim oversees the inn, which also serves as a popular watering hole and restaurant for both locals and loyal clientele who appreciate Shelter Harbor's simplicity and tranquility.

The fourteen bedrooms in the main house and new annex are large, light, cheerful, and immaculate. Some have their own balconies and fireplaces. All have modern baths and a sense of privacy. The furnishings are modern, belying the history and age of this handsome inn. There are ten more rooms in the barn, plus a conference center for executives who relish a country atmosphere. Downstairs in the main house, the original dining room looks more its age, with beam ceilings, large hearth, and Colonial colors. There are two more modern dining rooms, one with expansive windows overlooking the back yard (stone wall and all). The bar and another dining room are on the sun porch, a cozy place to congregate at night and a cheerful gathering spot during the day. The more intimate sitting room is always available for guests who want to relax in front of the fire or regroup after an active day outdoors.

One thing you can rely on at Shelter Harbor is a good meal. Inn guests are served delicious breakfasts every day, with offerings such as gingerbread pancakes with raisins, eggs any style, and granola with yogurt and fresh fruit.

Shelter Harbor is appealing during the winter when the only sounds heard at night are the howling wind and the crying sea gulls. Stately evergreens laden with snow surround the inn, and the sounds of cold-weather paddle tennis players might awaken you in the morning. Summer is equally inviting. Guests are given passes to a private beach, neighboring Watch Hill is home to one of the oldest carousels in the country, and Matunuck, a short drive away, is host to **Theater by the Sea** (Matunuck Beach Road, off Route 1, 401-789-1094).

Directions: From I-95, take exit 92 to Route 2 east. Go 1 mile, then turn right onto Route 78. Take a left onto Route 1 north. The inn is 4 miles along on the right.

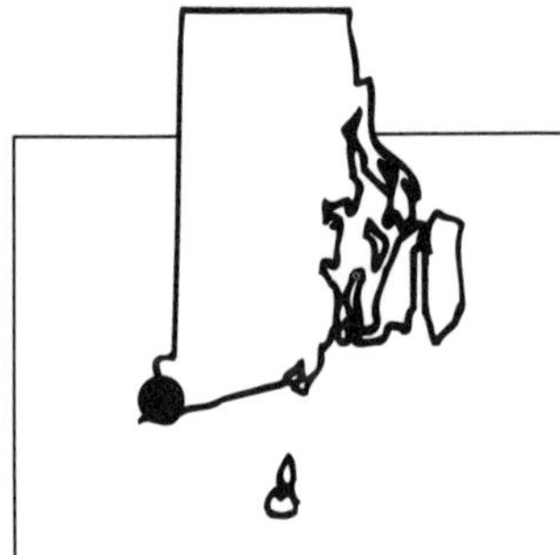

Shelter Harbor Inn
Route 1
Westerly, 02891
401-322-8883

All major credit cards
Open year-round
$80–$96

CONNECTICUT

BEDROOM COMMUNITY

Connecticut's bed and breakfast inns are the playground for travelers from New York and New Jersey. Many of them cater to the more sophisticated traveler, sometimes with a price tag to match. Featured in this chapter is a mixture of luxury inns and inns with a more countrified atmosphere, designed for guests who want to escape city-slicker life. Many are clustered in the Connecticut River Valley, and an equal number are located in the state's northeast and northwest corners. These inns are destinations in themselves—weekend escapes—rather than stopping-off points on an itinerary. You'll no doubt enjoy all of them, plain and fancy.

MANY CONNECTICUT INNS PROVIDE "WEEKEND ESCAPES" FOR NEW YORK AND NEW JERSEY TRAVELERS. ABOVE: GREENWOODS GATE, REVIEWED ON PAGE 210.

EASTOVER FARM TAKES ITS NAME FROM THE INN'S PREVIOUS LIFE AS A COLONIAL FARMHOUSE.

Bethlehem • **Eastover Farm**

It's a great place for young people to learn their barnyard manners, while the tranquil setting is restorative for their harried parents.

WHAT DO YOU DO when your grandmother wills you her 1773 farmhouse, a tennis court, a barn, and seventy acres of cows, pigs, chickens, and rabbits? Ask Erik and Mary Hawvermale for advice, and you'll probably end up with a rather rustic bed and breakfast inn, as they did.

When you're in the mood for a little gentrified farming, visit Eastover Farm for the weekend. Gentleman farmer Erik will introduce you to the subtle arts of animal husbandry, organic-style. It's a great place for young people to learn their barnyard manners, while the tranquil setting is restorative for their harried parents. When you approach the farmhouse, shaded by enormous maple trees, you'll feel as though you've entered another century. There's an authentic grandmotherly feeling to the house, with its two sitting rooms and older-generation decor in the seven comfortable bedrooms. An enormous Colonial fireplace (the original kitchen cooking hearth) commands the downstairs library; it's a welcome asset in the winter.

If you need literary diversion, the inn has plenty of books to keep you occupied. The charmer of the house is the game room, a sitting room paneled in barn siding, with a picture-window view of the surrounding acreage. The room doubles as a showcase for sporting trophies from Mary's New Zealand-born Pratt family.

The bedrooms are fairly modest. The loveliest is Granny's Room, serene in blue with a private bath and the impression that Grandmother Pratt has just

NOT ONE BUT TWO COMFORTABLE SITTING ROOMS AWAIT YOU AT THIS RELAXING INN.

left the room. There's also a snug single, the Cuckoo Room; the larger Pump Room, with a queen-size bed; the pretty upstairs Pine Room, with green trim and rag rugs; and the Summer Cottage, suitable for the entire family. Five of the rooms share baths, and all give you the childlike feeling that you're visiting your grandparents.

Breakfast is served in the sunny dining room, with its bay-window view of the farm's property. Summer guests congregate on the screened-in sun porch to dine. Mary's sister Nancy Smith does all the baking, with remarkable results. Her breads and coffee cakes are served with fresh fruit. After breakfast the kids can follow Erik and his young sons Jake and Nicky to do some barnyard chores. The tennis court, the farm's hiking paths, the inn's crafts shop, and nearby Woodbury, which is filled with antique shops, provide enough options to keep everyone busy.

Erik and Mary have a healthy, hearty look (as do their children), reflected in this unique inn, which is as relaxed and easygoing as they are.

Directions: From I-84, take exit 15 to Route 6 north. Turn left onto Route 47 west for 1 mile, then turn right onto Route 132. Four or 5 miles along, there will be a big bend in the road. The inn is .7 mile from the bend, on the right.

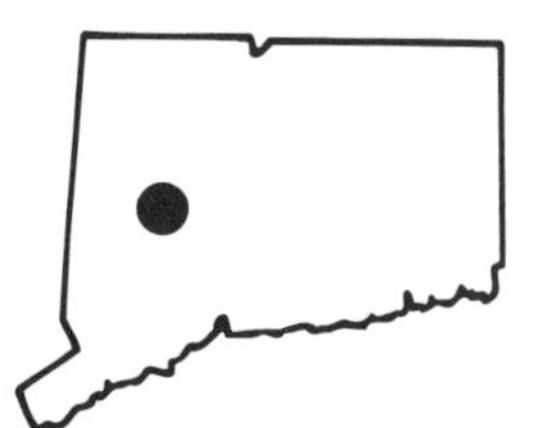

Eastover Farm
Guilds Hollow Road
(Route 132)
Bethlehem, 06751
203-266-5740

MC, V
Closed Christmas
Shared bath, $75; private bath, $85

Deep River • **Riverwind Inn**

RIVERWIND INNKEEPER BARBARA BARLOW INVITES YOU TO EXPERIENCE HER RELAXED LODGINGS.

RIVERWIND WINS THE bed and breakfast inn originality award hands down. Resourceful artisan Barbara Barlow has creatively restored an unprepossessing 1850s house, turning it into a highly personal museum of American primitives, folk art, and early American antiques. A self-taught restorer (she claims all her expertise comes from the public library), Barbara has left her imprint on every detail of this inn, from the wiring and bathroom tiling to the handmade, handcut stencils and innovative color selections.

It will take an entire weekend just to explore the visual crafts treats waiting you in the eight-bedroom inn. Quilts, antique kitchen gadgets, weather vanes, handmade baskets, and a treasury of handcarved objects are secreted away throughout the house. Everything from a menagerie on wheels and a miniature watermelon to sturdy pine antiques and handsome lighting fixtures have been chosen with a keen eye. And if you notice a predominant pig motif, Barbara will cheerfully exclaim, "My daddy's a hog farmer!" In fact, her family and southern upbringing have a strong presence at Riverwind; her grandmother's crockery, her great-grandfather's desk, and even her own childhood collection of Virginia arrowheads are part of the decor.

What makes this inn so special are Barbara and her husband Bob Bucknall's enthusiasm and friendliness. They are the first to tell you that they love restoring old houses. The inn reflects their philosophy: "There isn't anything in the house that could get hurt if you put your feet up and make yourself comfortable." They also place personal service high on their list. They do everything from making breakfast to making the beds.

Each of the eight rooms has its own look—and even its own guest book to record visitors. For honeymooners and romantics, the Barn Rose Room is as sweet as its crocheted lace canopy bed is comfortable. The private bathroom alone is worth a visit just to see Barbara's decorating touch. The Smithfield Room (named after her Virginia hometown) is a celebration in red, white, and blue, its centerpiece a massive maple bed. The Havlow Room, named after Barbara's family's farm, has exquisite stenciled borders to match the handpainted headboard. And Zelda's Room, central headquarters for the inn cat,

Riverwind Inn
209 Main Street (Route 154)
Deep River, 06417
203-526-2014

AE, MC, V
Open year-round
$85–145

Miss Hickory, takes a 1920s break from early Americana with a homage to F. Scott Fitzgerald's crazy wife. The new annex built by Bob (that's how Barbara met him!) houses four rooms, just as country-perfect as the rest of the inn. Champagne and Roses has a private balcony and soothing Japanese steeping tub. The Keeping Room downstairs showcases a twelve-foot cooking hearth.

There are many common rooms where guests can relax. The upstairs game room is crowded with useful antiques (the games are in the pie safe). The sun porch is filled with wicker and sunlight; the living room is a minimuseum filled with furniture and objects that are Barbara's old friends and family favorites; and the communal dining room, where Barbara and Bob prepare breakfast, is clearly the heart of the house.

Breakfast is prepared in the finest southern tradition. If you love Smithfield ham, you've come to the right place. Barbara's family ships up this delicacy, and she and Bob cook a sturdy breakfast of biscuits (in the shape of piglets), southern-style gravy, the family ham, homemade preserves, hot fruit curry in the winter, and fresh fruit compote in the summer. Whether it's the breakfast or Barbara's and Bob's own special brand of hospitality, guests have been found at the breakfast table at two in the afternoon, still forging new friendships.

A backward glance on your way out sums up what Riverwind is all about. Look for the heart-shaped patch on an upstairs window screen—proof that Barbara simply doesn't do things anyone else's way.

DECORATIVE CRAFTS ABOUND AT RIVERWIND—AND PIGS ARE A FAVORITE MOTIF.

Directions: From I-95, take exit 69 to Route 9 north. Take exit 4 (Deep River) and turn left onto Route 154 north (formerly Route 9A). The inn is 1½ miles along on the right.

East Haddam • **Austin's Stonecroft Inn**

ANTIQUE WINDOW GLASS AND CIRCULAR WOODPILES HELP TO GIVE STONECROFT ITS UNIQUE CHARACTER.

NEW OWNER BONNIE Baskin has given handsome Austin's Stonecroft Inn a decidedly feminine look and feel. A native of Seattle, Bonnie is a veteran in the bed and breakfast world, having run a successful inn there for several years. Her Victorian furnishings and down-to-earth friendliness fill Stonecroft and make this appealing inn all the more so.

The 1830s house is perfectly located near the **Goodspeed Opera** (203-873-8668), a popular excuse for people to visit East Haddam. It's also the reason Stonecroft is booked well in advance during opera season.

The five rooms, all with private baths, are comfortable, cheerful, and decorated with Bonnie's antique beds and furniture. Her collections of antique accessories are scattered throughout the house to carry out the Victorian theme. Fireside Room, downstairs, is decorated with pink-tone floral accents. It has a working fireplace, and its gentle glow will greet you when you stay here in the winter. Four Poster, the upstairs front room, also has a fireplace, the expected four-poster canopy bed and attractive decor. The spacious private bathroom completes this sanctuary. Although the other three rooms are smaller, they are no less welcoming. River Bend, in the back of the house, is especially appealing with blue and green detailing. On a clear day, you can see its namesake, the Connecticut River.

Bonnie serves a generous homecooked breakfast with fresh fruit, baked apples, cinnamon rolls, eggs Benedict, baked eggs with spinach, and shirred eggs—offered with plenty of bacon, sausage, and home fries. After breakfast, many guests prefer to relax in the charming Victorian parlor admiring

Bonnie's silver and china collections, or on the side porch overlooking the garden. And there is a windup toy collection in the second-floor sitting room, perfect for the child in all of us. You may be fortunate enough to meet Bonnie's mother, Betty, visiting from nearby Guilford. She is an engaging conversationalist and great fun.

One of the most charming aspects of Austin's Stonecroft Inn is the antique window glass throughout the house, which gives the back yard and side garden a slightly dreamy look. Bonnie has plenty of prestamped postcards for guests to send to friends to invite them to experience this and all the charms of Stonecroft Inn firsthand.

Bonnie Baskin's Victorian furnishings and down-to-earth friendliness fill Stonecroft. . . .

When you're ready to strike out and tour the area, visit a veritable treasure trove just down the road, **Black Whale Antiques** (Route 82, Hadlyme, 203-526-5073), the charming headquarters for owner Tom Rose's handpainted cabinets and bureaus. City meets country here with a collection of English and American antiques to suit all tastes and pocketbooks.

Another local attraction not to be missed is **Gillette Castle** (67 River Road, off Route 82, 203-526-2336). This structure can best be described as a highly personal architectural indulgence—a cross between a Norman fortress and the Los Angeles Watts Towers. It is popular among picnic-toting tourists in the summer and is loveliest during the holiday season (mid-October to December 22, when it is open on weekends). You'll also appreciate the panoramic view of the Connecticut River, with its Currier and Ives snowy banks and briskly moving ice floes.

Directions: From I-95, take exit 69 onto Route 9 north, then take exit 7. Turn left onto Route 154 and continue to the traffic light. Turn right at the light onto Route 149 and go over the Connecticut River on the East Haddam Bridge. Inn is the fourth house on the left. From I-90, take I-84 west to exit 55, which is Route 2 east. Take exit 16 and turn right onto Route 149 south. Inn is 11½ miles along on the right (Route 149 is also called Main Street here).

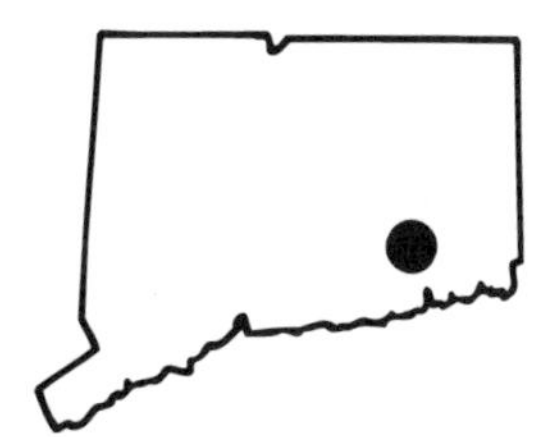

Austin's Stonecroft Inn
17 Main Street (Route 149)
East Haddam, 06423
203-873-1754

Cash or personal check only
Open year-round
$75–$90

Essex • **Griswold Inn**

EVEN IF YOU'RE ONLY remotely considering getting the blues, go immediately to the Griswold Inn on banjo night or sing-along night to join the happy throngs celebrating the end of another workweek. The energy level is as high as the crowd is cheerful, and you'll find plenty of opportunities to meet people or simply to enjoy the Dixieland jazz on your own. Music night, like the Griswold itself, is an institution in Essex and the surrounding area.

DETAILED AUTHENTICITY IS A HALLMARK OF THE GRISWOLD INN, WHICH DATES FROM 1776.

No doubt about it, the Griswold is the doyenne of country inns. It has been feeding and sheltering travelers and locals since 1776, a fact that's obvious when you're immersed in its authentic historic decor. Owners Bill and Vicky Winterer are sticklers for detail, and in their words, "You won't find any repro here." That leaves you with an inn filled with heritage lore, from the Revolutionary War to the present. If the walls could talk, you'd be privy to conversations that would give you an American history lesson. It also leaves you with low ceilings, snug rooms, and insulation just as it wasn't two hundred years ago. Be prepared to sing along in bed to "Anchors Aweigh" and "Yankee Doodle Dandy," since the joyous sound carries and the Griswold's guests are committed to having the time of their life.

The Griswold is essentially a classic country inn, a place to meet friends and to share food inspired by Colonial times. What the cuisine might lack in lightness, it more than makes up for in authenticity. The popular weekly Sunday Hunt breakfast will energize you for the entire day. Grits and cheese soufflé, fried chicken, and broiled kidneys are just a few of the tasty offerings. Overnight guests help themselves to breakfast in the library, with an assortment of teas, English muffins, fresh fruit, and attentive service to make them feel at home.

Dinner also is served at the inn and features the Griswold's own homemade sausage (made here since 1776), a variety of seafood, southern specialties such as fabulous red-beans-and-rice dish (compliments of eighteenth-century Abigail Griswold, the Louisiana-born wife of the inn's original owner), and a host of other recipes that have held up to the test of time. During the annual Christmas dinner, offered the entire month of December, the staff jumps into the spirit of things, sporting Colonial costumes and serving goose, venison, moose, partridge, cranberry pound cake, and custard-bread pudding, among many other eighteenth-century dishes.

Overnight guests have a selection of twenty-three rooms, guarded by the inn's marmalade cat, who appears to have eaten his fair share of Hunt Breakfasts and has all the energy of a doorstop. Most of the rooms have comfortable highboy four-poster twin beds, Colonial-print wallpapers, exposed beams, and a selection of period antiques. All have small, private baths. One of the prettiest rooms, Three, faces the street and is decorated in festive red. There are four lovely suites, perfect when you're in the mood to splurge a little. Their fireplaces take off winter's chill. All the rooms have telephones, the Griswold's only concession to the twentieth century, in deference to the increasing number of business travelers who can't leave home without them.

The Griswold is the doyenne of country inns. It has been feeding and sheltering travelers and locals since 1776.

The Griswold is an inn for all seasons. In summer the boat people invade the town and marina. The color palette is heightened with ice-cream-colored pants and deck shoes, and the inn's regulars say their good-byes to the staff, only to return in the fall when things have quieted down.

If Disney World were to create Colonial Land, Essex could no doubt serve as its model. Griswold owners Bill and Vicky Winterer have been active in the preservation of this town and in revitalizing the ecology of the Connecticut River through their work with the River Museum. While in Essex, you can tour houses along the back streets, sit peacefully by the dock (surrounded by camera-toting tourists and residents taking their constitutionals), browse through the local shops, or visit the **River Museum** (Steamboat Dock, at the end of Main Street, 203-767-8269). One of the most popular attractions in town is the **Valley Railroad** steam train, with its restored 1910 parlor cars and coaches, which winds its way north along the banks of the river. At the end of the rail line, a riverboat continues the journey, past the Goodspeed Opera House and Gillette Castle in East Haddam, before returning to the waiting train for the trip back to Essex (203-767-0104, or write Valley Railroad, P.O. Box 452, Essex, CT 06426).

Directions: From I-95 north, take exit 65 (Westbrook); make a left onto Route 153 and continue to Essex. Inn is on Main Street, on the right. From I-95 south, take exit 69 to Route 9. Take exit 3; turn left at the end of the ramp onto West Avenue, then left onto Main Street.

Griswold Inn
48 Main Street
Essex, 06426
203-767-1812

All major credit cards
Closed Christmas Eve and Christmas Day
$75–$170

Greenwich • The Homestead

For New York City's well-to-do, this was the place to stay while servants opened up summer homes farther up the coast.

IMAGINE YOURSELF SIPPING a cocktail in the twilight, surveying the tranquil landscape, immersed in wicker, and accompanied by overflowing flowering plants. In the words of innkeeper Nancy Smith, "Is there a more civilized way to end a summer weekend?" You might want to put yourself in this enviable position with a stop at the Homestead after your weekend in the country. Sunday evenings here are comfortable, languid, and not terribly crowded. Drinks on the side porch, followed by elegant French dining in a rarefied country-inn atmosphere, will cure whatever could possibly ail you.

If you are just discovering the Homestead, you'll agree with its fiercely loyal clientele that this is indeed an oasis of refined quality, perched on a hilltop in Greenwich, far from the corporate business crowd. You, too, will be impressed as you enter the driveway and approach this beautifully restored 1799 farmhouse. Fresh flowers, impeccable details, and professional service are there to greet you.

Nancy believes that country living should not be a struggle, and the Homestead is perhaps the best of both worlds. Everything has been chosen to make any sophisticated traveler feel at home—from the Hammacher Schlemmer spa towels and roomy terry cloth robes to the well-selected antiques and comfortable beds in each room. Televisions and telephones link guests to the outside world.

Each room is unique, and with the Independent House, eight additional rooms are waiting to please you. The names of the rooms are as whimsical as the rooms are charming. The Birdcage Room is especially enticing, with its canopy bed and heritage colors. The Nutmeg Suite (named in honor of Connecticut, the Nutmeg State) is lovely in blue, with its hexagonal windows in the snug sitting room. The General's Suite, in honor of the legendary Revolutionary War soldier General Israel Putnam, is as spacious and country-elegant as you could imagine. And the quaint Robin Suite, sporting the oldest stencils in Fairfield County, uncovered by accident during restoration, is a third-floor hideaway in the main house. Each room is a treat, and it will take you twenty-three visits to stay in all of them. The Independent House also features designer bathrooms, with the de rigueur French fixture, the bidet, provided no doubt for the many European travelers who make the Homestead their overnight home.

The Homestead
420 Field Point Road
Greenwich, 06830
203-869-7500

All major credit cards
Open year-round
$85–$175

THE HOMESTEAD, "AN OASIS OF REFINED QUALITY," OFFERS TWENTY-THREE ROOMS.

If you are fortunate enough to have Nancy herself give you a tour of the inn, you will be infected by her enthusiasm and energy. You will also discover all of her treasures from tag sales, learn about the history of the flagstone pathway, and see what was unearthed from the Homestead's barn. She and partner Lessie Davison have been in the business for twelve years, leaving no doubt that resourceful, middle-aged women need not fear the empty-nest syndrome. These two dynamos are living testimony to the notion that life might just begin when your last child leaves home.

The Homestead's history is filled with stories of the good life. For New York City's well-to-do, this was the place to stay while servants opened up summer homes farther up the coast. Today guests might meet fellow travelers from California, South America, corporate enclaves, and bridal parties, as well as house-hunters and relatives of Greenwich residents who have full houses during the summer.

Breakfast is served on the sun porch by white-jacketed waiters. You can enjoy freshly squeezed orange juice and homemade muffins, or you can select from an à la carte menu created by the inn's talented chef.

You owe it to yourself to indulge in a little country elegance and get away from life's exhausting routine. You can do just that when you settle into this private retreat, surrounded by acres of lush lawns and trees and a bevy of guests enjoying the rewards of hard work and success.

Directions: From I-95 north, take exit 3 (Arch Street). Turn left at the end of the ramp. At the second light, turn left onto Horseneck Lane. At the end of the street, turn left at the light onto Field Point Road. The inn is ¼ mile along on the right. From I-95 south, turn right at the end of the exit 3 ramp and follow the above directions.

Kent • The Country Goose

SET OFF THE ROAD, THE COUNTRY GOOSE IS A WONDERFUL PLACE TO RELAX.

IF YOU LIKE YOUR bed linens handpressed, your eggs blue-ribbon winners, and your hostess friendly and nurturing, then the Country Goose should be a part of your itinerary. Owner Phyllis Deitrich is proud of her attractive country inn, and with good reason. The beautiful Federal-style house sits off the road and looks as inviting as it does impressive. Phyllis has chosen to decorate the inn with a Victorian point of view; the results are eclectically handsome. Not surprisingly, there are more than a few country geese intermingled with the more formal furnishings, a touch that brings a sense of humor to the house.

Three of the four bedrooms (each shares a bath) are open and airy; the one single is petite and cozy. The Sheep Room — overlooking the picturesque sheep grazing out back — has handsome white mahogany furnishings; Colonial has a canopy bed, walk-in closet (to share with the single when both rooms are booked together), and an oversize scale; and Victorian has its expected period furnishings and a brass bed.

The true appeal of this place is the wonderful breakfast that Phyllis serves. She does all her own baking (with those prize-winning eggs) and is likely to serve coffee cakes, muffins, quick breads, and her own homemade jams. You may be lucky enough to sample her date-nut bread, another blue-ribbon winner from the Goshen country fair.

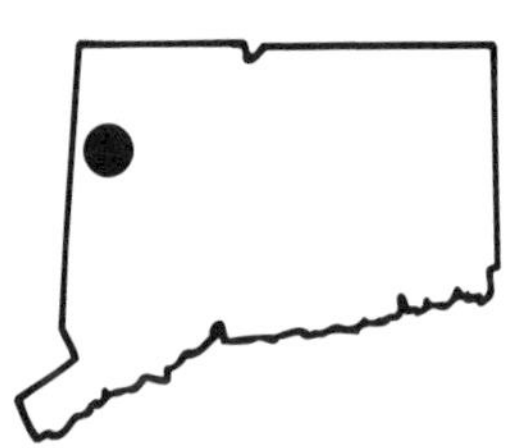

The Country Goose
211 Kent-Cornwall Road (Route 7)
Kent, 06757
203-927-4746

Cash or personal check only
Closed March through April 10
$80

SPACIOUS BEDROOMS MAKE THE COUNTRY GOOSE AN EVEN MORE PLEASANT EXPERIENCE.

When you're not relaxing in the parlor or formal sitting room, you may choose to take in the scenery from the gazebo. The inn commands a strong view of St. John's Ledges and the Appalachian Trail, with Phyllis's small orchards in the foreground. And wherever you situate yourself, you'll no doubt fall in love with Phyllis's afternoon chocolate chip cookies or apple squares—more good things from the Deitrich oven. And there's no fear of getting locked out of the inn, or your car. Phyllis's husband, George, is the Village Locksmith, and handy around the house, to boot!

Directions: From I-84, take Route 7 north. The inn is about 3 miles north of the Kent town monument, on the left.

Kent • **Flanders Arms**

FLANDERS ARMS IS A SUPERB EXAMPLE OF GOOD TASTE AND QUALITY

IT IS ALWAYS refreshing to find a country inn where restraint in decorating reflects the original strength of Federal-era architecture. Marc and Marilyn DeVoses' handsome 1738 inn is a superb example of good taste and a classy approach to creating an inn worth writing about. Actually, it's not surprising, considering the DeVoses have a sophisticated worldview, thanks to Marc's Belgian birthright and his former career in international advertising, a job that sent the family to Europe to live. The inn showcases stunning furniture, family memorabilia, the occasional collection (antique paperweights and exquisite handpainted plates, for example), and photographs of the four DeVos children, some of which are displayed in those timelessly stylish silver frames. It's the real stuff that Ralph Lauren dreams about.

The five rooms, all named for the color that sets the mood of the room, are handsome with the Devoses' restrained decorating touch and attention to detail. The Colonial-green Green Room has beautiful iron-and-brass beds, eyelet linens, and floral-print wallpaper. Terra Cotta is equally beautiful with its crewel-style headboard and botanical prints. Plum is just as pretty with its floral prints and Laura Ashley linens. The Blue Room has a Count Rumford fireplace, which gives the decor a sense of history, even

THE SIMPLICITY OF SHAKER CRAFTSMANSHIP COMBINES WITH THE HOSTS' EYE FOR DETAIL TO MAKE FLANDERS ARMS SPECIAL.

though it is only for atmosphere. The Shaker Room, the Devoses' latest renovation, is a beautiful homage to Shaker style, with handmade Shaker furniture, a print collection of the Shaker tree of life, and a trompe l'oeil bathroom door. Son David created the door. As a painter and jack-of-most-trades, his handiwork is evident throughout the inn. He chose a convenient trade in view of his parents' occupation.

Breakfast is served in the cheerful dining room, a simple but satisfying Continental affair of croissants with sweet butter. You are likely to share your breakfast table with parents of students at local Kent School and prospective students during interview season.

The DeVoses are an athletic couple who are as charming as they are savvy. This inn, with its pale blue exterior, is one of the most handsome in Connecticut, made even more so by Marilyn's down-to-earth good humor and global perspective.

Directions: From I-84, take Route 7 north. The inn is about 1.7 miles north of the Kent town monument, on the left.

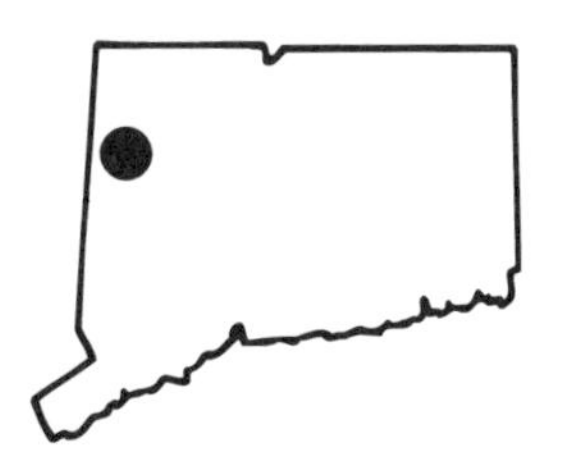

Flanders Arms
Kent-Cornwall Road
(Route 7)
Kent, 06757
203-927-3040

MC, V
Open year-round
$75–$85

Litchfield • Tollgate Hill Inn

The rooms are beautiful, with a true eighteenth-century feeling.

BOB NEWHART SHOULD have considered selling his show's Stratford Inn and relocating to the Colonial town of Litchfield. MTM Enterprises certainly would have saved money on back-lot and sound-stage costs. This lovely town is home to old Connecticut money and summer tourists who enjoy visiting the historical, Federal-period homes, taking audio-cassette tours by car. and stocking up on bulbs and flowering bushes at **White Flower Farm** (Route 63, 203-567-8789), nursery to upscale gardeners for whom price is of little concern. There's also the **Auction Gallery** (Route 202, 203-567-4303), the **Haight Vineyard** (Chestnut Hill Road, off Route 118, 203-567-4045), **White Memorial Conservation Park** (Route 202, 203-567-0015), and miles of rolling countryside to keep out-of-towners busy.

At the eastern end of the town, Fritz Zivic has set up shop in the picturesque Tollgate Hill Inn, one of the few inns with National Register landmark status. He could not have chosen a more appropriate spot; Litchfield is ideally located for New Yorkers taking day trips and for Connecticut locals who love the town for its quaint charm. The inn has a charm of its own; the barn-red building is nestled in a grove of pine trees and has retained a sense of authenticity.

In the main house the rooms are beautiful, with a true eighteenth-century feeling. High-post beds, beam

THE TOLLGATE HILL INN, IN BEAUTIFUL COLONIAL LITCHFIELD, IS A NATIONAL REGISTER LANDMARK.

TOLLGATE HILL BREAKFASTS ARE SERVED IN THE HANDSOME DINING ROOM.

ceilings, and authentic Colonial colors keep the heritage alive and well. Among the more attractive rooms are One and Two, which are large and airy and feature fireplaces. The three rooms on the third floor, snug under the eaves, are more contemporary in decor, with cozy bathrooms. There are four more rooms in the adjacent schoolhouse with tasteful country decor, cable television, and direct-dial telephones; the schoolhouse is connected to the inn by an underground tunnel. The new Captain William Bull House offers working fireplaces, VCRs, and queen-size beds in country decor in each of its ten rooms. There is also a new conference center in the lower level. A complete breakfast of waffles, hotcakes, and omelets is served in the handsome dining rooms.

The inn is well known as one of the better places to find a well-prepared country dinner. Fritz has created a warm atmosphere, appreciated by families, couples looking for (and finding) a romantic spot, old friends who enjoy good cooking, tourists, and inn guests. Fritz table-hops with his Hungarian joie de vivre to make sure everyone's happy. It's hard not to be cheerful here; the chef's cuisine is altogether pleasing. You'll be served a wonderful meal in a convivial setting, whether you dine in the paneled Tavern Room, warmed, perhaps, by a winter fire; in the Formal Room, lighter and brighter, surrounded by naïf prints of children sporting Colonial dress; in the large ballroom, with its mammoth fireplace and chandeliers to match, or outdoors on the shaded summer terrace.

Directions: From I-84, take Route 6 west to Route 8 north. Take exit 42 onto Route 118 to Litchfield Center. Turn right onto Route 202. Inn is 2¼ miles along on the left. From I-84, take exit 19 (Waterbury) onto Route 8 north and follow the above directions.

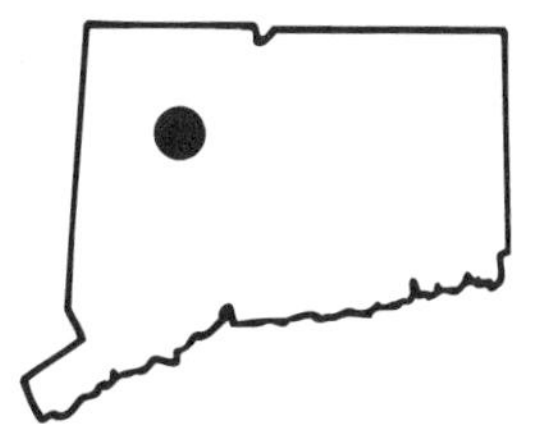

Tollgate Hill Inn
Route 202
Litchfield, 06759
203-567-4545

All major credit cards
Closed three weeks in March
$110–$175; incl. dinner, $175–$240

New London • **Queen Anne Inn**

You will be surrounded by beautiful woodwork and a selection of nautical paintings. . . .

THE QUEEN ANNE retains the immense charm that made this inn a real find. It's still the last thing you'd expect right off Interstate 95, in its little Victoriana neighborhood. This beautiful 1903 house has enormous rooms filled with antiques. Owner Captain Morgan Beatty has a penchant for authenticity, and he canvasses auctions and estate sales to furnish his inn. His finds are yours for the asking; all of the furniture and paintings at the Queen Anne are for sale.

This may be the only bed and breakfast in New England that offers lovely accommodations *and* the chance to take a sunset cruise. Morgan has a sparkle in his eye, is a bon vivant, is full of energy, and has been devoted to sailing for years. He and his daughter Kim will be happy to let you charter his forty-three-foot sloop *Sea Fever* for cruises—truly not your typical inn experience.

The Queen Anne also offers you afternoon tea on Thursdays, Fridays, and Sundays. You can indulge yourself with a feast of scones and finger sandwiches (curried chicken and walnut; cream cheese on date-nut bread; and the proverbial cucumber, radish, and watercress, popular with guests) followed by cakes, petits fours, and delicious macaroons. This elaborate tea is served in the dining room and foyer, with soothing music the classical accompaniment.

If you are traveling with an entourage, the Tower Suite on the third floor with the rooms Gables North and South is the place for you. The master bedroom has a king-size bed, a fireplace, and a kitchen. The other two rooms are perfect for friends or children (twelve or older). The oversize Jacuzzi will fit an overstressed family of four. The other ten rooms downstairs remain as pretty as ever with plenty of canopy beds, beautiful wallpapers, and private baths. The Rose Room is especially attractive with its brass bed and romantic look. The Artist's Room, equally spacious and tranquil in blue, has a painting and palette on display. The Bridal Suite has a novel floating canopy over its Victorian iron-and-brass bed as well as a working fireplace, popular with all guests, honeymooning or not. One of the most irresistible rooms is the Captain's Room—originally the study—on the first floor. The wood paneling plays handsomely in contrast with the lush green chinoiserie wallpaper print and large brass bed.

Breakfast is generous with homemade muffins,

Queen Anne Inn
265 Williams Street
New London, 06320
203-447-2600; 1-800-347-8818

AE, MC, V
Open year-round
$75–$135

fresh fruit salad, French toast, eggs, and breakfast meats. You will be surrounded by beautiful woodwork and a selection of nautical paintings, in homage to Morgan's first love, the sea.

Most of the dinner options near the inn have a distinctly franchise flavor. But there is a surprise around the corner across the street from the firehouse and next door to the Vac Shack. **Bayou Grill** (225 Broad Street, 203-443-4412) offers just above hole-in-the-wall decor and some good cooking. The Cajun cuisine here has a slight Jamaican accent. If you liked jerk pork in Port Antonio, you'll love it in New London.

THIS VICTORIAN DELIGHT IS A TRIP BACK IN TIME.

Directions: From I-95 south, take exit 84, turning immediately onto exit 84E, which becomes Williams Street. From I-95 north, take exit 83, which becomes Williams Street. The inn is up the hill, on the left.

New Preston • **Boulders Inn**

IN WINTER AND SUMMER, BOULDERS INN OFFERS A RANGE OF ACTIVITIES FOR OUTDOOR ENTHUSIASTS.

Boulders Inn
Route 45
New Preston, 06777
203-868-7918

AE, MC, V
Open year-round
Winter, $90–$100; (incl. dinner) $145–$150; summer (incl. dinner), $200–$225

THE BOULDERS' ENTHUSIASTIC new owners, Kees and Ulla Adema, have brought a fresh look to this popular inn. In summer, a profusion of flowers greets you in the newly landscaped entry gardens. The bedrooms have been refurbished, and the Ademas' personal touches are evident throughout the inn. The downstairs library is a cozy nook, filled with the expected collection of books and an unexpected collection of antique birdcages. The Lake Room is as impressive as ever with its uninterrupted view of Lake Warmaug and Kees's ship model on display, a visual memory of his former career as a ship broker. Ulla has a deft touch with pierced lampshades, and each room is a showcase for her exquisite work. The dining room now has romantic lighting, thanks to her pastel lampshades on the new wall sconces.

Upstairs, the six bedrooms have been repainted, there are plenty of new large beds, and each room reflects the Ademas' simple but tasteful decorating style. Southwest has lovely chinoiserie floral window seating and a sofa for afternoon relaxing; the large brass bed is the centerpiece of the room. Southeast has an oversize bed and private sitting room. North Middle has a Victorian bed and one of the Ademas' many quilts from their personal collection. Northwest is a particularly sunny room, offering guests twin beds. The new second-floor suite has a handsome sleigh bed and a king-size bed, as well as a pleasant sitting area.

The new carriage house has three more elegant rooms, each with its own fireplace. Out back, the eight cottages have been spruced up, making them snug weekend escapes, particularly when the landscape is laden with snow.

The Boulders continues in its tradition of serving award-winning cuisine. The Ademas offer a variety of internationally inspired dinner selections that are a cut above traditional country dining. Breakfasts are equally satisfying with generous servings of fresh fruit, yogurt, homemade müsli, coffee cake, Dutch babies (popoverlike pancakes), and French toast.

This 1895 country manor has a superb setting and offers plenty of activities to keep guests busy throughout the year: cross-country skiing, ice fishing, and snowshoeing in the winter, and loads of lake sports in the summer. The Lake Room and the outdoor terrace are perfect places to watch the last glimmers of another perfect sunset across the lake, no matter what the season.

The Boulders continues its tradition of serving award-winning cuisine.

Directions: From I-84 west, take the Farmington exit to Route 4 west. Take Route 4 west to Route 118 west, then continue to Route 202 west. Follow Route 202 west to Route 45 north. The inn is 1½ miles along on the right. From I-84 east, take exit 7 (Danbury). Follow Route 7 north to Route 202 east, then continue to Route 45 north. Follow the above directions.

GREENWOODS GATE, A COMPLETELY RENOVATED 1797 HOUSE, OFFERS FOUR ROMANTICALLY DECORATED ROOMS.

Norfolk • **Greenwoods Gate**

WHEN YOU WANT to experience life at its best and you know you deserve to be treated like royalty, prepare yourself for a visit to Greenwoods Gate. Without a doubt, this is the most romantic bed and breakfast inn in New England. You'll be pampered, befriended, entertained, and discreetly left alone by hostess-owner Deanne Raymond. She has an overflowing generosity of spirit, and you will leave this beautiful inn with fond memories and a new friend.

The energetic Deanne completely renovated her 1797 house, doing everything possible to create a decor that flatters the eye. From the gentle colors of the E. J. Trescott Suite, swathed in Ralph Lauren florals, to the honeymoon-ready oversize Jacuzzi in the cherry-paneled bath of the Levi Thompson Suite, to the heart-shaped waffles served with freshly whipped cream and strawberries, this place is designed for romance. Deanne has put considerable time and energy into making this four-bedroom inn a perfect little hideaway and a showcase for her talented design touch. The living room is a peaceful pale yellow, and guests are invited to share a drink before they leave for dinner.

You'll be pampered, befriended, entertained, and discreetly left alone. . . .

The upstairs bedrooms are a delight to explore. The Captain Darius Phelps Room shimmers with its silk-satin peach wallpaper, beautiful period sofa, vanity table, two three-quarter beds, and striking view of a birch tree framed by the oversize window. The bathroom has a superb Victorian tub, forged for extra-long travelers.

Next door the snug Lucy Phelps Room features a beautiful handpainted bureau, forest-green walls flecked with golden stars, and cabbage-rose print bed linens. The E. J. Trescott Suite, a tribute to Ralph

Lauren, is feminine, with its brass-and-iron double bed, large bathroom, and replica of Greenwoods Gate—a bed and breakfast dollhouse (inhabited by small bears and furnished with a collection of miniature antiques) that looks just like Deanne's house. The adjoining single room is perfect for parents traveling with a very well behaved older child; there's so much to look at that even the most curious child will be in heaven.

The pièce de résistance is the Levi Thompson Suite, Deanne's rendition of a storybook garret hideaway. This custom-designed room has a loft bed, beautiful Victorian stained glass window, and handcrafted cherry railings, floors, and headboard.

The decor is outdone only by Deanne herself. A super-achiever, she has a million ideas and the stamina to make all her dreams come true. If you want a piece of what makes Greenwoods Gate so special, you can browse through Deanne's tiny gift shop to find the perfect memento.

Deanne is also a fabulous cook. You'll be tipped off to this by a kitchen designed for serious eating. You can join her in her culinary headquarters for a cup of her signature coffee (a secret blend, touched with crème de noisette) and chat with her while admiring the sparkling tin ceiling, installed to complement her extensive collection of cookie cutters (Deanne is an inveterate collector of everything).

When breakfast is served, you'll dine in the formal dining room, fire blazing in the winter, feasting on her latest whim. You could be treated to leek-and-cheese omelets, eggs Benedict Florentine, apple-pear compote, frothed juices, or, if you're of the younger generation, paper-doll pancake cutouts.

When you're ready to leave, you'll know what month it is as you drive out. Deanne concocts displays in her front yard for every holiday. Handpainted valentines, shamrocks, a field of tiny American flags, Easter egg baskets—even miniature deer fashioned from logs—stand guard over Greenwoods Gate.

Directions: Take I-90 to Route 7 south. Then take Route 44 east for about 8 miles to Norfolk. Inn is ½ mile from the village green on the east side of the green.

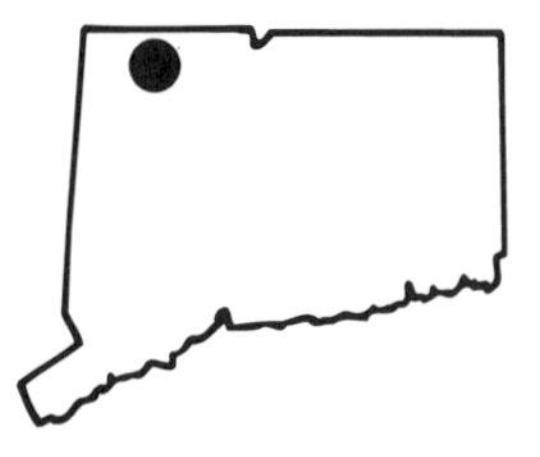

Greenwoods Gate
105 Greenwoods Road East (Route 44)
Norfolk, 06058
203-542-5439

AE
Open year-round
$125–$155

Norfolk • Manor House

The nine rooms, scattered on the upper two floors, are an exercise in Victorian nostalgia.

IF YOU APPRECIATE the taste of homegrown raspberries and strawberries, back-yard honey, fresh herbs, and garden vegetables (not to mention the effort it takes to grow them), the Manor House offers you the bountiful harvest of Diane and Hank Tremblay. This resourceful couple has created a Victorian bed and breakfast palace in their 1898 home. The imposing Bavarian-style house is set back from the road on five acres of property, complete with a brook.

The rooms are large and surprisingly airy, considering Victorian-era interior design sobriety. They also reflect the personalities of Manor House's well-traveled original owners, the Spoffords. The monumental frieze over the mantel evokes the Parthenon; the columns in the dining room, the Temple of Athena; the beam ceilings, Tudor England; and the cherry-paneled entryway, a country home in France. The dramatic focal point of the house is the collection of original Louis Tiffany leaded glass windows, housewarming gifts to the Spoffords. They are exquisite and in perfect condition, and they provide a glimpse of privileged life at the turn of the century.

The oversize living room opens its doors to a variety of special events, from weddings to receptions and private parties. The Tremblays also provide sleigh rides in the snow, carriage rides through the autumn foliage, and hay rides in the summer. Both children and adults are enthusiastic fans of these old-fashioned diversions. During warm weather, inn guests are invited to use nearby Toby Pond for canoeing and swimming.

The Tremblays trade off breakfast-cooking assignments, and you'll be treated to their culinary creativity in the large formal dining room (with Tiffany fish-and-fowl windows and a vintage Victorian ceramic fireplace), in the smaller breakfast room, or on the summer porch. Wherever you sit, you'll feast on original creations such as freshly baked blueberry, rhubarb, or pumpkin bread; orange waffles; poached eggs with lemon-chive sauce; and French toast stuffed with garden-fresh raspberries. Their garden also provides cut flowers, which are arranged throughout the house (the seeds for the hollyhocks hail from Monet's sanctuary in Giverny).

The nine rooms (seven with private baths), scat-

Manor House
Maple Avenue (off Route 44)
Norfolk, 06058
203-542-5690

AE, MC, V
Open year-round
$70–$165

tered on the upper two floors, are an exercise in Victorian nostalgia. The romantic French room, La Chambre, is dominated by a brass bed, a wall of feminine fashion prints and photographs, and an art nouveau bathroom with a large footed tub. The beautiful Spofford Room, with its king-size canopy bed and large fireplace, is a luxury of spaciousness. The Lincoln Room has a sleigh bed, and the Morgan Room has its own direct-stop elevator and private balcony. The third-floor Chalet Suite offers a secluded place to stay with its own sitting room. There are also two very large third-floor rooms that give guests a welcome sense of openness. All have delicate lace curtains and Victorian furnishings, in keeping with the personality of the house.

WINTER SLEIGH RIDES HELP MAKE MANOR HOUSE A SPECIAL PLACE.

When you find a moment to wrest yourself away from the personable Tremblays and their idyll, visit **Hillside Gardens** (515 Litchfield Road, Route 272, 203-542-5345), renowned for its stunning perennial gardens and landscaped grounds.

Directions: From I-84 west, take the Route 4 (Farmington) exit. Turn onto Route 179 north, then take Route 44 west to Norfolk. In Norfolk turn right onto Maple Avenue across from the village green. Inn is 100 yards along on the left. From I-90, exit onto Route 7 south (Great Barrington-Canaan exit). In Canaan take Route 44 east to Norfolk. Turn left onto Maple Avenue. Follow the above directions.

COBBSCROFT IS A DELIGHTFUL DISCOVERY, ACROSS THE BORDER FROM BUSTLING STURBRIDGE, MASSACHUSETTS.

Pomfret • **Cobbscroft**

WHEN YOU COME TO Cobbscroft, in addition to staying in a beautiful room and enjoying a tasty breakfast in an elegant dining room, you may well walk out with an original watercolor. The best part about this very special bed and breakfast inn is its owners, Tom and Janet McCobb. You might get the impression that the soft-spoken Tom, with his quiet wisdom and balanced sense of humor, has seen it all in life. He probably has! A retired international executive, he has the spirit of a man who has come to terms with life. He also has come to painting as a new career, a conduit for a creativity that lay dormant for many years while he rose to the top of the business world. Today he paints, teaches, lectures, and loves to share his art with guests. In fact, Tom conducts workshops, so you can come to Cobbscroft and learn to paint!

This immensely appealing house doubles as a gallery, and many of Tom's works are on display. The McCobbs have opened a gallery in the former cow barn and chicken coop out back, which also houses their framing business. The inn also is sprinkled with works by some of Tom's favorite watercolor artists and a marvelous collection of animal sculptures by friend E. B. Cox, an octogenarian Canadian sculptor. You'll be tipped off that Cobbscroft has an artistic bent when you enter the house on a pathway strewn with Cox's outdoor sculptures, which compete for attention with the McCobb's three real-life dogs.

Tom is a great raconteur, and he'll gladly discuss art and just about anything else with you.

Cobbscroft is the perfect place to stay if you want to get away from the commercialism of Sturbridge (across the border in Massachusetts), if you're visiting students at the nearby Pomfret or Rectory prep schools,, or if you're simply touring this gorgeous section of Connecticut. The house is an artistic haven even beyond the obvious artwork; the McCobbs have a collection of antiques that are true treasures. The Queen Anne lolling chair in the gallery is testimony to their well-educated eye and love of quality. The gallery itself is large, sunny, and cheerful in lemon yellow. The living room is equally appealing with a traffic-stopping handmade Windsor bench. This five-wood piece was made by a young, local woodworker and looks every bit as sensational as an original.

This immensely appealing house doubles as a gallery.

The downstairs double room is handsome in red, and the adjacent single room is snug in blue-and-white wicker. Upstairs, the bridal suite has its own fireplace, Empire-style furnishings, and a bathroom that is the talk of the Pomfret plumbing world, with stunning gold fixtures and an elongated "Napoleonic" bath that will make you feel every bit as regal as you deserve. You won't be disappointed by any of the rooms or their beautiful private baths.

The dining room is country-elegant, with a Queen Anne table and chairs, a collection of lovely antique clocks, and a stunning eighteenth-century dresser. Janet serves a different breakfast each morning according to the "spirit of the cook." You can expect to be served homemade coffee cake, hot apple crisp, almond puff pastry, waffles, pancakes, sausage quiche, fresh strawberries or pineapple, or any of her other breakfast specialties.

This inn is one of the most delightful places you could visit. The town of Pomfret is every bit as charming as the inn, and Tom's personal style will make you an instant friend—and possibly a collector of his lovely watercolors.

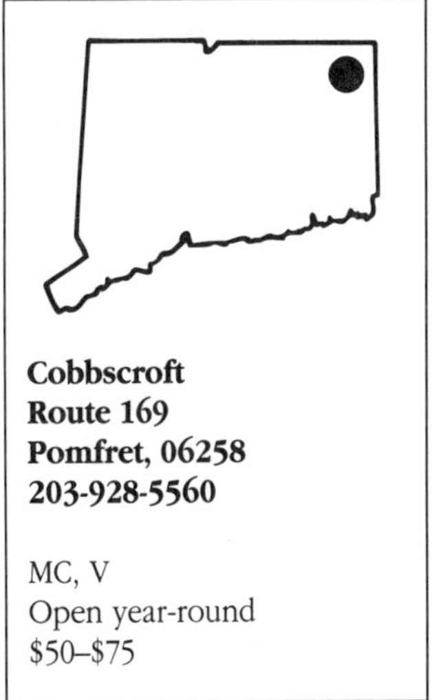

Cobbscroft
Route 169
Pomfret, 06258
203-928-5560

MC, V
Open year-round
$50–$75

Directions: From I-395, exit at Route 101 west (exit 93), then take Route 169 north for 2 miles. Inn is on the right. From I-90, take exit 10 onto I-290 south. Take I-395 to exit 97 onto Route 44 west. Turn left onto Route 169 south at the red blinking light. Go past the Rectory and Pomfret Schools. Inn is on the left.

Warren • Evie's Turning Point Farm

JOE AND EVIE GROSSI TURNED TO INNKEEPING AFTER RETIREMENT FOR "A NEW CHALLENGE."

Evie's Turning Point Farm
Route 45
Warren, 06754
203-868-7775

Cash or personal check only
Closed Thanksgiving and Christmas
$75–$85

ONE OF THE unexpected surprises along the back roads of northern Connecticut is this beautiful farmhouse, lovingly restored from the ground up by Evie and Joe Grossi. Evie and Joe found themselves postretirement innkeepers after their three daughters announced, "You need a new challenge!" Not ones to slack off later in life, these youthful grandparents bought a run-down, two-century-old farmhouse, complete with barn and eleven acres of rolling countryside. Today it is the house that Joe built, with Evie's revision. She explains that she closed her eyes and visualized how she wanted the house to look, then Joe created it for her room by room.

They have every reason to be proud of the results, particularly since Joe, a former electronics engineer, had never built anything in his life. Now he's an expert at installing baths, rebeaming ceilings, moving walls, adding rooms, and building cabinets. Recent triumphs are the lovely back porch and upstairs balcony. Without a doubt, Turning Point Farm proves that marriage, after over forty years, only gets better. You'll be touched by the Grossis' enthusiasm and loving friendship.

The farm is a work in progress, evolving as Evie's vision changes and Joe's prowess strengthens. He is constantly honing his restoration skills on new projects. The completed bedrooms are charming, with rough-hewn beam detailing reminiscent of a seventeenth-century French farmhouse. There is an assortment of antiques and family furniture in each of the three upstairs bedrooms, and the entire house is decorated with oil paintings and ceramic works by one of the Grossis' daughters. The loft room with its upstairs sitting area, the double room with its high-back headboard, and the twin-bedded cherry room are all delightful. All also share a bathroom, professionally installed by the master carpenter/plumber himself. The upstairs common room is perfect for relaxing and admiring the landscape through its oversize window.

Evie is a seasoned cook, and breakfasts are another bright spot that keeps guests returning to the farm. Specialties such as German pancakes with apples and sausage, grits pudding with zabaglione, sautéed cornmeal cakes served with coconut and maple syrup, bulgur-wheat pancakes, and molasses bread certainly

THIS EIGHTEENTH-CENTURY FARMHOUSE IS A "WORK IN PROGRESS."

will whet your appetite. Guests are served in the country-elegant dining room, with Evie's lace tablecloth, cut-glass collection, and Colonial pine furniture. The kitchen is the most welcoming room in the house, with Joe's handmade display shelves housing Evie's china, beautiful European tile work, and enough cooking space to entertain both guests and the Grossis' grandchildren, who are frequent visitors. In her spare time Evie will take you on a tour of her beehives and show you her handcrafted dried-flower arrangements and the garden of flowers currently drying in the barn.

Turning Point Farm is appropriately named. The inn represents a turning point in the Grossis' lives, and a visit here may be a turning point in your life as well, as you will no doubt want to come again and again to enjoy the wonderful relationship of this exceptional couple.

Directions: From I-84 east, take exit 8 in Danbury onto Route 7 north. Then take Route 45 south for 2½ miles to the inn. From I-84 west, turn onto Route 8 north. Then take Route 202 south to Route 45 north. Inn is about 10 miles from the intersection of Routes 202 and 45.

IF YOU HAVE CAUSE FOR CELEBRATION, COTSWOLD INN MAKES A DELIGHTFUL SPLURGE.

Westport • **Cotswold Inn**

THE STOCK MARKET is bullish. You're in line for a promotion. Your son made the dean's list. It's your twentieth anniversary. Your youngest child is finally moving out of the house into an apartment. Your great-aunt's inheritance just came through. You looked younger than all your classmates at your school reunion. Your first grandchild was just born. Your insurance premiums finally went down. Your tax refund is higher than you expected. You made it through another birthday.

If any or all (or none!) of these is true and you want to celebrate, be good to yourself with an overnight visit to the Cotswold Inn. This elegant inn is on the scale of a doll's house, with four beautiful bedrooms, a stunning living room, an eat-in kitchen, and an expense-account tariff. The inn is extremely popular among business travelers, but you will also see weekender couples who come here to enjoy its quality and beautiful ambiance. The inn also has been home to Broadway and Hollywood stars who have stayed here during the **Westport Country Playhouse**'s eleven-week season (25 Powers Street, 203-227-4177). You'll find their autographs in the inn's guest ledger.

Cotswold Inn
76 Myrtle Avenue
Westport, 06880
203-226-3766

AE, MC, V
Open year-round
$175–$225

Each of the four rooms is a Laura Ashley showcase, combining country colors with contemporary design flair. All the furniture is superb reproduction quality, and the overall effect is charming, without looking new or modern. The Bedford Room is a symphony of slate blue, with light pine furniture and white rag rugs. The Jesup Room is a study in green, with signature Ashley wallpaper and matching fabrics. Sherwood, the smallest room but by no means petite, is cozy in dark blue. And the Wheeler Suite is a knockout in apricot, with a canopy bed, fireplace, and daybed in the sitting room (a perfect hideaway for a traveling family). Each room is equipped with a fabulous modern bathroom, discreetly concealing color television, and telephone.

The inn has been home to Broadway and Hollywood stars who have stayed here during the Westport Country Playhouse's eleven-week season.

Partners Richard Montanaro and Lorna Smith are on hand to make your stay pleasant and comfortable. They serve a generous Continental breakfast, as befits the pricey atmosphere of this jewel-box inn. You will be treated to fresh pastries and breads, yogurt, cereals, and fresh fruit—all served in the casual kitchen or outdoors in the garden during warm weather.

A classical harpist provides mood music on weekends in the living room, accompanied by complimentary wine and cordials. The Cotswold is a favorite destination for discriminating travelers who appreciate a first-class approach to life, even if it's just for the weekend.

Directions: Take I-95 to exit 17. Turn north onto Route 33, then right onto Post Road (Route 1). Turn left onto Main Street. At the top of Main Street, turn right onto Avery Place. At the end of Avery, turn right again onto Myrtle Avenue. Inn is 300 feet along on the left, at the end of a pebble driveway.

About the Author

DEBORAH PATTON, former editor of the Gault Millau/America travel book series, is an experienced travel writer and restaurant reviewer. Of her own wanderings, she writes:

> I've loved to travel ever since I was a child. Summers on Lake Michigan and at Martha's Vineyard (the whole family drove from landlocked St. Louis), car trips with my grandparents, drives across the country during college and since then—the secondary roads always revealed some new discovery or surprise, other than the obvious of getting lost a lot. Even my travels in Europe are on the back roads, guidebooks and road maps in hand.

She has made a career in creative and promotional services in consumer magazines such as *Seventeen, Reader's Digest,* and *HG.* She is currently Marketing and Promotion Director of *M, Inc.* magazine. She is also the author of Morgan Fairchild's *Super Looks* beauty book and a contributing editor to Gault Millau's *The Best of New England.*

She lives in New York City with her husband, Jon Montgomery, and their sons Max and Sam who also love to travel and mercifully fall asleep the moment they get into the car.